An Illustrated History of
SOUTHERN WAGONS

Frontispiece: In 1935 100 standard covered goods wagons (Diagram 1428) were taken into Eastleigh shops and converted for use on the Dover-Dunkirk train ferry service. Here we see 20 of them nearly finished but still lacking their safety chains and tare weights. *R. Chorley collection*

An Illustrated History of
Southern Wagons

by
G. Bixley, A. Blackburn,
R. Chorley and M. King

Volume 4 - The Southern Railway

Oxford Publishing Co

AUTHORS' NOTES AND ACKNOWLEDGEMENTS

It is a sobering thought, but it was nearly 40 years ago that two of the present team first discussed the possibility of writing a history of the Southern wagon. Nothing like it had ever been attempted before, and we doubted if there would be enough interest, so for the time being it remained a dream. In 1970 came *The British Wagon*, and Ray contributed to what was to become a standard work on the subject that is unlikely to be bettered. *Southern Wagons* nearly happened in 1971, but families, careers and other interests then took their toll of our time, and it was not until 1984 that a team which now numbered five people saw publication of the first volume of a work that had grown to include the pre-Grouping companies as well. Volume Two followed in 1985, but about this time John Newton (our original 'South Eastern man') had to drop out for personal reasons, and the project might have stopped there had it not been for Gerry and Mike. Gerry tackled the Chatham wagons, and in truth only Mike was interested in things South Eastern & Chatham, but with much hard work Volume Three was eventually finished in 1999.

This volume deals with the Southern Railway designs and their BR developments, and is largely the work of Ray, as was originally intended — and, as a former Lancing apprentice and Eastleigh C&W draughtsman, who better? Later in his career it fell to Ray to introduce Computer Aided Design to the C&W Drawing Office at Derby, so now, with this first book of CAD wagon drawings, things have come full circle for him. It was also Ray who, many years ago, saved the originals of a lot of the drawings used in this series and many of the photographs, but that, as they say, is another story.

In Volume One we stated that it was not our intention to write a technical history, and we have not attempted to do so, but some reference to technical matters will be found in this volume. The reason for this is that we are now, in many cases, dealing with wagons that still exist, and, during the course of preparing this volume, we have probably had at least as many questions asked by those who are working on the restoration of former SR wagons as those wishing to build models of them. Happily a significant number of Southern wagons have found their way into preservation, but readers should always obtain permission before going to look at them — even a heritage railway can be a dangerous place.

We now come to the hardest part of our work, and that is to thank all those who have helped us over the years, and in some cases urged us not to give up. How can one remember every one over such a long period? Many old colleagues did not always realise they were helping, and sometimes it was better they did not know, for in the railway industry there is a very fine line drawn between respect and contempt for railway enthusiasm, and one must never forget that, for most, it was a none-too-well-paid job and far from being a hobby.

Our enthusiast friends know who they are, but there are three people whom we must mention by name: Terence Barry, Roger Silsbury and Adrian Swain. Terence was probably the first person to study the Southern Railway's rolling stock in detail, and in the early years his help and notes were invaluable. Roger was one of the few people at the time to take an interest in BR wagons, and he has filled a gap in our knowledge. Adrian has very carefully checked many of the drawings and prevented some silly mistakes. For those not mentioned by name, you are not forgotten, and we thank you all. We hope you enjoyed our efforts — we have done our best.

Gerry Bixley, Alan Blackburn, Ray Chorley, Mike King.
April 2002

Main References

The SR Wagon Registers formerly in the Rolling Stock Office at Eastleigh
The SR Wagon Registers formerly in Southern House, Croydon
The SR Wagon Diagram Book
The BR Wagon Diagram Book
The Public Record Office at Kew
The National Newspaper Collection, Colindale
The Library of The Model Railway Club
Hampshire County Library Winchester Railway Collection
Kent County Library Ashford Railway Collection
Fyffes PLC

Books:

Sir Herbert Walker; C. F. Klapper
War on the Line; Southern Railway
Ashford Works Centenary; Southern Railway
The Southern Railway Magazine; Southern Railway
The Railway Wagon Theory & Practice; L. Lynes
British Goods Wagons; R. J. Essery, D. P. Rowland, W. O. Steel
A History of GWR Goods Wagons; A. G. Atkins, W. Beard, D. J. Hyde, R. Tourret
A Pictorial Record of LNER Wagons; P. Tatlow
The LMS Wagon; R. J. Essery, K. R. Morgan
British Railways Wagons; D. Rowland
HMRS Livery Register No 3: LSWR and Southern.

Title page: **Plate 1** What advertising people would call an 'Express goods': a Southampton Docks-Feltham Yard fully fitted goods, seen on the Addlestone curve in the late 1930s. There are a couple of LSWR refrigerator vans next to the engine followed by two Southern insulated vans, three or four containers and a further string of vans of various types.
F. Foote collection

First published 2002

ISBN 0 86093 564 7

Published by Oxford Publishing Co

an imprint of Ian Allan Publishing Ltd, Hersham, Surrey KT12 4RG.
Printed by Ian Allan Printing Ltd, Hersham, Surrey KT12 4RG.

Code: 0207/A1

Contents

Above:
Plate 2 No hanging about! A typical South Eastern section goods train from Bricklayers Arms bound for Ashford via Tonbridge, seen near Chislehurst in September 1948. Three or four vacuum-braked wagons form a 'vac-head' on the front, the first a Southern van in ex-works condition; the roof looks white but is almost certainly light grey 'Ruberoid', a rubberised material much used on these vans in later years. *E. R. Wethersett*

Left:
Plate 3 Another train from Bricklayers Arms in good health, this time seen from the bottom of H. C. Casserley's garden in Bromley in May 1938 and bound for Dover via Swanley and Sevenoaks. Again there is a 'vac-head' of at least four vehicles including three Southern container wagons loaded with SR containers. *H. C. Casserley*

Chapter 1.
General Introduction

A Background to the Southern Railway's Goods Traffic

Most readers will no doubt have read the previous volumes in this series and so will know that, almost uniquely in Britain, the three pre-Grouping companies that went to make up the Southern Railway earned more from their passenger receipts than they did from the carriage of goods. It follows, therefore, that the same was true for the Southern, but a few figures will explain the position more clearly. In 1923 the Southern Railway's goods receipts were roundly £6m — about £156m at today's prices. That figure represented only about a quarter of the figure earned by the passenger traffic, but was still a very large sum of money. Looked at nationally, the Southern's overall share of the railways' combined goods traffic was on average just 6%, but that only underlines the vast amount of traffic handled by the railways in those days.

But this situation was about to change: the motor lorry had emerged from World War 1 as a serious challenger, and by the late 1920s it was making significant inroads into the railways' business. The railways, led by the LMS, endeavoured to retain their business by introducing railhead distribution schemes offering cheap rates to those who used them, and followed this with road-rail containers offering door-to-door transit. The GWR introduced 'Express goods trains' with booked connections, and

the LNER developed this theme in its 'Green Arrow' service. All these initiatives the Southern dutifully followed. In only one area of the freight business could the Southern be said to lead the other companies, and that was in terms of the actual speed and general sharpness of its operating practice — a requirement dictated more by the need to avoid delaying the passenger services than by anything else, it must be said, but no other railway in Britain timed its goods trains more tightly than the Southern.

The years of the depression were difficult, of course, and several items of major expenditure were postponed. However, the Southern was not quite as badly affected as the other companies, because the bulk of its goods traffic consisted of the day-to-day domestic requirements of the community, whether the economy was in recession or not. The mid- to late 1930s saw the Southern emerging as a very well-run business. The electrification schemes were paying dividends, the trunk freight-train services had been greatly improved by the introduction of part- and fully-fitted trains, the Southampton Dock extensions had been completed despite the slump and the Dover-Dunkirk train ferry was promising great things. But, above all, the railways had purchased a controlling interest in most of their road competition, and as a result this period saw the nearest thing this country has yet seen to an efficient transport system. Sadly this promising situation would not last for long.

Plate 4

S.R. EXPRESS FREIGHT SERVICES TO AND FROM LONDON

A SERVICE of express freight trains for the conveyance of merchandise and perishable traffic is run every weekday to and from London, serving all principal stations on the Southern Railway.

Traffic handed in at the London Goods Stations by 5.0 p.m. (Mondays to Fridays), 12.30 p.m. (Saturdays), is scheduled to arrive at all chief stations during the early hours of the morning following the day of loading, and at all other destinations before noon on the day following the day of loading.

Traffic handed in at Provincial Stations for London during the late afternoon Mondays to Fridays, and 1.0 p.m. Saturdays, is scheduled to arrive in London during the early hours of the morning following the day of loading.

Deliveries to the London Markets are made throughout the night. (See page 25.)

The arrival times in London and at some of the chief provincial stations are as shown on these pages.

Arrival from London. (NINE ELMS)	Stations.	Arrival in London. (NINE ELMS)	Arrival from London. (NINE ELMS)	Stations.	Arrival in London. (NINE ELMS)
6 20 a.m.	Aldershot ...	1 31 a.m.	6 0 a.m.	Haslemere ...	1 31 a.m.
7 23 ,,	Amesbury ...	3 34 ,,	9 22 ,,	Holsworthy ...	12 51 ,,
12 35 ,,	Andover ...	3 34 ,,	6 13 ,,	Honiton ...	12 51 ,,
6 59 ,,	Axminster ...	12 51 ,,	7 52 ,,	Ilfracombe ...	12 51 ,,
7 0 ,,	Basingstoke...	11 0p.m.*	7 15 ,,	Launceston ...	12 51 ,,
9 50 ,,	Bere Alston...	12 51 a.m.	4 40 ,,	Okehampton ...	12 51 ,,
8 28 ,,	Bordon ...	1 31 ,,	6 20 ,,	Plymouth Friary	2 58 ,,
5 42 ,,	Bournemouth (Centl. Gds.)	3 34 ,,	5 19 ,,	Poole ...	3 34 ,,
6 23 ,,	Barnstaple ...	12 51 ,,	6 38 ,,	Reading ...	4 58 ,,
7 7 ,,	Bideford (Goods)	12 51 ,,	6 41 ,,	Ringwood ...	3 34 ,,
			7 4 ,,	Salisbury (Milford)	2 58 ,,
7 15 ,,	Bude ...	2 58 ,,	8 4 ,,	Seaton ...	12 51 ,,
11 38 ,,	Callington ...	12 51 ,,	7 29 ,,	Semley ...	2 58 ,,
6 37 ,,	Chard Jct. ...	12 51 ,,	6 18 ,,	Sherborne ...	12 51 ,,
7 9 ,,	Crediton ...	12 51 ,,	8 5 ,,	Sidmouth ...	12 51 ,,
6 0 ,,	Crewkerne ...	12 51 ,,	5 0 ,,	Southampton ...	3 6 ,,
5 55 ,,	Devonport ...	2 58 ,,	10 54 ,,	South Molton Road	12 51 ,,
6 27 ,,	Dorchester ...	3 34 ,,	8 29 ,,	Swanage ...	3 34 ,,
5 0 ,,	Exeter (Central)	12 51 ,,	8 15 ,,	Tavistock ...	12 51 ,,
7 12 ,,	Exmouth ...	12 51 ,,	7 30 ,,	Torrington ...	12 51 ,,
10 9 ,,	Eggesford ...	12 51 ,,	8 48 ,,	Wadebridge ...	12 51 ,,
7 55 ,,	Gillingham (Dorset)	2 58 ,,	6 42 ,,	Wareham ...	3 34 ,,
			5 30 ,,	Winchester ...	11 3p.m.*
4 20 ,,	Guildford ...	1 31 ,,	6 13 ,,	Weymouth ...	3 34 a.m.
8 32 ,,	Halwill ...	12 51 ,,	7 5 ,,	Yeovil ...	12 51 ,,

* Same night.

Arrival from London. (BRICKLAYERS' ARMS)	Stations.	Arrival in London. (BRICKLAYERS' ARMS)	Arrival from London. (BRICKLAYERS' ARMS)	Stations.	Arrival in London. (BRICKLAYERS' ARMS)
2 38 a.m.	Arundel ...	11 12p.m.*	6 40 a.m.	Herne Bay ...	5 40 a.m.
2 5 ,,	Ashford (Kent)	12 52 a.m.	12 31 ,,	Horsham ...	11 12p.m.*
3 30 ,,	Battle ...	5 40 ,,	2 22 ,,	Lewes ...	1 55 a.m.
5 55 ,,	Bexhill Central	1 55 ,,	6 25 ,,	Littlehamp'n	2 35 ,,
6 10 ,,	Bognor ...	2 35 ,,	6 12 ,,	Maidstone West	1 52 ,,
12 18 ,,	Brighton ...	12 16 ,,			
5 55 ,,	Broadstairs ...	5 40 ,,	5 0 ,,	Margate ...	12 52 ,,
4 12 ,,	Canterbury W.	12 52 ,,	6 30 ,,	Midhurst ...	11 12p.m.*
3 15 ,,	Chatham ...	2 35 ,,	6 20 ,,	Newhaven ...	1 55 a.m.
3 19 ,,	Chichester ...	2 35 ,,	3 13 ,,	Portsmouth & S'sea	2 35 ,,
7 30 ,,	Deal ...	12 52 ,,			
4 55 ,,	Dover ...	12 52 ,,	6 5 ,,	Ramsgate ...	12 52 ,,
4 25 ,,	Eastbourne ...	1 55 ,,	5 5 ,,	Red Hill ...	4 10 ,,
6 2 ,,	East Grinstead	12 16 ,,	4 38 ,,	Sevenoaks ...	1 55 ,,
3 45 ,,	Faversham ...	5 40 ,,	6 54 ,,	Shalford ...	11 55p.m.*
4 15 ,,	Folkestone ...	12 52 ,,	4 0 ,,	Sittingbourne	5 40 a.m.
6 45 ,,	Gravesend West Street...	5 40 ,,	9 35 ,,	Steyning ...	11 12p.m.*
			5 10 ,,	Tonbridge ...	5 40 a.m.
4 10 ,,	Hastings ...	4 40 ,,	2 20 ,,	Tunbridge Wells	5 40 ,,
1 26 ,,	Haywards Hth	12 16 ,,	3 58 ,,	Worthing ...	12 16 ,,

* Same night.

➤ *Greatly accelerated deliveries of Goods traffic, both "Small" and "Full Truck Load" Consignments, have been secured by revising a large number of services, together with a general speeding up in the running of various important freight services and any of the Area Representatives listed on page 36 will be glad to tell you of these in detail.*

Above:
Plate 5 A view of Feltham Yard from the clock tower looking towards London, *c*1939. Hounslow Heath is on the left with a Southern van just going over the Up hump. From left to right are the up-side brake-van road, 18 departure roads, the C&W repair depot, the down arrival roads (10) (just visible) and beyond that the 'Loco'. Feltham Junction 'box, controlling the London end of the yard, is out of sight, beyond the steam to the left of the C&W. In the foreground are the two cattle-dock roads and the line used to transfer traffic from the up side of the yard to the down side, with a South Western 'new van' bringing up the rear of a train of transfers. Under the coaling tower can be seen the Down hump with a train being propelled over it, the hump point box with two wagons just passing, and a shunter about to drop the brake on the first one. (There was not enough room to fit wagon retarders at Feltham.) Beyond is the down-side brake-van road and the throat of the 20 down-side departure roads.
F. Foote collection

Above left:
Plate 6 A freight heading for Feltham, this time from Reading. Again, the photograph was taken in the late 1930s. No freight from Reading was complete without its fitted head of 'Partos' — vans with specially fitted partitions to protect the Huntley & Palmer biscuits they carried. The 'H16s' were used a lot on these Reading jobs. *Authors' collection*

Left:
Plate 7 We could not resist this photograph, because in truth it portrays a very common sight, a Southern goods train without so far as we can see a single Southern wagon in it! The brake van is probably a Southern vehicle, but it must be said that SR wagons could be rare birds. The train is a loose-coupled load of coal from Feltham to Woking, seen approaching its destination in May 1947. The train has got about '30 on' — about all the driver of a 'Charlie' would want without a fitted head. *Ken Nunn collection*

Below:

Plate 8 Looking in the opposite direction from Plate 5 we see the west end of the yard and Feltham itself in the distance. The down hump is out of sight behind the photographer on the left. From the right are the two running lines (Waterloo-Windsor). Feltham East 'box, just visible in the far distance, controlled the country end of the yard and the entrance to the eight up reception roads. It must be around mid-morning, for there is only one train waiting to be humped on No 4. A train of transfers is being pulled off the country end of No 8, this being the only up reception road with a connection to the down side. Next is the line which connected the cattle docks etc to the down side of the yard. Over the grass are the 20 departure roads, and, although about nine trains are being made up, only one SR wagon can be seen. Next comes No 21 road, which connected the 'Loco' to the West end. Beyond that there are the eight 'grid' roads, provided for shunting wagons into train order, and, just visible in the top-left corner of the photograph, the beginnings of the seven 'Military sidings' used to store wagons awaiting orders.
F. Foote collection

SOUTHERN RAILWAY
MAP OF RAILHEAD DISTRIBUTION CENTRES

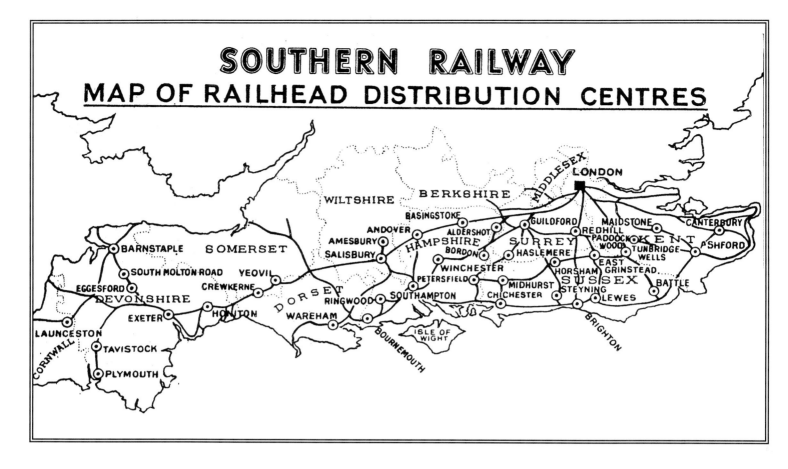

To help you to get the best from

SOUTHERN RAILWAY "SERVICE"

RAILHEAD DISTRIBUTION

YOU NEED NOT SEND TO THE STATION
The Station will send to you

THE Southern Railway has pleasure in distributing this booklet to traders, farmers, estate owners, etc., with a desire to bring to their notice the advantages to be obtained from using the modern S.R. freight services (see details on pages 12-15), and the Railhead Distribution scheme in force all over the districts served by the Southern Railway (see pages 10 and 11).

What exactly is Railhead Distribution? In a word it is this—A rail and road service, under which the Railway Company will collect and deliver all descriptions of goods from and to your premises, unpack consignments and place in shops, collect and repack empties, issue Credit Notes, deliver on to site if you are building, and provide storage accommodation where required. Under the scheme a trader can send his goods in full truck loads by express freight trains at low rates, to be stored for

a short or long period according to the circumstances, and then delivered to the local client by Southern Railway lorry as and when the sender instructs. In many cases a comprehensive charge is made to cover all the services provided, *i.e.*, collection, rail transit, handling and delivery.

The Southern Railway feels confident that once people realise that such a service exists at their doors, it will soon become an indispensable feature of modern country life, and prove of considerable benefit, especially to manufacturers and the whole agricultural community.

The Railhead Distribution scheme is essentially designed to deal with traffic consigned *in bulk* for delivery to a number of consignees. It gives a collection and delivery service from and to all places situated within a 10-mile radius of selected stations for full loads, such as grain, cake and meal for cattle and poultry feeding, fertilisers, etc., in sacks, but it is applicable to almost any kind of article or commodity, though a small additional charge is made in the case of Bricks and materials requiring extra handling, *e.g.* :—

The rate for the delivery of Oil Cake, Grain, etc., in sacks in 4-ton loads to a farm five miles distant from the Railhead Centre is 4s. 6d. per ton (see scale on page 8), but for the delivery of Bricks and other traffic conveyed loose, additional charges are made to cover the extra labour involved in loading and unloading, varying from 1s. 0d. per ton, according to circumstances.

Bulky, but relatively light articles, such as Reapers and Binders, Hay Mowers and other Agricultural Machines, are also delivered, for which quotations will be made on application to the local Station Master or Goods Agent.

To Estate Owners, Farmers and others, the scheme is far more economical than keeping a lorry for occasional use with its heavy annual charges for taxation, depreciation and insurance, and its steady cost in maintenance and labour.

SMALL CONSIGNMENTS.

A special scale of charges is applicable to small consignments (see page 8) and this will be found helpful when you have purchased a few drums of paint, sectional poultry houses or some wire fencing, etc., weighing, say, eight hundredweights—such consignments will come under this Scale and will be delivered up to 4 miles for four shillings.

Goods can be purchased in London, Liverpool or any other Provincial Centre, and delivery to your premises is assured. All you have to do is to arrange for your traffic to be consigned to the nearest Southern Railway Company's Railhead Distributing Station (see list on page 10), give the local Station Master or Goods Agent a standing order to deliver, and we will do the rest.

The outbreak of World War 2 in September 1939 found the Southern at the height of its success, and by this time there was probably no more efficient railway in the country. It was not long before the Southern found itself literally in the front line, but this actually had the effect of producing some spare capacity, and for a time the Southern was in a position to loan locomotives and rolling stock to the other companies. However, as the course of the war unfolded, this situation changed and, by the time the preparations were being made for 'D-day', the Southern freight services were in many areas stretched to the limit of their capacity. Feltham Yard alone was said to be handling 7,000 wagons a day on occasion — a lot of wagons, even by the standards of the large northern yards.

A few words about Southern freight working in general. The Southern, unlike the other three companies, did not have separate classes of goods train. The Signalling Bell codes did provide for fully fitted trains, but this description was used for parcel and van trains, not goods services. The Company's goods trains did not carry a separate tail lamp unless the train concerned was going to run over another company's lines. Normally Southern goods trains ran with two side lights only, and one of these served as the tail lamp to indicate that the train was complete. As any old Southern man will confirm, the Company never wasted a penny on anything that could be dispensed with, and that is being polite about it! The engine, of course, carried a route code in the same way as a passenger train. Double-heading of freight trains was almost unknown, as was banking, except where specially authorised, such as Exeter St David's-Exeter Central and New Cross Gate-Forest Hill.

Finally, a word about nomenclature. The advertising department liked the word 'freight', which was thought to be modern. The term was also widely used elsewhere, but it never entirely replaced 'goods', and both words appear in this book as appropriate.

Left:
Plate 9 Nine Elms-Southampton Docks on the down local between Walton and Woking in the mid-'Thirties. The first four vans next to the engine are all LNER banana vans on loan to the Southern. The engine, a rebuilt 'River', was common enough on the South Western, but a 4-6-0 would have been more usual for such a heavy train as this. *Authors' collection*

The CMEs and some of their Staff

The evolution of the Southern Railway's management structure was not an easy one, and it was not until the end of June 1923 that the Company was able to announce who its senior officers were to be, the Southern being the last of the 'Big Four' to do so. In the meantime the organisation of the three old companies continued (in theory, at least) until the end of that year.

Richard Maunsell became Chief Mechanical Engineer and established his office at Waterloo. He had two Assistants — G. H. Pearson, who was responsible for locomotive matters, and Surrey Warner, who was responsible for carriages, wagons and road vehicles. Pearson was one of Maunsell's old team at Ashford, and he remained there. Surrey Warner was the former LSWR C&W Superintendent and also remained in his old office, at Eastleigh. Albert Panter, the former LBSCR C&W Superintendent, was appointed as his assistant, but there is no further mention of him after 1924, so it would seem that for one reason or another he left the service.

Of the three senior C&W draughtsmen, Lionel Lynes at Ashford came up to Waterloo as one of a small Head Office team that Maunsell established there. There must have been some Drawing Office people left at Ashford, but the only subsequent wagon design work known to have been carried out there was in connection with a ramp wagon design built in 1940 for the Army.

Lynes' post was that of 'Chief C&W Draughtsman'. With that title, one might have expected him to have answered to Surrey Warner, but this does not seem to have been the case. It is known that Maunsell laid down strict lines of responsibility, ensuring that everyone understood their position, but it must have called for some tact on several people's part, for Surrey Warner had his own long-established and respected Chief Draughtsman at Eastleigh, Mr W. H. Beckley, whom most railwaymen would have considered senior to Lynes at the time of the Grouping; he had been longer in his post, was older and had served the larger railway. Mr Beckley's thoughts on this are not recorded, but he continued in charge of the C&W Drawing Office at Eastleigh until his retirement in the late 1930s.

If one might make an educated guess at Lynes' position, it would be that he laid down the principles of what was required, and the Drawing Office people then produced the detailed drawings. It is very unlikely that Lynes actually drew anything at this stage of his career.

Mr H. Thorpe was in charge of the Drawing Office at Lancing. He is first recorded as the Chief Draughtsman there in 1920, and he remained in that post until he retired c1949. In the Southern's early days his office did some new design work, but from about 1929 this was all concentrated at Eastleigh.

In May 1929 Surrey Warner retired and his post was abolished. There is no reason to believe that his position had ever been supernumerary; on the contrary, there was much to do in 1923, especially on the carriage side, but by 1929 the Southern had settled down, and saving money was the order of the day.

Maunsell retired in October 1937, being succeeded by Oliver Bulleid. It would be hard to imagine two CMEs with more different approaches to the job: Maunsell, strong on good management, delegation and proven design; Bulleid, happy to delegate the management side of his duties but keenly interested in design and development and full of new ideas. However, before very much could be done there were changes in the top team. Assistant CME G. H. Pearson retired in 1938, and in due course he was replaced by E. A. W. Turbett, formerly Works Manager at Eastleigh. Harold Holcroft became Technical Assistant (Locomotives), and Lionel Lynes now became Technical Assistant (C&W), a title which probably more accurately described his former position as well.

The changes must have been quite hard at first for Lynes, whom Maunsell had left alone to get on with the detailed decisions; now, in Bulleid, he had a chief with a great deal of C&W experience and who wanted to get personally involved. In the event the two men seem to have worked very well together, and in due course they jointly took out at least one patent concerning the design of wagon underframes, of which more anon. Bulleid left the Southern Region (as it had become) in September 1949 for the CIE in Ireland, and Lynes retired not long after.

All those mentioned so far were very senior, but it is only proper to recall the majority of the C&W workforce. In 1947 the main works employed roundly 3,600 people and the 'outdoor' organisation another 1,000. These were the men and women who kept the wheels rolling on a daily basis. For some it was a very responsible job, often carried out in dangerous and unpleasant circumstances; for others it was a matter of skill and knowledge; for most it was simply hard and frequently dirty work. All deserve to be remembered with respect.

The Workshops

One of the benefits expected of the Grouping was that the new companies would be able to save considerable sums of money from the rationalisation of duplicate facilities.

The workshops were amongst the most expensive of the railways' overheads, and Maunsell lost no time in looking to see what savings could be made on the Southern. Eastleigh C&W Works had been built some 30 years previously but was well laid out and fully utilised. The oldest buildings at Lancing were only 12 years old and were also operating efficiently and to capacity. Ashford, of course, he knew all about: some of the buildings were very old, but, on average, most of the C&W buildings were quite new and again fully utilised. On the Isle of Wight there were two small works — one at Newport and the other at Ryde; both were very cramped and were overworked due to the age and variety of the rolling stock.

However, savings there had to be, and on 31 October 1923 Maunsell came up with recommendations that were accepted by the Board. These were that Eastleigh build approximately two thirds of all new carriage bodies, whilst continuing to maintain all the former South Western C&W stock. Lancing would build the remaining new carriage bodies and all new carriage underframes, and in addition would continue to maintain all the former Brighton C&W stock. Ashford would build all new standard goods stock whilst continuing to maintain all the former South Eastern C&W stock. On the Isle of Wight, Newport would be converted into a paint shop, whilst all the repair work would be concentrated at Ryde; the overall workload would be reduced by the introduction of standardised rolling stock.

Wagon matters were to remain largely unchanged for the next five or six years, but it was soon decided that Eastleigh should build all new carriage bodies, and Lancing completed its last 'all built' coach in October 1925. However, it cannot have been long after this that it was realised that substantial savings would be made if all the Company's carriages could be repaired at one

central location. Lancing was the works most suited to the task and in December 1928 began what was known there as the 'Progressive Carriage Repair Scheme'. This was based on a similar scheme introduced at Crewe some two years before and entailed moving the carriages progressively around the shop as the work proceeded. To provide enough space for this, Lancing's wagon-repair work was transferred to Ashford, but this too was no doubt seen at Waterloo as advantageous.

When Lancing repaired its last wagon is not known, but former LSWR open goods No 7439 was renumbered there in July 1929, so it would seem there was some reluctance to lose this work. It is interesting to note the presence of a South Western wagon at Lancing, but in practice it had not been unusual for all three works to repair stock from another section when it was convenient to do so.

Eastleigh continued to repair South Western stock, including some carriages, but the withdrawal of older vehicles saw its traditional workload begin to tail off. To compensate, it was decided that Eastleigh should build and repair the Southern's new containers, and this it continued to do into BR days.

As intended, Ashford built the vast majority of all the new standard wagons, the only major exception being 1,500 open goods wagons built by outside contractors in 1926/7.

Normally the Southern only went outside for non-standard vehicles that it adjudged cheaper and less trouble to purchase. The reason for purchasing the opens seems to have been two-fold — firstly a need to replace a large number of obsolete wagons and secondly a desire to take advantage of the very low prices available from the trade at that time. One tender in 1926 attracted no fewer than 19 quotations. Placing work outside also helped to put pressure on the railway's own works to keep their costs down. One way of doing this was to utilise sound recovered material — especially wheelsets — from withdrawn stock, and the Drawing Office at Eastleigh came up with a whole range of designs that took advantage of this long-established practice. These wagons were officially known as 'Rebuilds', but among the men in the works they were known as 'Shareholders wagons', as these were the people this policy was designed to keep happy. One of these designs, Diagram 1400, even went so far as to provide for the replacement of the 'last turned' wheels it was built with, and this replacement work started before some of these wagons were more than two years old!

Of interest are a few examples of actual costs (approximate 2002 prices in brackets). A 1927 contractor-built 12-ton open cost £169 (£4,536), an 8-ton bogie open for the L&B line £196 (£5,260), ditto covered £230 (£6,173) and a contractor-built 20-ton ballast wagon £189 (£5,073); at the top end of the scale, a 40-ton bogie 'Crocodile' cost £700 (£18,788).

Whilst Ashford built the standard Railway Clearing House (RCH) wagons, Lancing constructed most of the goods brake vans. Lancing also built many other non-standard vehicles, such as machinery and well wagons, tank cars and 'Warwells' for the Ministry of Supply, and a whole range of special wagons in BR days.

Eastleigh did not normally build wagons unless they were of LSWR design, such as stone trucks or bogie bolsters etc. It did, however, build bodies for underframes provided by Ashford, and it also carried out special rebuilding projects such as the ferry-train wagons and the first bogie goods brakes.

Before leaving the workshops, mention must be made of their contribution to the war effort. All the Southern workshops were called upon to produce all manner of items, from landing barges to the tails of Horsa gliders, but Ashford, despite its proximity to the enemy in France, was one of the works selected to continue with the construction of goods rolling stock. Ashford's normal peacetime production was about 1,000 wagons a year, but through increased efficiency and overtime this was more than doubled, and in the six years 1940-5 it produced roundly 14,000 wagons. In this time the works built wagons for all four main-line companies and the Ministry of Supply.

Policy & Records

Each spring a committee known as the Rolling Stock Committee met at Waterloo under the chairmanship of the General Manager to review the current rolling-stock position and to propose the next year's production, which in theory commenced on the first day of the new year. This review covered the whole range of rolling stock, including locomotives and road vehicles. The CME was always present, as were various other interested senior officers and other key people such as the Chief Rolling Stock Clerk.

The actual proposals put before the Rolling Stock Committee would have been worked out beforehand in accordance with what was required for new traffic and to replace obsolete stock. The extent of any discussion that may have taken place is not known, because the Minutes record only the decisions. Proposals for the Engineer's rolling stock were dealt with separately by the Engineering & Estates Committee. The combined requirement then went before the Directors' Rolling Stock Sub Committee for approval. There does not seem to have been any occasion when this final approval was not given, but there are several instances of later amendments, so despite the system's apparent formality it obviously had some flexibility and provides a good example of the complete trust the Directors had in their General Manager.

As soon as the Directors had approved what was proposed, the CME allocated the jobs to the appropriate works and issued what were known as Head Office Works Orders. These orders were numbered sequentially and were not confined to rolling stock, including as they did such items as furniture or, indeed, anything that a railway works could manufacture.

When a wagon was built its details were recorded in the Wagon Registers with the Works Order number recorded alongside the relevant entry. The Southern did not use Lot numbers. Each works kept its own copy of the Wagon Registers, and a master copy was kept in the HQ Rolling Stock Office. The information was exchanged between all parties by correspondence, and, as might be expected, there were a number of small discrepancies between the copies, mainly concerning dates.

The Designs

What was destined to become the Southern's first standard wagon design was a 20-ton machinery wagon. This had been designed by Lynes whilst he was still at Ashford but none was built until 1923. It was a straightforward, modern vehicle, and

further batches were built in 1928 and 1942.

It was to be three years before the first Southern Railway-designed wagon appeared. In the meantime, Maunsell was content to continue building various pre-Grouping designs as required. This made good sense, for the three works all had orders outstanding at the time of Grouping, the designs being built were all satisfactory and everyone knew what they were doing. The Brighton opens were a little dated, but in this case there were a large number of non-standard wheelsets to use up, and it all helped to keep the costs down at a time when every penny was needed for electrification schemes.

In 1923 the RCH had issued new specifications for the design of wagons, and the Southern's new standard wagons were built in accordance with these. The first appeared in January 1926 as a part of two orders placed with contractors in June 1925 for a total of 500 12-ton, eight-plank open goods.

It would seem that the Commercial Department was very keen to carry on with high-sided wagons similar to those built by the SECR and LSWR. The former had a capacity of 500cu ft on an underframe 17ft long, with seven-plank sides; the latter were somewhat bigger, with a capacity of 625cu ft on an underframe 18ft long, with eight-plank sides. The new standard underframe was 17ft 6in long, and it was decided that it should have eight-plank sides, giving an official capacity of 593cu ft. It was designed at Eastleigh, and, although it had some resemblance to both the previous designs, cannot really be considered as a direct development of either. The Rolling Stock Office gave the new design a Diagram number following on from the SECR version, but it is thought the Chief Clerk there was a former South Eastern man who, with Lynes 'in charge', assumed them to be a development of the SECR design. Waterloo referred to these wagons as the 'Standard 12-ton RCH open wagon', although it is doubtful whether the other 'Big Four' companies regarded it as such.

The theory was that the new design should serve as a general-purpose wagon as had its round-ended predecessors, and to emphasise this the *Southern Railway Magazine* dutifully noted how useful they were for the Kent coal trade. The problem was that most of these wagons were 'common user' and as such tended to leave the Southern system to be replaced by other railways' nominal five-planks, so their usefulness to the Southern was largely lost. It is difficult to understand why this situation was allowed to continue, but the Southern remained faithful to the type until their construction was stopped in 1939 with the outbreak of war.

Right:
Plate 10 The Southern did not generally favour the use of shunting trucks, but this is a nice photograph of one of the two provided for passenger shunting at Clapham Junction. Notice the three-link couplings on the hook. Clapham Junction was the only location on the Southern Railway where the loose shunting of passenger stock was permitted. *F. M. Gates*

The next standard design did not appear until March 1927. This was a 25-ton goods brake van, and, although it had a new underframe, it was definitely a development of Lynes' SECR design. Also new in 1927 were two designs — a bogie open and a bogie van — for the L&B line. A third was for a 40-ton bogie 'Crocodile' well wagon.

On the evening of 24 August 1927, 'River' class tank No A800 became derailed near Sevenoaks, with the loss of 13 lives. That the 'River' class tanks were rebuilt as 'U' class Moguls is well known, the effect of the accident on the Southern Railway's permanent way rather less so. It was decided that all main lines on the South Eastern and Central sections would be re-ballasted using stone from Meldon Quarry in Devon, this being the only source of good-quality track ballast on the railway. To carry this stone a number of new wagons would be required, and, in order that they could be worked over the West of England main line without delay to the passenger services, it was essential that they should be suitable for running at some speed and be fitted with an automatic brake. All these new wagons were built by contractors, and the first arrived on the Southern in June 1928. The design was a 20-ton five-plank open, built on the 21ft 6in version of the standard RCH underframe — the first time the Southern had used this.

Four months later there appeared the first of a new design of 40-ton vacuum-braked bogie ballast hopper. These followed the general concept of the LSWR design described in Volume One but differed considerably in detail. The design was to prove very successful, and there were to be several developments, culminating in the BR 'Sealion' and 'Seacow' wagons. When one of your authors was asked to write the specification for these in 1970, he based it on the 1947 Southern design because it represented almost exactly what was wanted, and because nothing better had been developed in the meantime. To complement the 1927 hoppers, Lynes updated his 1914-designed ballast plough brake, but these did not appear until 1932.

It seems that someone with influence did not like the design of the 1927-built goods brakes, complaining that the body was unnecessarily large for the accommodation of one man and that it lacked side duckets, enabling the guard to observe his train from within the protection of the van. As a result, Lancing was asked to redesign the body, and the result was the well-known 'Pill box', the first of which appeared in April 1928. Unfortunately the new body went from the sublime to the ridiculous, and it used to be said that it was full with a wet raincoat in it! It nevertheless had a very good brake, and with various modifications this design continued in production until 1948.

Also new in 1928 were six refrigerator vans designed and built at Eastleigh. They featured the new standard 17ft 6in underframe; the bodies were not unlike their South Western predecessors, although they differed in external appearance.

The next design appeared in May 1929, and this was another of those prepared at Lancing. This was the 12-ton covered goods van, featuring the 'Lynes roof'. As noted in the previous volume, this roof was prone to leak, so it is worth quoting Lynes himself on the subject. 'It is the general practice in this country, but not abroad, to build covered wagons with camber roofs. The slight curving of such a large surface as a roof imparts but little to its resistance to flexing. Undue flexing tends towards the early breaking down of the roof canvas or other similar medium, when the wagon is running. When the shape of the roof is elliptic these disadvantages do not apply equally. Incidentally, a better use of the load gauge arises with this form of design, which is certainly less dated.' (This also implies that Lionel Lynes took his holidays in Switzerland — the only country to make common use of an elliptic roof for its goods stock!) The design went through many variations in detail, and in the war years it was built for both the LMS and the GWR, the latter well aware that Lynes was originally trained at Swindon.

It was not until April 1930 that a Southern-designed cattle van appeared, but this was little more than the previous Lynes SECR timber-framed design adapted to a new steel underframe. Also in 1930 came a small batch of 10-ton open goods, the only 'Standard five-plank opens' built by the Southern in Maunsell's time.

In January 1931 a van for fresh meat was introduced. This had the 'Lynes roof', but the following month an insulated van appeared with a body based upon the 1928 refrigerator van; this had a single-radius roof.

New designs were now appearing at fairly frequent intervals. No fewer than four versions of container wagon were introduced in 1932, and these were followed in 1933 by 12- and 20-ton minerals. These wagons were built for the Kent coal trade and were seldom found very far from that area.

A noteworthy event in 1933 was the introduction of the first of the Southern's well-known bogie 'Express goods brake vans'. These were rebuilds of redundant 'AC' electric motor luggage vans. They quickly became very popular with the goods guards, and a new-build version followed shortly after.

In 1935 a decision was made to lengthen the wheelbase of the standard RCH 17ft 6in underframe (from 9ft to 10ft) to make it more suitable for the higher speeds that were now being run by the newly introduced express-goods trains. The open-goods, covered-goods and container-truck designs were all amended accordingly. The first new SR design to incorporate this development was a banana van introduced in August 1935. The body of this again had much in common with the previous refrigerator and insulated designs but had horizontal (instead of vertical) planking. Also introduced to traffic in 1935 were a number of standard 9ft-wheelbase open and covered goods that were converted for use on the Dover-Dunkirk train-ferry service. There was also a new 21ft 6in open goods wagon for this service developed from the 20-ton mineral design.

It would seem that things were now slowing up a little in the Drawing Office, and it was not until January 1937 that the next new design appeared. This was a 64ft, 40-ton-capacity bogie rail wagon, required to carry the newly standardised 60ft rails. The requirement for normal bolster wagons on the Southern fell rapidly, and the only other bolster wagons the Company needed to build were the dual-purpose South Western design or 'Bertram Mills' wagons, as they were later known. Another new design for the Civil Engineer to appear in 1937 was a 15-ton, four-plank version of the 1928 20-ton design. These wagons lacked the vacuum brakes of the earlier design — a retrograde step it is difficult now to understand. Also in 1937 there arose an urgent requirement for a further 125 banana vans, and this was met by adapting the standard covered goods design. That October, O. V. S. Bulleid took over as CME, and from this point onwards one can detect his hand in C&W design matters.

Although World War 2 did not start until September 1939, it had been apparent for some time that such an event was likely. One of the precautions the railway industry took at this time was to consider the effect that a war would have on the supply of timber, and how the best use could be made of such supplies as might be available. At the end of 1938 various types of Southern van began to appear with alternate pairs of normal and narrow planks. This arrangement allowed the use of smaller sections of wood that would otherwise have been too small for C&W work. It has proved impossible to find any official reference to this feature, but we elieve it to be an example of the aforementioned prewar planning.

Elsewhere, others had been busy in the field of wagon design, and in 1939 a new version of the standard RCH underframe appeared. This differed from the earlier versions in that continuous drawgear was abandoned in favour of a non-continuous design. Lynes' standard SECR 1915 design had non-continuous drawgear but had a long drawbar pulling on a middle cross-bearer in the GWR manner, whereas the new design pulled on the headstocks. The underframe itself was strengthened to take this load by additional longitudinal members at each end. Almost certainly a committee sat at the RCH to consider this important change, and almost certainly Lynes would have represented the Southern on that committee.

Right:
Plate 11 The standard RCH axle-guard as used for most 12-ton and some 10-ton wagons. *Authors' collection*

One development the war did not stop was the building of the Southern's first shock-absorbing open goods wagons. This class of wagon was first introduced on the LMS in 1937, and the Southern was a little late in catching up on this development. For the time being, the SR could build only 12 of these wagons, but 38 more followed in 1949, and later Ashford was to build large numbers for BR, to a modified Southern Railway design.

In 1944 the Southern collaborated with the English Steel Corporation in the design and construction of 11 20-ton well wagons. This was a novel design in the best Bulleid tradition, with the object of saving weight. This it did, and, although construction was somewhat complicated, the overall result was a very successful wagon.

Bulleid's next experiment, carried out with the whole-hearted assistance of Lynes, was even more innovative and involved nothing less than challenging the whole concept of the standard RCH underframe, which they considered to be both too heavy and lacking in strength; to address these problems they together designed and patented a version of a triangulated underframe. Such underframes featured in three wagons built for the Southern — an open goods that went into traffic for a while and two experimental wagons that never did, all three ending up as 'internal' departmentals. The design was too radical for BR, but Bulleid took it with him to Ireland where the CIE was not troubled by existing standards. Whether or not it was a success in the long term it is difficult to say.

A much more normal design introduced in 1945 was a very standard 13-ton, eight-plank mineral. Only 100 were built for the Southern, but no fewer than 1,850 followed for the LNER; the latter built some very similar wagons, and this may actually have been an LNER design.

The last three Southern designs were all built in BR days. First, in 1949, came two very similar 'all-dropside' open goods — quite unlike anything that had gone before, but then Bulleid was in charge! The first was a three-plank, but the second had five-plank sides and, even with the door springs provided, these proved too heavy for any reasonable number of men to lift. Bulleid may well have had the big doors of the LNER brick wagons in mind when he passed this feature, but, either way, the Traffic Department refused to accept them, and they were 'loaned' to the CCE, where they were no more happily received.

Bulleid's final design also suffered from heavy sides — so heavy, in fact, that they required a crane to lift them. This design was a 20-ton steel-sided ballast wagon built on underframes recovered from 20-ton minerals. They were actually designed to work with a small mobile crane inside them, but in later years they entered general use; their sides made them very unpopular, and eventually many of them were rebuilt with new fixed sides.

Details

Wheels
Both solid and split-spoke wheels were used for new wagons until the 1930s, whereafter disc with three holes were more common. Goods brake vans were always fitted with disc wheels, some of which had very small holes; such wheels looked very similar to those used on other vehicles but were in fact specially manufactured in order to withstand the heat generated by prolonged braking.

Axleboxes
The normal, divided RCH axlebox was standard for most types. The 'Rebuilds' usually retained their original 'boxes, but their bearing pads could be fitted into the RCH 'box so one sometimes found that used. Wagons designed in pre-Grouping days were built with their original design of 'box but with the letters 'SR' cast on them. In Bulleid's time the LNER open-front fabricated type was much used.

Brakes
Hand brakes: the first 2,000 12-ton opens had the normal Morton arrangement, but thereafter two independent sets of brakes were used — an arrangement the Southern called the 'Freighter brake'.

The Southern used three different types of vacuum-brake arrangement The first seems to have been reserved for those wagons expected to spend much of their time running in fast fitted trains. This used eight brake blocks arranged in clasp mode, with the brake cylinder on the wagon centre line. One cylinder was used, and this might be either a 15in or 18in model. The second design used four brake blocks and a lift link, as per SECR and LSWR practice; one cylinder was normally used, but some of the covered goods and the brake vans built for the Army had two, again either 15 or 18in models. As far as is known, the Southern was the only railway to use two cylinders on a four-wheel vehicle.

Both the previous arrangements were unique to the Southern. The third used four brake blocks and a Morton clutch with a single 18in cylinder. This design was used latterly by the Southern, but BR used it a great deal for fitting wagons in the 1950s. A point modellers may find helpful: brakes with a cross-shaft normally push on the wheels at an angle of 90° to the shaft; those without a shaft push at right angles to the wheel tread. (Wheel treads are turned to an angle of 1 in 20.)

Buffers
Standard RCH 18in buffers were used for unfitted wagons. Early fitted wagons used these mounted on a 2½in wooden packing piece; later a design with a 2½in-longer guide was

Left:
Plate 12 The SR lift-link brake as used on most fitted wagons with four brake blocks. *Authors' collection*

Right:
Plate 13 The SR brake arrangement as used on most fitted wagons with eight brake blocks. *Authors' collection*

Left:
Plate 14 The SECR standard self-contained buffer used by the SR for several types of wagon and the goods brake vans. *A. Blackburn*

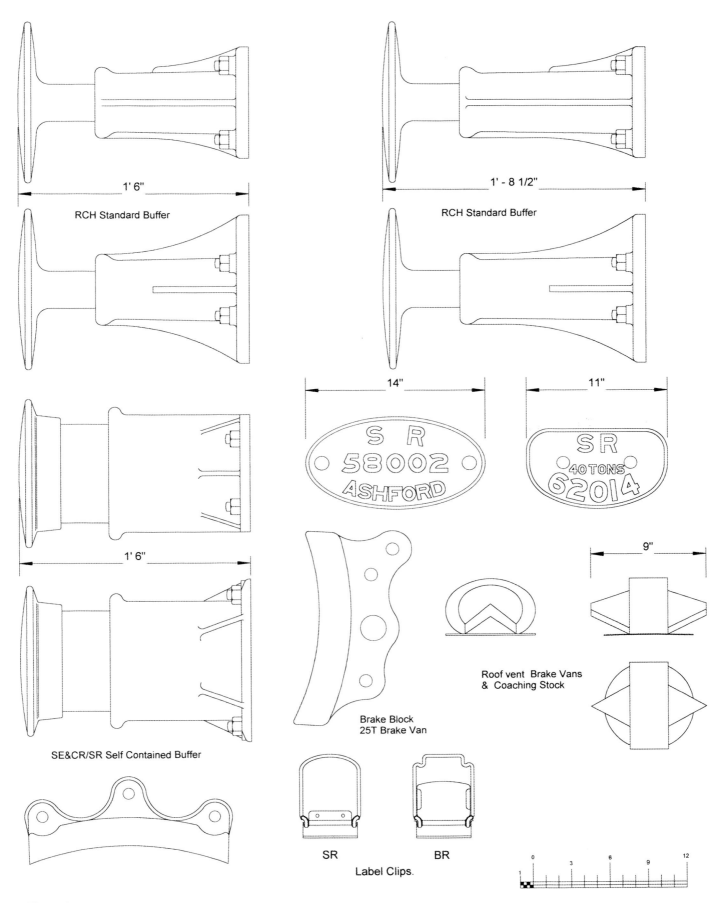

1' 6"

RCH Standard Buffer

1' - 8 1/2"

RCH Standard Buffer

1' 6"

SE&CR/SR Self Contained Buffer

14"

S R 58002 ASHFORD

11"

SR 40 TONS 62014

Brake Block
25T Brake Van

9"

Roof vent Brake Vans
& Coaching Stock

SR   BR

Label Clips.

Figure 1

used. As an exception to this, the fitted ballast wagons had 18in buffers. Some Borails had fabricated buffer guides. Brake vans, machinery wagons, ballast hoppers and 'Borails' were provided with self-contained buffers, some of SECR design, others SR.

Couplings
These were standard RCH three-link for unfitted wagons, screw for the fitted ones. Instanter couplings were not used by the Southern, although BR employed them extensively on the SR wagons it fitted.

Bogies
Up until 1946 the Southern used the diamond-frame design used by the LSWR. In that year Bulleid introduced the Association of American Railroads (AAR) three-part cast-steel bogie; at the time, this was referred to in the press as being of the 'Coil Elliptic' double-truss type. Built in England by the English Steel Corporation, presumably under licence, this design was widely used in the USA; in terms of reliability, it was far in advance of anything used in Britain at the time and, indeed, remained so until the Gloucester design of the 1970s. In a perfect world it should without doubt have become the BR standard freight bogie, but the 1950s were not noted for advances in British wagon design.

Bodywork
In Maunsell's time the capping strips, used to protect the top planks of open wagons, were secured by long counter-sunk bolts that passed right through the top plank to its bottom, access to the nut being by way of a notch cut out of the wood on the inside. The opens built during the war with thin sheeting generally lacked capping on the sides, but it was normally fitted to the top of the doors and the ends, and this was normally secured by the more common 'U'-clip arrangement. At least one batch of Bulleid opens seem to have had capping all round, secured by wood screws. It is thought that most of the opens built with 1⅜in-thick hardwood sheeting had this replaced with the normal 2½in softwood in later years.

Also in Maunsell's time, the side and end planks of open wagons did not overlap one another but ended against a vertical corner post. This allowed individual planks to be removed for replacement without interfering with any others. On some of Bulleid's opens, the three middle boards of the five planks were secured by internal steel strips rather than the conventional bolts. This might have been a good idea for the side planks but was found not to suit the ends, as these could be burst open for lack of sufficient fastening. A similar idea was to retain the floorboards by an external light metal strip; this proved a success and was later adopted generally for both new stock and repair work.

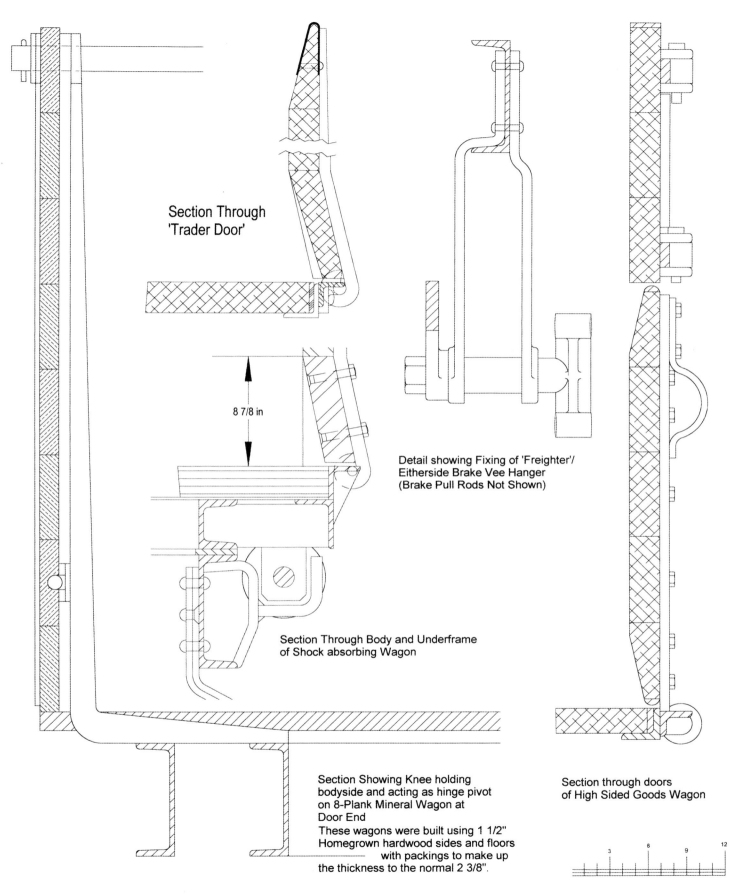

Section Through
'Trader Door'

8 7/8 in

Detail showing Fixing of 'Freighter'/
Eitherside Brake Vee Hanger
(Brake Pull Rods Not Shown)

Section Through Body and Underframe
of Shock absorbing Wagon

Section Showing Knee holding
bodyside and acting as hinge pivot
on 8-Plank Mineral Wagon at
Door End
These wagons were built using 1 1/2"
Homegrown hardwood sides and floors
          with packings to make up
the thickness to the normal 2 3/8".

Section through doors
of High Sided Goods Wagon

3   6   9   12

Figure 2

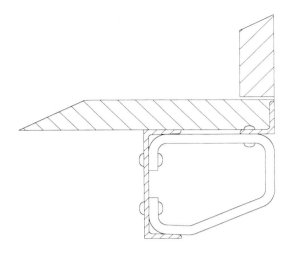

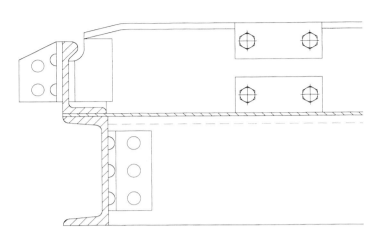

Detail showing Solebar Bracket Supporting Curb Rail
SR Open Goods Wagons & Covered Goods Vans

Section Through Solebar & Bodyside rail
of 40 Ton Bogie Rail Wagon

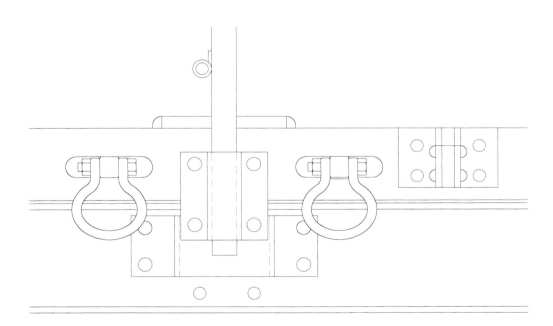

View showing Detail around Stanchion Pocket
on 40 Ton Bogie Rail Wagon

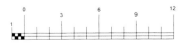

Figure 3

Chapter 2.
Liveries, Diagrams and Numbering

Liveries

The basic colours chosen for the Southern Railway's wagons were the same as those used by the LSWR, namely dark brown for the great majority of vehicles, buff (or 'stone', as it was described) for insulated vans etc and red oxide for the ballast wagons. There does not seem to be any record as to how or when this decision about the livery was made, but it has been said that Lancing used up supplies of the LBSCR carriage umber (brown) on wagon work. The actual specification for making up the brown does not seem to have survived, but the official name for the colour was 'Goods stock umber'; this leads to speculation that it was based on Brighton umber, rather than the South Western colour. (Wondering what the Brighton umber looked like, one of your authors asked this of the Lancing paintshop foreman in the 1950s and was told, without hesitation, 'Same as Pullman umber'.) However it was, the two colours seem to have been very similar. Like all paints at that time, it was mixed from the basic ingredients as required, and, in order to ensure that the finished product agreed with what was required, colour sample boards were issued for guidance.

It has been said that Ashford's version of the brown colour varied from that used elsewhere, but there seems no reason to dwell too much on that; given the method of production, it was perhaps inevitable that there would be the occasional variation. Basically the colour was a dark 'plain chocolate' brown, without any trace of red in it, but weathered over the years to a lighter shade.

More interesting is the style of lettering used and its layout. A Brighton open was repainted at New Cross Gate as early as 16 January 1923 with the letters 'SR' on it (see Plate 26 of Volume Two), so this basic point must have been settled at a very early date. These things are not done without authority and take time to implement, so it would be very interesting to

know when this decision was made and by whom. Company initials aside, the wagon in question was lettered and numbered in the normal Brighton manner. The standard Southern layout, when it appeared, closely followed the later SECR style, but the relevant drawing was actually produced at Lancing, a point that in itself is not without interest.

To deal with matters of detail, we will first describe the manner in which the majority of the wagons were painted, and then deal with the exceptions.

The body, headstocks and solebars were painted brown. All running-gear, wheels, draw- and buffing-gear were black, although sometimes the buffer guides were brown, especially when repainted. Roofs were initially white, later grey. The insides of new open wagons in prewar days were painted 'lead colour', but the insides of wagons were not painted upon general repair. During and immediately after the war, the painting of the bodywork of open goods and mineral wagons was discontinued, and it was noted at the time that the unpainted woodwork had a not unpleasant yellow hue. The ironwork of these wagons was painted black. Nothing has been recorded about the painting of the other new stock at this time, but from photographs it would seem that they were painted brown etc as normal. There are one or two prewar reports of Southern wagons painted grey; there is no obvious explanation for this, other than the possibility that some component of the original colour was unsound, leading to serious discolouration. (Something similar occurred in the 1970s, when some BR departmentals painted olive green turned a light brown colour.)

The lettering was in white. There was a wide range of sizes available to suit various kinds of wagon (see Fig 4), but the normal 1923 standard called for the letters 'S' and 'R' to be painted 18in high, one either side of the door, halfway (or just over halfway) up the side of the wagon. The number and wagon capacity were painted in characters 5in high — the

Right:
Plate 17 The standard SR wagon livery as used from 1923 to 1936. The exact position of the writing was left to the painter and depended on the location of various obstructions such as bolts and cleats etc.

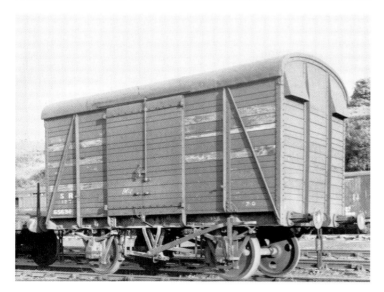

Above:
Plate 18 A view taken at Dover *c*1937, showing well the differences between the original and the '1936' style. The vehicle on the end is one of the two reach trucks built for use in loading and unloading the train ferry. *A. B. MacLeod*

Left:
Plate 19 Covered goods No 48916 (Diagram 1458) built in March 1937, showing the '1936' writing as applied to a van. *R. Chorley collection*

Lower left:
Plate 20 Covered goods No 65636 (Diagram 1455) built in 1943 and showing the '1942' writing. *Authors' collection*

number on the bottom plank at the left- hand end of the wagon, the capacity normally at the same level towards the right-hand end, with the tare weight underneath it in 2½ in characters on the floor or crib rail. If there was no crib rail, as in the case of the very numerous 'eight-planks', the capacity was normally moved up a plank.

An RCH numberplate was bolted to the solebar, and this carried the Company's initials, the carrying capacity, the number and sometimes the name of the works that built the wagon (or, perhaps more accurately in some cases, the works that had built the underframe). The numberplates were painted black with white letters. Pre-Grouping stock had their numberplates reversed and the new SR number painted centrally on the back, with the letters E, A, B or D under the number to indicate their origin, all the characters being 2½ in high. There was quite a lot of writing etc on the solebar. Towards the left-hand end appeared the paint date in ¾ in block figures. If vacuum brakes were provided, a 3in star was painted over the release cord. Towards the right-hand end appeared 'DATE OILED AND DISTRICT' in 1in and ¾ in letters, together with a 5in x 4in black patch for chalking on the actual date. At the extreme right-hand end came the depot reference number and 'floating' date in 1in figures. Wagons which were not included in the national 'common user' pool were denoted by the letter 'N', which was painted 4in-high on each end of the wagon side, towards the bottom of the body, very often on the corner plates.

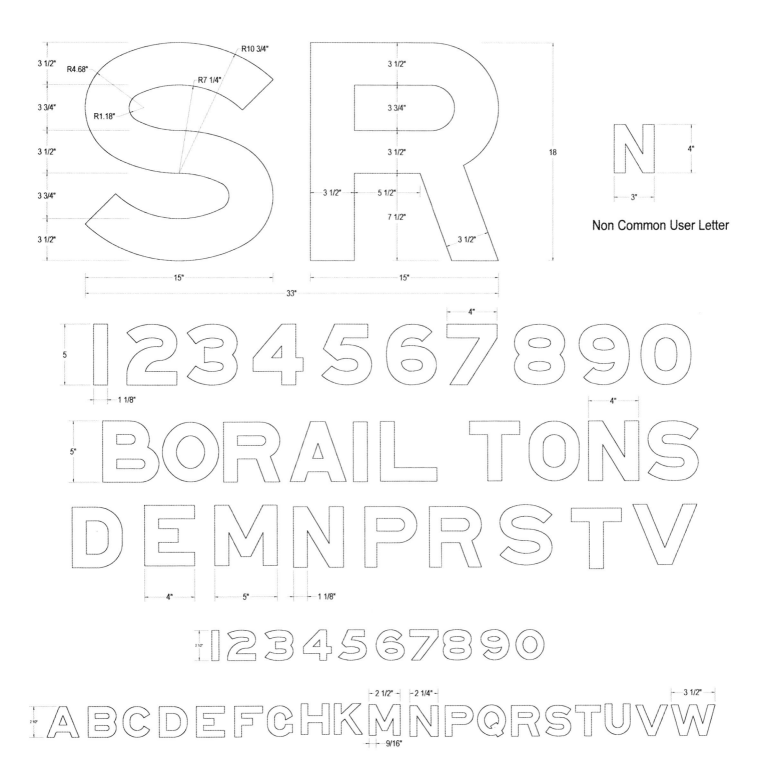

Figure 4

In 1936, in agreement with the other companies, the Southern decided to standardise and simplify wagon lettering. All characters were reduced in size — the Company's initials and wagon number to 4in, the carrying capacity and tare to 3in. The layout was also completely rearranged: at the left-hand end of the wagon, towards the bottom, were arranged, in descending order, Company initials, carrying capacity and number; at the right-hand end, level with the number, was the tare weight.

In 1939 it was decided to uprate the carrying capacity of all standard 12- and 20-ton wagons by one ton as a wartime move to increase the total wagon capacity; no alterations were made to the wagons other than alteration of the figures, but a careful note was made of those vehicles dealt with and this was reflected in the annual rolling-stock returns, for details of which see Appendix 4.

In 1942, as part of wartime economies, the size of the lettering was again reduced — the Company's initials and the

FOR S.R.
LOCO COAL
ONLY

Board used on
20 Ton Mineral wagon

1936 Style Lettering

SR

ED

15 T

63001

TARE 8.19.0

Alterative Early Style for Tare

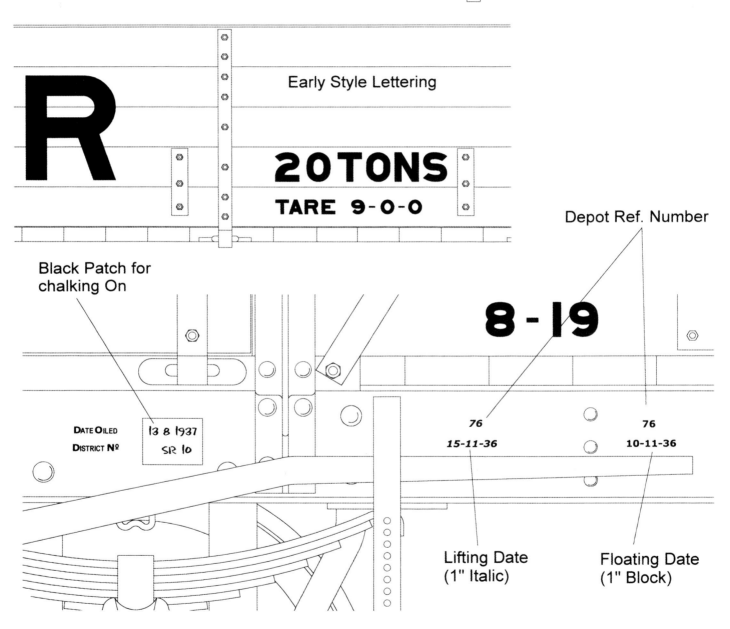

Early Style Lettering

R

20 TONS

TARE 9-0-0

Depot Ref. Number

8-19

Black Patch for
chalking On

Date Oiled — 13 8 1937

District Nº — SR 10

76

15-11-36

76

10-11-36

Lifting Date
(1" Italic)

Floating Date
(1" Block)

Figure 5

wagon number to 3in, the tonnage and tare to 2in, all now to be painted on a black patch to make them more visible.

Brake vans

These were painted in the same way as most vehicles, except that the headstocks, veranda ends and the inner body ends were painted Venetian red. The buffer guides were usually red, but some were black. The lids of the sandboxes on the bogie brake vans had the word 'SAND' painted on them 1¾in high, and this feature may have been found on the similar four-wheeled vehicles. The interior of the guard's compartment was painted purple brown up to 3ft 2in above floor level and stone above, with a 1½in black band between the two colours.

Refrigerator, Insulated, Meat and Banana vans

The body and headstocks of these were stone (buff) and the lettering Venetian red, except the 'N' letters, which were white. Solebars were officially brown, but there are several reports of them painted black, so possibly both colours were used; after a period in traffic, the difference would be academic. In 1941 it was decided to change the main body colour to red oxide, with lemon lettering, but, on the basis that a wagon is normally given a heavy overhaul every seven years, it is doubtful whether all were repainted thus.

The seven-year overhaul period was probably adhered to fairly closely before the war. Thus one might conclude that any wagon built before, say, 1932 was probably repainted properly in the 1936 style, whilst those built later would have fallen due for overhaul during the war years, when probably only the essentials were dealt with.

Engineer's Department stock

Livery was similar to that of most vehicles, except that the brown colour was normally replaced by red oxide and that the letters 'ED', 5in high, were painted above the number, usually above the first two or three characters but sometimes in the middle. There is little doubt that all the ballast hoppers were originally painted red oxide, but some of the older ones were certainly painted brown at the time of their withdrawal, and

some of the newer ones may also have been brown before they were repainted black by BR. The 1947 Ashford-built hoppers were definitely red, not brown as might be surmised from certain photographs.

During the war, grey was used for some service stock, including the first of the 'utility van' conversions and the wartime-built cranes. When freshly applied it was a medium shade of grey, but it quickly weathered to a very light colour that was nothing like the original.

Containers

Generally these were painted in a similar way to the wagons: the ordinary open and closed types were brown with white lettering, the insulated types stone with Venetian red letters. There were, however, exceptions to this. Furniture containers Nos K590-639 and B791-855 were painted in what was described as 'sea green' — basically a light green, with the zig-zag motif adopted by the 'Big Four' for their household-removal promotion. The colour of the lettering was complicated: the Company initials, lesser lettering and the zig-zag were 'standard green' (presumably the standard carriage colour) and the legend on the panel was officially Portland stone (noted as yellow), with a ¼in outline in orange. Fresh meat containers Nos M640-59 were painted in a silver colour when new, again with 'standard green' lettering. (These were the containers Hornby made a model of, and its portrayal of the livery was really very good — as, indeed, was its version of SR wagon brown, although this could vary.)

Wagon sheets

Very little is known about this subject, the drawings being based on the standard RCH layout. The big question is: 'What colour were they?' As a youngster your writer remembers that wagon sheets came in two colours, black or a red-brown colour. The only clue so far uncovered appears in *The LMS at War*, where there is mention of 'red wartime wagon sheets', so it is probably safe to assume that the Southern's wagon sheets were normally black, with possibly some red ones making their appearance during the war. (In BR days there were also grey sheets, but that, as they say, is another story.)

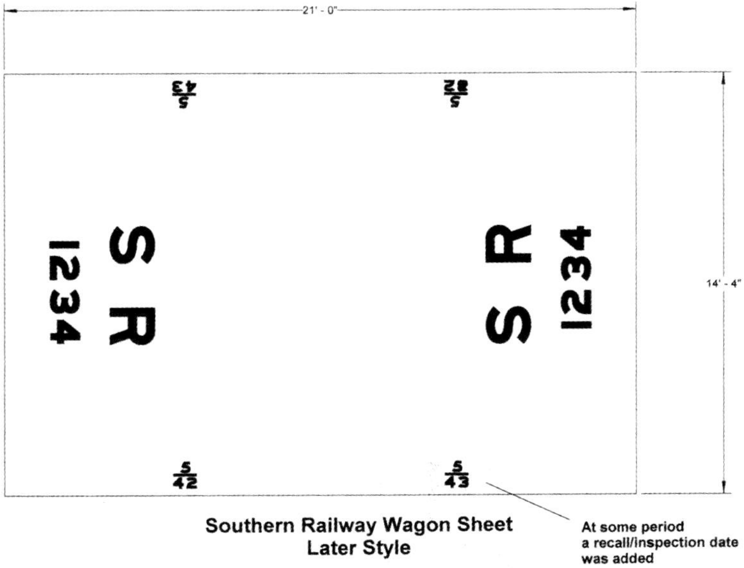

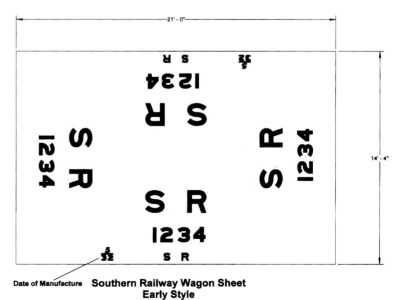

Southern Railway Wagon Sheet
Later Style

At some period a recall/inspection date was added

Date of Manufacture   Southern Railway Wagon Sheet
Early Style

Figure 6

Figure 7

Diagrams and Numbering

As noted in previous volumes of *Southern Wagons*, the SR issued a diagram for what was considered to be a dimensionally different design of wagon, as seen from the user's point of view. So far as the pre-Grouping wagons were concerned, these diagrams were more-or-less copies of the original companies' diagrams, and such errors as appeared in them were generally repeated. The diagrams were issued by the Rolling Stock Office, which, until it was evacuated to Brighton during the war, was situated in the offices at Grosvenor Road sidings, near Victoria. A Mr C. W. Pepper was the Chief Rolling Stock Clerk in charge there and he held this position for the whole of the Southern Railway's separate existence. It is of interest to note that the Head Office of the Outdoor C&W Assistant was also located at the same address.

Returning to the diagrams, these, like the running-numbers of the wagons, were arranged in blocks according to the railway of origin, the LSWR always coming first, followed by the SECR, LBSCR and finally the L&BR. The Isle of Wight companies did not issue diagrams, and it seems the Southern did not consider it worthwhile to make any, although it did get so far as to have all the Island wagons measured. The South Western prepared a diagram for the two Plymouth, Devonport & South Western Junction Railway (PD&SWJR) brake vans, but no Southern version has been uncovered. All the pre-Grouping diagram blocks were filled consistently, but there were gaps at the ends of each block, and, where appropriate, new SR or pre-Grouping designs rebuilt by the Southern followed. Generally, however, the new Southern designs were issued with diagrams numbered beyond the LBSCR blocks, re-using most of the old L&BR numbers. There were nevertheless one or two oddities, and one wonders why, for instance, the 1936 bogie brake vans were given the diagram number of 1550 rather than 1582, which at the time was the next spare number in the brake-van series. The plot thickens in the case of the number 1550, because this number had already been used for a pair of Diagram 1541s modified for use on the Canterbury & Whitstable line. One is left to conclude that, in this case, a mistake was made. The use of diagram numbers 1598/9 is a little odd, but perhaps these wagons were seen to be a development of the Diagram 1597.

The clerical mind moved in its own way in these matters, and no doubt Mr Pepper could explain all, were he alive today. Table 1 (*below*) gives the basic information.

The allocation of running-numbers was carried out in a very similar manner to that used for the diagrams. All pre-Grouping wagons were renumbered, the numbers being allocated in groups by origin, type, size and carrying capacity, and finally by order of their pre-Grouping numbers — all very logical. It took some time to work all this out, and it was not until the autumn of 1923 that wagons began to appear with SR numbers. Once the renumbering got underway the work proceeded quite quickly, and the majority of the wagons had been dealt with by the late 1920s, the last being a mixture of the later pre-Grouping vehicles and older ones that had become lost. It was not unusual for wagons (especially older ones) to become lost; sometimes they were forgotten in isolated locations, some were destroyed in unreported accidents, some fell into deep water (likewise not reported) and others were effectively stolen by industry. Sometimes, for various reasons, a wagon might exchange identities with another; no one would ever know — except, perhaps, a railway enthusiast! The last wagon recorded as being renumbered was LSWR No 9818, an eight-plank open goods ('South Western Top'), renumbered 7901 at Eastleigh in May 1932.

SR-designed wagons were normally numbered in new blocks that started well clear of the pre-Grouping wagons, but there were many cases of wagons taking the numbers of withdrawn pre-Grouping vehicles. Some of these were wagons built on renewal account, or so-called 'rebuilds' that used varying amounts of material from withdrawn wagons but certainly not all, and again there are cases of 'rebuilt' wagons being given new numbers. One is left with the feeling that there was a policy as to whether a wagon received a new or previously used number, but it would require a lot of work to get to the bottom of it. Besides the main number series there were two sets of numbers used for various miscellaneous service vehicles. The main series included locomotives, cranes, specialised wagons, stores vans and the like. These had a number suffixed 'S', and many of them had diagrams in the 18xx series. The second list was used for dock and similar old open wagons, these being prefixed by the letter 'O'. These are not covered, other than a cursory look at the commercial hand cranes.

Table 1: SR Wagon Diagrams

Type	Ex-LSWR	Ex-SECR	Ex-LBSCR	Ex-L&BR	SR
Open goods	1301-18	1324-60	1363-7	1391-5/7	1319-20/62/74-92/6/8-400
Covered goods	1401-13	1419-27	1433-6	1453	1428-30/52/4/5/7-60
Insulated	1461-5	-	1471	-	1475/7-9
Meat	1481-5	1489-91	-	-	1486
Cattle	1501-8	1512-8	1527/8	-	1529/30
Brake vans	1541-8	1552-60	1564-77	1589-90	1549/50/61/70/8-82
Timber	1591-7	1601-10	1616-21	-	1598/9
Cartrucks	1641-50	1654-7	1661	-	-
Special vehicles	1671-6	1678-81	1684-9	-	1682/90/1
Gunpowder	1701	1703	1705	-	-
Miscellaneous	1711	-	-	-	1712-7
Ballast	1731-7	1741-8	1751-9	-	1749/60/71-5
Sleeper and rail	1781-91	1794-6	1798-803	-	1787

Chapter 3.
Open Goods Wagons

This chapter is divided into three parts, dealing respectively with the various pre-Grouping designs built by the Southern, the SR designs built in Maunsell's time and the Bulleid designs.

Part One
Pre-Grouping designs constructed by the Southern Railway

These have all been described in detail in previous volumes but for completeness are summarised here. Full details of running-numbers etc will be found in Appendix 1.

Pre-Grouping designs fall into two categories: those already on order in 1923 and those ordered by the Southern. In the first category were two SECR orders — the first for 70 10-ton five-plank 'Rebuilds' (SR Diagram 1347) and the second for 10 12-ton seven-planks (SR Diagram 1355). The 'Rebuilds' incorporated a small amount of second-hand material but were otherwise brand-new wagons. Both were to the current Lionel Lynes design, and both entered traffic in 1923 with SECR numbers. Also already on order were two batches of the current LBSCR 10-ton five-plank design (SR Diagram 1369). Both batches were for 125 wagons — one lot described as 'Partial Renewals', the other as 'Complete Renewals'; both were built to the same drawing, so the physical difference (if any) must have been in the amount of new material used. These wagons entered traffic in late 1923 and early 1924. LBSCR numbers were allocated to these wagons but are not thought to have been carried, because 20 went new to the Isle of Wight in 1924, and, although there is a record of their intended Brighton numbers, there is no reference to their having been renumbered.

Right:
Plate 21 This is the only available new photograph of a wood-framed SR-built Diagram 1316, showing No DS9290 as a C&W departmental at Eastleigh c1958. (For a better photograph in original livery see Plate 39 in Volume One.) *A. Blackburn*

Open goods wagons built or purchased by the Southern Railway

Pre-Grouping open goods wagons on order 1/1/1923

Diagram	Order	Date	Quantity	Construction	Numbers	Examples of Tare weights	Notes
1347	SECR	?	70	2/23-3/23	14401-70	NR (Diagram tare 5-14-2)	'Rebuilds'
1355	SECR	?	100	6/23-7/23	14897-996	NR (Diagram tare 6-6-1)	
1369	LBSCR	30/12/22	125	11/23-1/24	25934-26058	NR (Diagram tare 5-16-0)	'Complete Renewals'
1369	LBSCR	30/12/22	125	2/24-4/24	26059-183	NR (Diagram tare 5-16-0)	'Partial Renewals'

Pre-Grouping open goods designs ordered by the Southern Railway

Diagram	Order	Date	Quantity	Construction	Numbers	Examples of Tare weights	Notes
1369	L8	3/5/23	250	5/24-4/25	27462-27711	NR (Diagram tare 5-15-0)	LBSCR design, 'Partial Renewals'
1316	E9	3/5/23	100	10/24-1/25	9141-9240	9141 6-19-1, 9191 6-19-1, 9240 6-19-1	LSWR design
1347	A15	3/5/23	150	10/25-11/25	19079-19228	19079 5-14-2, 19104 5-13-3, 19228 5-15-0	SECR design
1369	L27	17/3/24	350	6/25-7/26	18729-19078	19078 5-15-2 (last LBSC- design wagon built)	LBSCR design, 'Partial Renewals'
1355	A28 Pt	17/3/24	500	2/26-6/26	28501-29000	28501 6-8-2, 28756 6-8-2, 29000 6-6-0	SECR design. Order originally for 800 amended 7/10/25
1316	E77	26/1/25	100	10/25-12/25	9241-9340	9241 6-19-1, 9291 6-19-1, 9340 6-19-1	LSWR design

Note: NR = No record

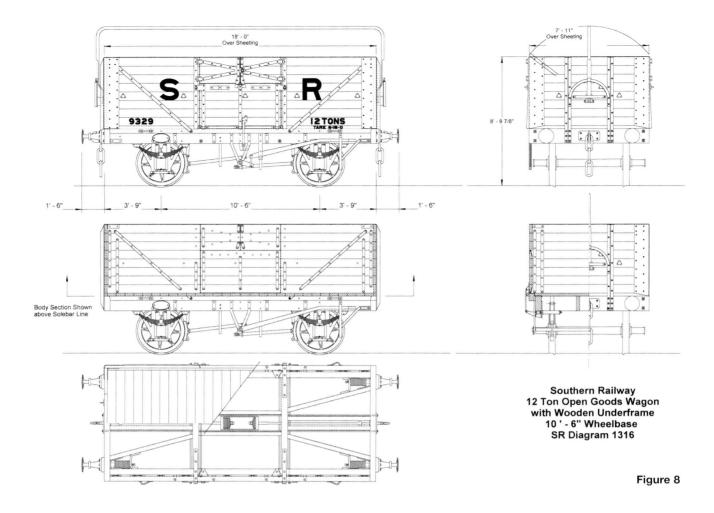

Southern Railway
12 Ton Open Goods Wagon
with Wooden Underframe
10 ' - 6" Wheelbase
SR Diagram 1316

Body Section Shown
above Solebar Line

Figure 8

Pre-Grouping designs ordered by the Southern Railway

New open goods wagons were urgently required and pre-group designs were built as a matter of convenience until the new standard designs were ready and Ashford was organised to build them. The first three orders were placed in May 1923. These were for 250 LBSCR 10-ton five-planks (SR Diagram 1369); again described as 'Partial Renewals', they were built to the same drawings as the pre-Grouping wagons but were built 'square ended'. Next there was an order for 100 LSWR 12-ton eight-planks (SR Diagram 1316). Rather interestingly, these wagons were not built to the latest Eastleigh 17ft design for such a wagon but followed the earlier 18ft design. There were also 150 SECR 10-ton five-plank 'Rebuilds' (SR Diagram 1347).

These were followed by orders placed in May and June 1924 for what was to be a final batch of 350 Brighton 10-ton five-planks and 800 SECR 12-ton seven-planks. In the event, the last 300 of this order were built to the new standard SR design. The last non-standard open goods order was placed in January 1925, for 100 LSWR-type 12-ton eight-planks to Diagram 1316. These wagons differed from the earlier examples of this design in that they were built on a wooden underframe.

Part Two

Brief mention must first be made of the design produced in 1926 for the narrow gauge Lynton & Barnstaple line. This was an 8-ton, four-plank bogie wagon and is described fully, along with all the other L&B stock, in *Southern Wagons: Volume Two LBSCR and Minor Railways*.

Standard SR Maunsell designs

There were 10 of these, but there were basically only three types — a 17ft 6in eight-plank open that came in eight versions, a five-plank version of one of the former and a 21ft 6in eight-plank built specially for ferry-train traffic.

The story begins with the Diagram 1379, an eight-plank open built on a standard RCH 17ft 6in underframe. This design first appeared in January 1926, and production continued until May 1933, by which time a total of 7,950 had been produced, making it numerically by far the largest SR design built. They were virtually identical, except that the first 3,000 built had Morton brakes and the remainder what the Southern called the 'Freighter brake', consisting of two brake blocks and a lever either side. Why the brake design was changed is not known, but it may well have had something to do with paying royalties.

Right:
Plate 22 Open goods No 29306, one of the first Diagram 1379s to be built. The builder's title board states 1925, though none was delivered before January 1926.
Authors' collection

SR standard open goods designs — 'Maunsell period' (For full details of running-numbers see Appendix 1)

Diagram	Order	Date	Quantity	Construction	Numbers	Examples of Tare weights	Notes
1396	L110	6/4/25	4	8/27	28316-9	NR (Diagram tare 6-1-1)	Lynton & Barnstaple line (1ft 11½in gauge)
1379	A28 Pt	7/10/25	300	9/26-12/26	29001-300	29251 7-0-0, 29300 7-0-0	Morton brake
1379	MRCW	7/10/25	250	1/26-3/26	29301-550	29301 6-18-0, 29306 6-16-3, 29426 6-18-0	Morton brake
1379	GRCW	7/10/25	250	1/26-3/26	29551-800	29551 6-18-1, 29676 6-18-0, 29800 6-18-0	Morton brake
1379	A128	7/10/25	800	1/27-?/27	29801-30600	29801 7-0-0, 30200 7-0-0, 30600 7-0-0	Morton brake
1379	A164	8/7/26	400	?/27-3/28	31601-32000	31601 6-16-0, 31696 6-16-0, 31801 6-16-0	Morton brake
1379	BRCW	17/3/27	125	1927	30601-725	30601 6-19-1, 30725, 6-19-1	Morton brake
1379	BRCW	17/3/27	125	1927	31101-225	31101 6-19-0, 31225 7-0-1	Morton brake
1379	MRCW	17/3/27	125	1927	30726-850	30726 6-18-1, 30850 6-16-3	Morton brake
1379	MRCW	17/3/27	125	6/27-?/27	31226-350	31226 6-17-2, 31350 6-17-1	Morton brake
1379	MetCW	17/3/27	125	?/27-6/27	30851-975	30851 6-19-2, 30975 6-19-1	Morton brake
1379	MetCW	17/3/27	125	5/26-?/27	31351-475	31351 6-19-0, 31475 6-19-0	Morton brake
1379	GRCW	17/3/27	125	1927	30976-31100	30976 6-19-0, 31100 6-19-0	Morton brake
1379	GRCW	17/3/27	125	1927	31476-600	31476 6-19-0, 31600 6-19-0	Morton brake
1379	A255	7/4/27	1250	3/28-1/29	32001-33250	32001 6-16-0, 32400 6-16-0, 33551 6-6-0	'Freighter brake', as were all later unfitted opens
1379	A342	6/6/28	750	1/29-11/29	33251-34000	33453 6-16-0, 33551 6-12-0, 34000 6-14-2	
1379	A466	17/5/29	1150	11/29-?/30	34001-35150	34401 6-12-0, 34527 6-14-2, 34805 6-15-0	
1380	A469	17/5/29	300	?/30-6/30	9341-9640	9341 6-2-0, 9491 5-19-0, 9640 6-3-1	Rebuild Type 1; LSWR wheels etc
1379	A575	16/5/30	1200	?/30-4/31	35151-36350	35151 6-15-2, 35551 6-17-2, 36350 6-11-0	
1380	A576	16/5/30	550	5/31-7/31	9641 etc	9641 5-17-2, 10205 5-18-0	Rebuild Type 1; LSWR wheels etc
1380	A577	16/5/30	50	7/31	10206/7 etc	10206 5-17-2, 10256 5-19-0	Rebuild Type 1; LSWR wheels etc
1379	A637	14/4/31	600	7/32-5/33	36351-950	36351 6-12-2, 36651 6-15-2, 36950 6-13-0	
1381	A638	14/4/31	200	9/34-10/34	10258 etc	10258 6-10-2, 10359 6-10-0, 10471 6-10-2	Rebuild Type 3; SECR wheels etc
1381	A668	18/7/31	400	3/32-5/32	10472 etc	10472 6-8-2, 10673 6-10-0, 10472 6-8-2	Rebuild Type 3; SECR wheels etc
1381	A737 Pt	7/10/32	100	10/34	26200 etc	26200 6-9-0, 26307 6-12-0	Rebuild Type 3; SECR wheels etc
1381	A737 Pt	7/10/32	400	8/35-10/35	26308 etc	26308 6-12-2, 26507 6-13-0, 26718 6-15-2	Rebuild Type 2; LSWR wheels etc. Sheet supports?
1385	A759	21/4/33	100	10/-11/33	36951-37050	36951 7-3-2, 37050 7-0-2	Rebuild Type 1; LSWR wheels etc,. AVB 1 x 18in cylinder, four brake blocks, sheet supports
1387	A823	3/8/34	30	?/35-5/35	36352 etc	NR (Diagram tare 7-10-0)	Diagram 1379 rebuilt ABV 1x8in four brake blocks, WP. Sheet supports 1947 onwards
1388	A826	13/8/34	20	4/36	40981-41000	40981 9-18-2, 41000 9-18-2	AVB 1 x 18in cylinder, eight brake blocks, WP. Sheet supports 1947 onwards
1398	A864	30/4/35	250	12/35-1/36	37051-300	37051 7-5-0, 37200 7-8-0, 37300 7-8-0	AVB 1 x ?in cyl four brake blocks. Sheet support
1400	A865	30/4/35	650	8/36-1/37	26719 etc	26719 6-13, 27301 6-16, 27417 6-11	Rebuild Type 4; SECR wheels?
1378	?	?	60	4/36-4/37	29079 etc	NR (Not stated on Diagram)	Dia 1379 rebuilt to carry cable drums, many more later
1400	A914	3/4/36	750	8/37-11/37	10912 etc	10912 6-14, 11178 6-12, 11302 6-11	Rebuild Type 4 SECR wheels?
1398	A915	3/4/36	100	7/37	37301-400	37301 7-8, 37350 7-7, 37400 7-8	AVB 1 x ?in cyl, four brake blocks. Sheet support
1377	A968	6/5/37	500	10/38-6/39	37401-900	37401 6-16, 37651 6-16, 37900 6-16	
1377	A1033a	14/6/38	250	11/39-12/39	37901-38150	37901 6-16, 38026 6-16, 38150 6-16	'Traders door'. Order originally for 500 wagons

Note: NR = No record

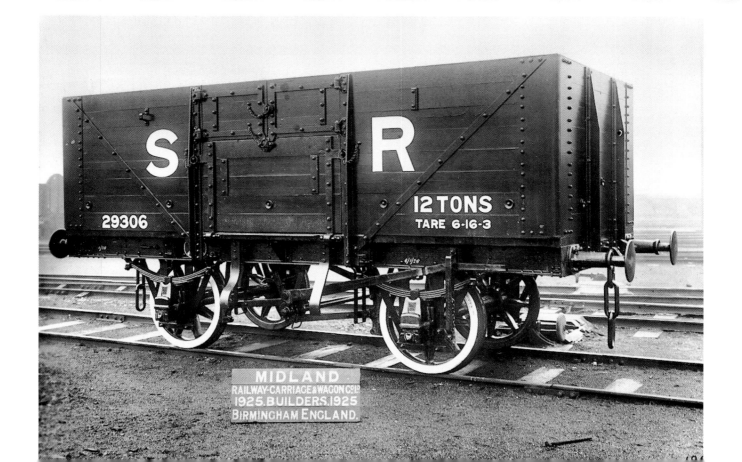

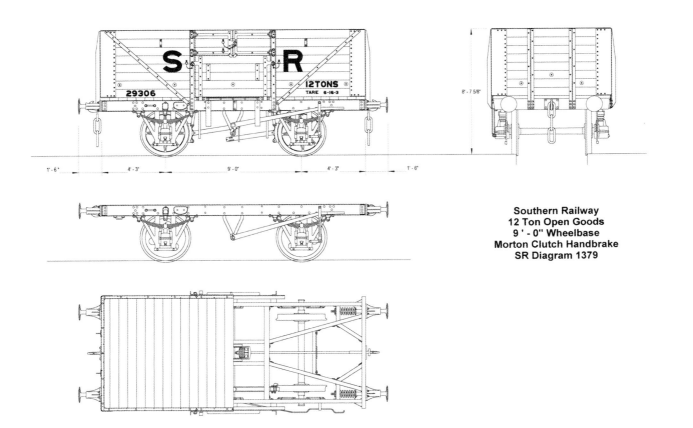

Southern Railway
12 Ton Open Goods
9 ' - 0" Wheelbase
Morton Clutch Handbrake
SR Diagram 1379

Figure 9

Above:
Plate 23 A typical Diagram 1379 after overhaul in 1948. One or two minor but common alterations are apparent: capping clips on the end, in place of the long internal bolts used originally, and the removal of the sheet cleat from the middle plank (if it ever had one — only the early wagons were built with them). The livery is that adopted by Ashford, prior to the introduction of the standard BR livery: body, solebars, buffer guides and headstocks SR brown, writing white on black patches.
National Railway Museum, York

The next design — Diagram 1380 — appeared in 1930 and is best described as a five-plank version of its predecessor. However, this wagon made use of the wheels, springs and axleboxes of withdrawn LSWR 10-ton wagons and was thus itself of 10 tons capacity and officially described as a 'Rebuild Type 1'. Like nearly all the 'Rebuilds' we shall describe, these wagons had their solebars spaced at 6ft 5in — 2in further apart than the standard RCH design — in order to accommodate the LSWR wheel sets, which, like the SECR examples, had 6ft 8in journal centres rather than the RCH-standard 6ft 6in. In later years some of these — and other SR 'Rebuilds' — were converted to take standard 6ft 6in wheels. This was accomplished by packing the 'W' irons out with 1in steel strips, standard RCH axleboxes being fitted at the same time. No fewer than 900 of the D1380s were built, the last in July 1931.

In March 1932 what might be described as an eight-plank version of the D1380 appeared as Diagram 1381. There were 400 built using LSWR wheels etc (known as 'Rebuild Type 2') and 700 using SECR wheels etc ('Rebuild Type 3'). The standard LSWR 10-ton bearings were 9in x 4in, the SECR versions 8in x 3¾in; both would fit in a standard RCH axlebox, and some rebuilds had these. Construction was spread over

several years, but in October 1932 this design spawned a vacuum-fitted version (Diagram 1385) as a part of the programme of accelerated freight trains. These wagons were provided with sheet supports. The Southern did not normally fit such items and, indeed, following a decision made by the other companies, had been progressively removing them since 1924, but presumably these vehicles were seen as a special case. They used LSWR wheels etc and were called 'Rebuild Type 1', like the five-plank Diagram 1381 examples.

Somewhat similar were 30 D1379s converted (to Diagram 1388) for use with the Dover-Dunkirk train ferry service. These were provided with vacuum brakes, air pipes etc and were ready for traffic in June 1935. The service did not, however, begin until October the following year, and it would be interesting to know what these wagons did in the meantime. None was lost during the war, and in 1947/8 they were somewhat belatedly equipped with sheet bars. They remained as ferry wagons until withdrawn from this service in April 1954 but were reinstated in December 1956 and continued to be used as ferry wagons until 1964, when they were officially returned to normal use. As a point of interest, Dunkirk was considered to be a Southern depot, and there were Southern staff employed there to examine and repair stock.

Above:
Plate 24 No 9509 (Diagram 1380) seen here at Dowlais in October 1937. This was the only SR-designed five-plank type built in Maunsell's time and was officially known as a 'Rebuild Type 1', using LSWR wheels and buffers etc.
P. Tatlow collection

Above:
Plate 25 Another Diagram 1380 in early BR days. This wagon seems to have Southern 1942-style writing, with the 'R' of 'SR' painted out and no black patches. Many of these wagons became internals later, and some were sold to the Port of Bristol Authority along with many examples of Diagrams 1347, 1355 and 1379. *R. S. Carpenter Photos*

Left:
Plate 26 A Diagram 1380 after overhaul in 1948. This wagon has capping clips and another very common modification, dating from Bulleid's time — the use of a light metal strip to hold the floorboards in position in place of the individual bolts used previously.
National Railway Museum, York

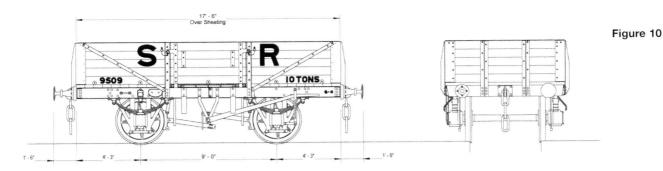

Figure 10

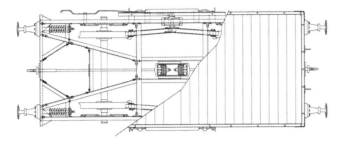

**Southern Railway
10 Ton 5 Plank Open Goods Wagon
9 ' - 0" Wheelbase
SR Diagram 1380**

Livery shown depicts the Wagon as it was in 1937
When New it would have had the Load painted
one Plank higher and the tare painted
on the lower plank :-

TARE 6-4-0

Right:
Plate 27 No 26675 of Diagram 1381. This wagon is a 'Rebuild Type 2', with LSWR wheels, axleboxes etc. The wagon has the full range of the Bulleid period modifications, including small metal patching plates. *National Railway Museum, York*

Below:
Plate 28 A Diagram 1381 in as-built condition. This wagon is a 'Rebuild Type 3', with SECR wheels and axleboxes. *HMRS*

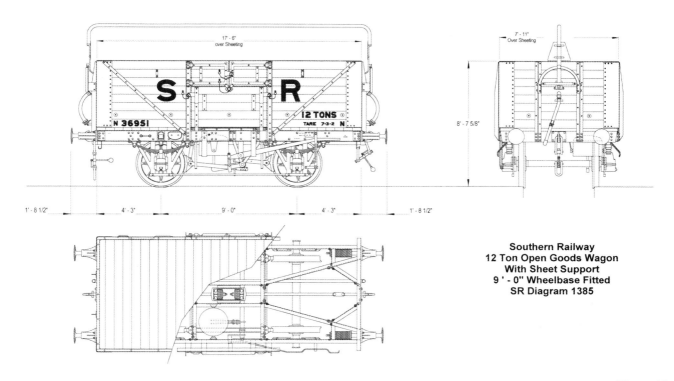

17' - 6"
over Sheeting

S R

N 36951
12 TONS
TARE 7-3-2 N

7' - 11"
Over Sheeting

8' - 7 5/8"

1' - 8 1/2"   4' - 3"   9' - 0"   4' - 3"   1' - 8 1/2"

Southern Railway
12 Ton Open Goods Wagon
With Sheet Support
9 ' - 0" Wheelbase Fitted
SR Diagram 1385

Figure 11

To complement the D1388s the Southern built 20 eight-plank 20-ton ferry opens on standard 21ft 6in RCH underframes, to Diagram 1387. These were basically open goods versions of the 20-ton mineral design and in fact were originally ordered as minerals. One of these wagons was lost overseas in 1940, but it was eventually found and it re-entered BR stock in July 1950. Like the 13-ton ferry opens they were fitted with sheet supports in 1947/8. This design was one of the very few Southern Railway designs to be adopted as the basis of a BR standard, although the BR version (BR Diagram 1/055) was 18in longer. The latter was designed at Eastleigh, 20 being built by Lancing in 1954 and a further 20 in 1956.

In 1935 the wheelbase of the standard 17ft 6in underframe was increased to 10ft, and the first open goods with this feature were the Diagram 1398s. They were fitted, had sheet supports and were intended for use on the newly introduced fast freights. In all, 350 were built between December 1935 and July 1937. An unfitted version was introduced in August 1936, and these became Diagram 1400. They were 'Rebuilds Type 4', but, although built with second-hand 10-ton wheelsets, they had their solebars set to the standard RCH width of 6ft 3in and were designed with the intention of their being converted to standard 12-ton wagons. In many cases the wheels they were built with were on their last turning, and many (if not most) were converted to 12 tons, some within two years of their construction. They totalled 1,400 in number, and construction continued until November 1937.

In 1936/7 60 of the unfitted eight-planks were converted to carry cable drums in connection with the Portsmouth electrification scheme. This entailed the fitting of a frame to carry the cable drum, the removal of certain end planks and the cutting of hand- and foot-holds in the sides. These particular wagons are thought to have been returned to normal use in 1939, but they had proved their worth for such duties, and there were later to be quite a large number of more elaborate and permanent conversions that involved taking out some portions of side plank etc. The number and details of the wagons concerned are conflicting, so it is impossible to say exactly how many were involved, but there were certainly more than the original 60. In later years, quite a number of these wagons were used for a variety of departmental duties, and some were cut down to five planks. This work was done very neatly, but they could be identified for what they were by the wider end corner straps — all the genuine five-planks had narrow straps. One, at least (No 33819), was noted in 1961 with its top doors through-planked, making it a 17ft 6in mineral.

In October 1938 what was destined to be the last of the eight-plank designs appeared, built to Diagram 1377, and 750 were built before construction ceased in favour of a five-plank design. The last 250 differed from all the previous opens in that the drop door was modified to the so-called 'Trader's door' design. This featured a tapered top plank which, when dropped on a platform, made it easier to push a sack trolley over, and this was used on all later five-plank designs. The 'Trader's door' seems to have originated on the LNER and was adopted by all four post-Grouping companies; the Southern was the last to do so, and this was probably the first sign of Bulleid's influence in wagon work. The last 250 also had the centre solebar bracket replaced by a gusset, as normally found on the underframes of vans; some of the Diagram 1398s (Nos 37051-300) also had this detail, and, again, it became a standard feature on the five-planks.

Above:
Plate 29 No 36639 (Diagram 1387), one of the 30 Diagram 1379s converted in 1935 for the Dover-Dunkirk train ferry service. The brake work was identical to the Diagram 1385 type introduced two years previously. The Southern Railway did not have a Photographic Department until one was set up at the outbreak of the war, primarily to photograph bomb damage. Prior to this, various arrangements were made when photographs were required. At Ashford the local firm of De'Ath & Condon was used for some years, and this is one of that firm's excellent photographs. *R. Chorley collection*

Above:
Plate 30 A nice end view of No 36639. Alterations include the provision of brake pipes, safety chains, screw couplings, lamp irons and sheet rings instead of cleats, the latter removed to a position one plank down. Otherwise the end is that of a standard Maunsell eight-plank open. m*R. Chorley collection*

Figure 12

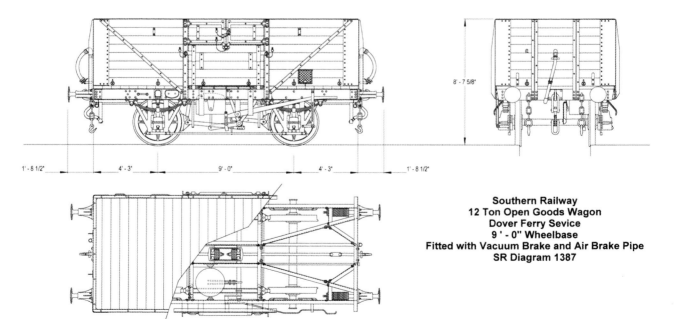

**Southern Railway
12 Ton Open Goods Wagon
Dover Ferry Sevice
9 ' - 0" Wheelbase
Fitted with Vacuum Brake and Air Brake Pipe
SR Diagram 1387**

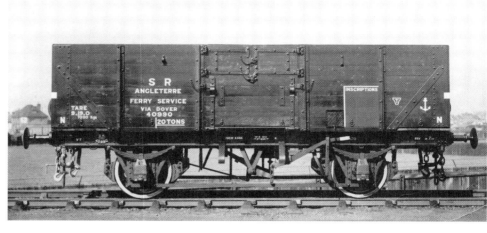

Right:
Plate 31 No 40990, a Diagram 1388 posed for its official photograph in Kimberley Yard at Ashford. Note that the floor planks either side of the door are retained by metal plates, this feature being unique to these wagons prior to its general introduction in the war years. This wagon was lost in France in 1940, but in July 1950 it returned to British use. Where, one wonders, had it been in the meantime? *R. Chorley collection*

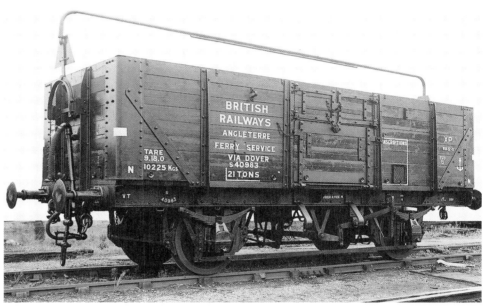

Right:
Plate 32 A Diagram 1388 as overhauled in 1948 and uprated to 21 tons. All the ferry opens were provided with sheet bars in the years 1947-51, other modifications including capping clips and sheet cleats instead of rings. *National Railway Museum, York*

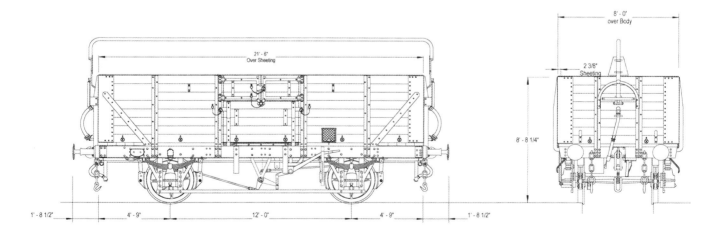

Southern Railway 20 Ton Open Wagon Dover Ferry Service
12' 0" Wheelbase Fitted with Vacuum Brake and Air Brake Pipe
Figure 13   **SR Diagram 1388**

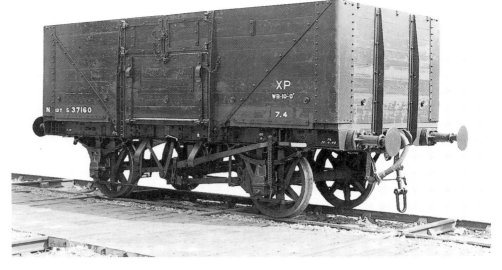

Right:
Plate 33 An example of Diagram 1398. These wagons were a 10ft-wheelbase version of Diagrams 1385/7. A feature of this diagram was that the bracket on the centre line of the solebar was of the type normally used on vans. Why these wagons had them is not known, but they reappeared on Diagram 1377 in 1938 and were used on all subsequent five-plank opens. *National Railway Museum, York*

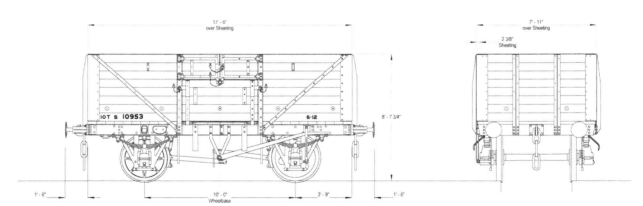

Left:
Plate 34 No S10953 of Diagram 1400, a 10ft-wheelbase version of Diagram 1381. It has acquired floorboard-retention plates but is otherwise as built. Unlike many other members of this diagram, it is still (1948) a 10-ton wagon with SECR wheels but, like many rebuilds, has RCH-type axleboxes. *National Railway Museum, York*

Figure 14

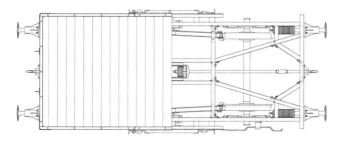

Southern Railway
12 Ton Open Goods Wagon
Type 4 Rebuild
10 ' - 0" Wheelbase
SR Diagram 1400

These Wagons were built using secondhand wheel sets with wheels of 3 ft - 0 1/2"dia. From 1939 on the wheels were replaced with standard dia wheels 3 ft - 1 1/2" dia. and the load increase to 13 Ton.
The left end of the side view shows 3ft - 0 1/2" dia wheels with 5/8" packing under the spring shoes and spring stop.
The right end of the side view shows 3 ft - 1 1/2" dia wheels with the packings removed.

Right:

Plate 35 No DS1674, formerly No 29924 (Diagram 1378A). No suitable photograph was available of one of the original 60 conversions, this being one of those converted in 1949. The originals had the hand-holds and portions of the second plank up removed, but the photograph shows the typical condition of the postwar wagons. The maximum size of cable drum that could be carried was 8ft 6in in diameter and 4ft 4in wide. These wagons carried a wide variety of liveries, the prewar examples being brown and those converted in 1948 having unpainted woodwork with black steelwork. This one is probably light grey, but many later ones were black, and one or two later still were 'gulf red' or olive green.
A. Blackburn collection

Right:

Plate 36 No S37815 (Diagram 1377). This was the final design of eight-plank open and is seen virtually as built, except for the livery. Most (if not all) eight-plank opens were built with spoked wheels, in some cases several years after disc wheels had appeared on other types of wagon.
National Railway Museum, York

Right:

Plate 37 No S38048 (Diagram 1377). This is one of the final batch of these wagons, fitted with the 'Trader's door', probably at Bulleid's behest. Seen in typical BR condition, it has been fitted with automatic brakes; the bottom end planks have been replaced by steel channels, the axle guards have been changed to the 1947 design and it has LNER-type open-front axleboxes. The livery is bauxite brown. The top end plank has lost its capping and has suffered accordingly. *Authors' collection*

Part Three

Bulleid designs

The Rolling Stock Committee Minutes do not reveal why the eight-plank type was discontinued, but the decision was almost certainly dictated by the need to save timber in the face of a possible war, which, indeed, broke out just as the last eight-planks were being finished. Henceforth, construction would be of what at the time were referred to as 'small-bodied' opens.

The last order for eight-planks had been for 500 wagons, but this was cut back to the 250 mentioned above. Of the balance, 238 were built as a five-plank version (Diagram 1375) of what had gone before; there was one small difference, however, the headstocks being cropped short to save steel, and this remained a feature of all wartime-built opens. Most had been built by the beginning of 1940, but construction was then interrupted, and the last few were not built until the end of 1942. The remaining 12 were built as a 'Shock-absorbing' open goods (Diagram 1376), six of which were fitted. These were built in April and June 1940.

In 1937 the LMS had invented the shock-absorbing wagon, this being a very important development in wagon design, aimed at protecting the load from the worst of the shocks it could receive in the course of normal rail freight movement. Basically the body of the wagon was not attached directly to the underframe but to a number of horizontal springs attached to the solebar. The Southern design generally followed that of the LMS very closely but differed in that steel springs were used for the main shock-absorbing unit rather than the rubber used by the LMS. The new wagons were given prominent coverage in the technical press at the time, and a detail mentioned was the use made in these wagons of home-grown

Above:
Plate 38 No 38392 (Diagram 1376), one of the unfitted version of the 'Shock-opens', seen at Waterloo in September 1940. This was one of the first wagons built to what might be called 'austerity' standards: it has thin planks, and the headstocks are cropped off square, just beyond the solebar gusset. Note the tare weight is quoted to the last quarter; this was not called for in the 1936 writing scheme and was probably put on for the photograph. The telegraph code 'Saw' was altered to 'Shock' in 1943. *A. Blackburn collection*

hardwood timber. This resulted in the sides and floor being only $1^3/_8$in thick (instead of the more normal $2\frac{1}{2}$in), dimensions that remained typical of all the wartime-built opens. Seen from above, the thin sides would have been very apparent (a detail modellers should bear in mind).

The next batch of five-planks to be built were something rather special and consisted of an order placed by the Ministry of Supply in September 1941 for 1,000 opens required (it was said) for use in Persia, where a supply route was being opened up to Russia. These wagons were the first opens to use the 1939 RCH 17ft 6in underframe, which differed from the 1923 design in that it had non-continuous drawgear and additional end longitudinals to suit. They were followed almost immediately by an order for a further 600. In the event it seems that these wagons did not go to Persia but were used instead on a new railway built by the Army between Haifa and Tripoli. Some may not have gone abroad at all, because, in 1949, 144 of them were taken into London Midland Region stock, but where these came from is not known.

SR standard open goods wagons — 'Bullied period' (For full details of running-numbers see Appendix 1)

Diagram	Order	Date	Quantity	Construction	Numbers	Examples of Tare weights	Notes
1375	A1033b	6/2/39	238	1/40-9/42	38151-388	38151 6-11, 38270 6-11, 38388 9/42	S/H softwood sheeting
1376	A1063	18/1/39	12	4/40-6/40	38389-400	38389 8-0-2, 38394 7-18, 38395 8-7	Shock-absorbing design, 38395-400 AVB 1 x 8in cyl, four brake blocks
1375	A1192	1/5/40	350	1/43-2/43	38401-750	38401 6-9, 38576 6-9, 38750 6-9	38418-28/32 built AVB 1x18in, four brake blocks (see Diagram 1389).1½in sheeting
1375	A1720	11/9/41	1000	9/41-11/41	SR1-SR1000	NR	Supplied as sets of parts to Ministry of Supply
1375	A1731	1/10/41	322	2/43-3/43	6801-7122	6801 6-9, 7122 6-9	7116-20 built AVB (see Diagram 1389). 1½in sheeting
1389	?	?	18+	1/43-1960?	Wide range	38418 6-18, 38428 6-18	Ongoing AVB conversion of Diagram 1375 into BR days 1 x 8in cyl, four brake blocks
	A1831	10/12/41	600	12/41	?	NR	WP supplied to Ministry of Supply
1375	A2301	9/11/42	500	9/43-11/43	5601-6100	5601 6-8, 5851 6-8, 6100 6-8	1½in hardwood sheeting
1375	A2505	13/4/43	350	9/44-5/45	6101-6450	NR	1½in hardwood sheeting
1375	A2516	15/4/43	400	3/44-7/44	NE262463 etc	NR	1½in hardwood sheeting
1375	A2533	4/5/43	465	1944	LMS 417610-8074	NR (Diagram tare 6-7)	LMS Lot 1371
1375	A2854	19/4/44	501	1944	5400-5572	5400 6-7, 5486 6-7, 5572 6-7	Softwood sheeting. Order originally for 502 wagons, including 52 as replacements for vehicles lost to enemy action
					6452-6779	6452 6-5, 6616 6-7, 6779 6-7	
1391	L3094	15/11/44	1	9/45	6780	6780 5-11	Triangulated underframe British Patent No 584858
1375	A3217	4/5/45	600	2/46-3/46	12001-12600	12001 6-6, 12301 6-8, 12600 6-8	1½in hardwood sheeting, middle three planks not bolted
1375	A3305	21/8/45	153	1/48-2/48	11848-12000	11848 6-8, 12000 6-8	2³/₈in softwood sheeting
1375	A3352 Pt	15/4/46	373	1/48-3/48	12601-12973	12601 6-8, 12751 6-8, 12973 6-8	2³/₈in softwood sheeting
1375	A3352 Pt	15/4/46	527	3/48-4/48	12974 etc	12974 6-10, 13082 6-10, 13496 6-10	1½in hardwood sheeting, middle three planks not bolted
1375	A3443 Pt	1/8/47	762	5/48-9/48	5153 etc	51153 6-10, 13503 6-10, 13820 6-6	2³/₈in softwood sheeting
1392	A3443 Pt	1/8/47	38	1/49-3/49	14033-14070	14033 8-2, 14052 8-11, 14070 8-10	Shock-absorbing design, 14052-70 AVB 1 x 18in cyl four brake blocks
BR1/33	A3444	1/8/47	100	12/49	B457000-99	NR (Diagram tare 6-17)	SR Nos 4901-5000 allocated. Renumbered B483650-749
BR1/16	A3447	1/8/47	100	11/49-12/49	B457100-99	NR (Diagram tare 6-4)	SR Nos 3941-4040 allocated
BR1/34	BR	?	600	12/49-12/50	B477050-649	NR (Diagram tare 6-10)	Southern Region development of Diagram 1375
BR1/35	BR	?	500	1/50-5/50	B720425-924	NR (Diagram tare 8-14)	Southern Region development of Diagram 1392

Note: NR = No record

The first wagons to be built for the Southern to what might be described as the 'austerity' version of Diagram 1375 appeared in late 1942 and were the remainder of the original batch previously mentioned. These were followed by a complete order for 350 built in January and February 1943.

These had been ordered back in May 1940, which serves to demonstrate how much the demands of the war had disrupted normal production. Eventually 5,076 were built, including the 1,600 for the Ministry of Supply, 400 for the LNER and 1,815 for BR.

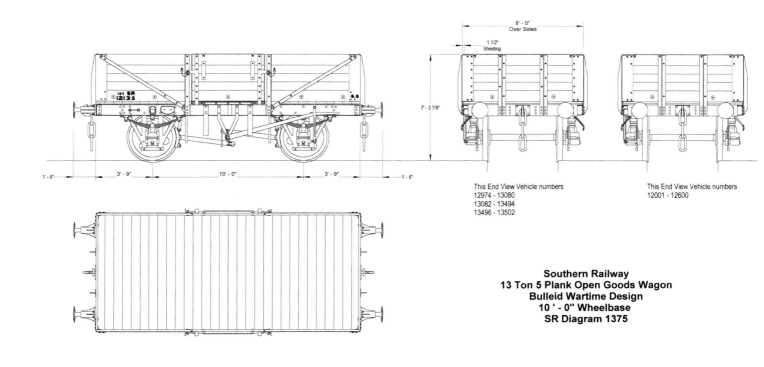

This End View Vehicle numbers
12974 - 13080
13082 - 13494
13496 - 13502

This End View Vehicle numbers
12001 - 12600

Southern Railway
13 Ton 5 Plank Open Goods Wagon
Bulleid Wartime Design
10 ' - 0" Wheelbase
SR Diagram 1375

Figure 15

Plate 39 No NE262463, built at Ashford in 1944. This photograph is the best available of an austerity Diagram 1375 as built. Note the short headstocks and thin boarding, packed up in the case of the floor to maintain the standard height. Like that in the previous photograph, this wagon also has quarters quoted in its weight. The colour of the ironwork is interesting; in theory it should be black, but grey looks more likely. *R. Chorley collection*

Construction ceased in September 1948. All the Diagram 1375 wagons were built with handbrakes only, but in April 1942 six wagons were equipped with vacuum brakes as a part of modifications made to enable them to carry light anti-aircraft guns as protection for passenger trains. The Germans had made several aerial attacks on trains in the past, but the RAF was currently pursuing a policy of attacking trains in France, and it was feared the enemy might retaliate. The plan was to run these wagons in passenger trains over various routes in Kent, as these were thought to be in most danger. The gun, a 'Bofors', was mounted in the middle of the wagon, the floor at each end being raised to assist the crew in serving the gun; there was also some sort of canvas screen at each

end to protect the crew. Once these weapons had been provided, it was then decided not to use them! They were placed in sidings around Ashford, and after a time the guns were dismounted and used as a part of the works' anti-aircraft defence. The wagons themselves reverted to normal use but retained their vacuum brakes and became Diagram 1389. By 1948 the total of this diagram had risen to 18, and in BR days there would be many more as the Diagram 1375s were steadily equipped with vacuum brakes as a part of the modernisation programme.

There is only one known instance of a five-plank open wagon being rebuilt, No 13443 being cut down in BR days to a fixed three-plank crane-test-weight truck.

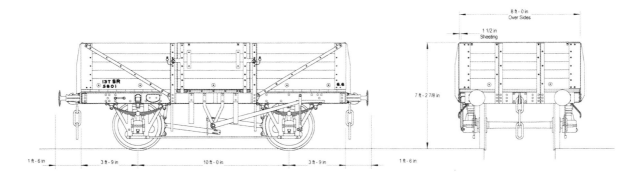

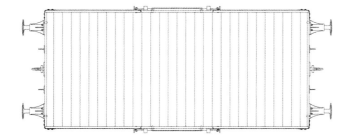

Southern Railway
13 Ton Open Goods Wagon
10 ' - 0" Wheelbase
Bulleid Design (400 supplied to LNER)
SR Diagram 1375

Figure 16

Above:

Plate 40 No S38422 (Diagram 1389), one of 18 Diagram 1375 wagons built in 1943 with vacuum-brake equipment recovered from covered goods vans sold to the WD for use in workshop trains. This was one of a number of wagons put into departmental service between the main works in the war years. They were not, however, 'Service stock' in the sense that they appeared in the Departmental wagon register. *National Railway Museum, York*

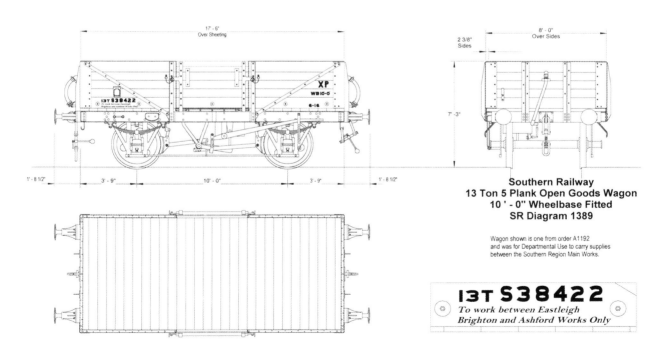

**Southern Railway
13 Ton 5 Plank Open Goods Wagon
10' - 0" Wheelbase Fitted
SR Diagram 1389**

Wagon shown is one from order A1192
and was for Departmental Use to carry supplies
between the Southern Region Main Works.

13T S38422
*To work between Eastleigh
Brighton and Ashford Works Only*

Figure 17

Left:
Plate 41 No S7120 (Diagram 1389). This very normal-looking wagon is one of the six altered to carry light anti-aircraft guns in 1943. The pattern of bolts on the corner plates indicates that this was one of the wagons originally built with unbolted middle planks. *T. A. Barry collection*

Left:
Plate 42 No S12134, built in 1946 to Diagram 1375, HO Order No A3217. The wagons built to this and all later orders reverted to a full-length headstock cropped to an angle at the ends. This is one of the wagons with the middle three planks held in position with clips instead of bolts. The livery seems to be brown timber with black ironwork — the only wagon observed so painted. *National Railway Museum, York*

It was at some time during the war that Bulleid and Lynes turned their attention to the standard RCH underframe design, which, they felt, could be improved upon. Ashford was finding that an increasing number of comparatively modern wagons were coming into the shops with badly deformed headstocks and solebars, and the problem became so serious that special tools were developed to straighten these out without removing them from the wagon. Lynes had a detailed study made of what was happening, and as a result he and his chief came up with a triangulated underframe design that was both stronger and lighter than the RCH design. This was tried out on three new wagons, one being a mineral (discussed in Chapter 5). The first to be built was a 'high'; this was of normal dimensions but had 2ft 9in wheels. Finding any details of its body construction has proved impossible, but it is believed to have had a wooden body. It was built by Lancing, carried the number 6780 and entered Departmental service in September 1945, running between Eastleigh, Brighton and Ashford. With a tare weight of 5 tons 11cwt it was about 14% lighter than a conventional 'high'. It was, it would seem, quite a successful design, and an order was placed in November 1948 for a further 500 for BR's Eastern and North Eastern Regions. Later this order was officially cancelled on the grounds that the design was non-standard. No 6780 was later renumbered 1430S, and it spent the remainder of its life as an internal in Lancing Works.

A second high-sided wagon was built c1948 with a modified version of the triangulated underframe, and this had a steel body. It does not seem to have had an HO Order number and was probably regarded as an experiment; it was built at Lancing and carried the number 1429S. It had a capacity of 14 tons, a tare weight of 5 tons 17cwt and seems to have spent its entire life as an internal at Lancing.

There were to be no more open-wagon developments built in Southern days, but a '1939' underframe version of the shock-open appeared in 1949. This was Diagram 1392, of which 38 were built, half of them fitted. Two more Bulleid designs appeared towards the end of 1949, for two very similar drop-side open goods — one of three planks, the other five. The Southern had never built such vehicles in the past, and it is difficult now to see what they were intended for. The three-plank entered service without comment, but the five-, which had originally been authorised as an order for 21-ton minerals, was refused by the Traffic Department because the side, even though it was equipped with door springs, was too heavy for a reasonable number of men to lift. No other four-wheeled, all-drop-side five-plank wagon had ever been built for a British railway, but the LNER had built something similar on bogies for brick traffic, and Bulleid would have known all about those. It has been suggested that these Southern wagons were built to carry bricks, but there seems to be no written evidence of this, and most spent their entire and unpopular lives 'on loan to the Southern Region CCE'.

Above:
Plate 43 No S14064 of Diagram 1392, the postwar version of Diagram 1376. The only differences from the earlier wagons seem to be the use of standard 2½in softwood timber, slightly different buffer castings and a different position for the numberplate. Although these wagons were ordered in August 1947, none of them was built before January 1949. Note that the non-'common user' letter 'N' is still being used. In later years the shock springs were covered by a protective plate. The BR-ordered and built Diagram 1/35 wagons were very similar. *D. Cullum*

Figure 18

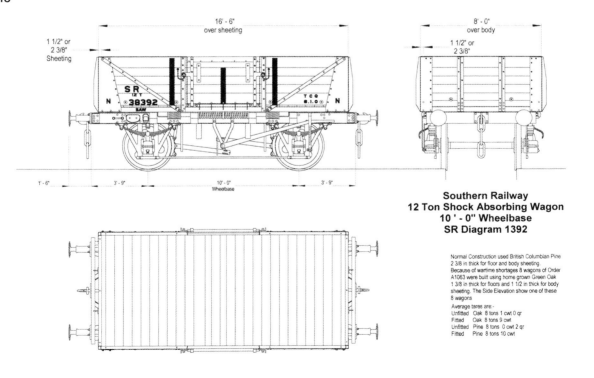

**Southern Railway
12 Ton Shock Absorbing Wagon
10 ' - 0" Wheelbase
SR Diagram 1392**

Normal Construction used British Columbian Pine
2 3/8 in thick for floor and body sheeting.
Because of wartime shortages 8 wagons of Order
A1063 were built using home grown Green Oak
1 3/8 in thick for floors and 1 1/2 in thick for body
sheeting. The Side Elevation show one of these
8 wagons
Average tares are:-
Unfitted Oak 8 tons 1 cwt 0 qr
Fitted Oak 8 tons 9 cwt
Unfitted Pine 8 tons 0 cwt 2 qr
Fitted Pine 8 tons 10 cwt

Plate 44 This photograph is of a triangulated underframe seen at Ashford in August 1947 and thought to be similar to that used under the Diagram 1391 open wagon built in September 1945. Note that the side springs follow the line of the solebar and that the axleboxes have unequal-length sides to suit. In the background are three vans in skeletal form and two Diagram 1379s undergoing conversion to cable wagons. Notice that they have completely new timber. *National Railway Museum, York*

Plate 45 A photograph taken in August 1949 of an all-steel 'high', believed to be the one that never had a diagram or traffic number. The underframe is of all-welded construction and has the running-gear arranged under a subframe, thus allowing the use of conventional axleboxes. The brake gear is another innovation and is of a type used by Bulleid for his Irish triangulated-underframe wagons. The headstocks are reversed — unusual for Britain but quite normal on the Continent. *R. Chorley collection*

It will have been noticed that very few of the opens built in Bulleid's time were equipped with automatic brakes. This was purely on account of a shortage of materials at the time, and Bulleid is known to have been of the opinion that all freight wagons should have been so fitted.

This chapter concludes with mention of two versions of open wagon built for BR in 1950. These were not ordered by the Southern Railway but they were designed in Bulleid's time and built at Ashford. Diagram BR1/034 was very similar to the SR Diagram 1375, and BR1/035 was very similar to SR 1392.

Above:

Plate 46 No DB457182 (BR Diagram 1/16), built at Ashford in 1949 — a very normal three-plank dropside, almost indistinguishable from hundreds of LMS examples, except for the headstocks and end stanchions. Note the open fronted axle boxes and the 1947 strengthened axle guards. This wagon is one of 1,500 open goods of various designs transferred to the Southern Regions Chief Civil Engineer in 1966 to meet the ever growing demand for ordinary open wagons brought about by mechanised track laying methods in connection with the laying of continuous welded rail. Most of these wagons were distinguished by green triangles painted on their left hand end. *Authors' collection*

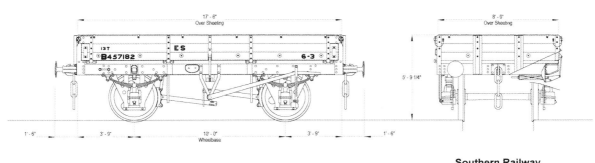

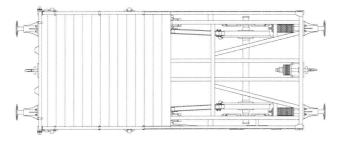

**Southern Railway
13 Ton Drop-sided Open Wagon
10 ' - 0" Wheelbase
BR Diagram 1/16**

Figure 19

Above:

Plate 47 No B483671 (BR Diagram 1/33), built at Ashford in 1949 as No B457021 and later renumbered. It is seen here at New Cross Gate in 1961, but it is in virtually as-built condition. Those who designed these wagons must have realised how heavy the doors would be. If they were really were designed for Brick traffic as some maintained, then the door weight would not have mattered too much as there would always have been a fair number of people about to handle them, at the time, the work of loading and unloading bricks was all done by hand. *A. Blackburn*

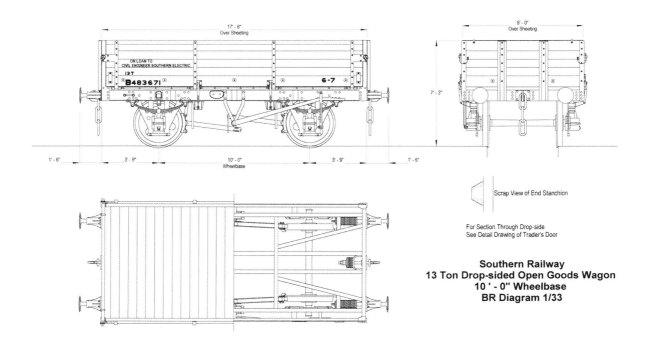

Southern Railway
13 Ton Drop-sided Open Goods Wagon
10 ' - 0" Wheelbase
BR Diagram 1/33

Figure 20

Chapter 4.
Container and Road-vehicle Trucks

The first wagons to be mentioned are 15 LBSCR vehicles ordered in 1920 (Diagram 1661). The Brighton company referred to these as 'Machinery wagons', but they were in fact very typical road-vehicle trucks classified by the Southern as 'Cartrucks' or 'Rucks'. As a class they are of interest in being amongst the last LBSCR wagons to remain in service (on the mainland); some were still in use in the early 1950s, and at least one acquired full BR grey livery. (These wagons are described fully in Volume Two.)

The first railway containers introduced on the Southern Railway in 1928/9 were various designs intended to carry meat from Southampton Docks to Smithfield Market. They were carried initially on the LSWR road-vehicle trucks that had been used for this traffic when it was carried in horse carts, and it was not until 1932 that it was found necessary to design special wagons for the conveyance of containers, by which time the containers themselves had diversified into a whole range of types travelling far and wide.

Containers and Road-vehicle Trucks

Pre-Grouping road-vehicle trucks on order 1/1/1923

Diagram	Order	Date	Quantity	Construction	Numbers	Examples of Tare weights	Notes
1661	LBSCR	Jun-20	15	1923	15 of 60423-545	NR (Diagram tare 5-12-0)	LBSCR Machinery truck. SR 'Ruck' or 'Cartruck'

Standard designs

Diagram	Order	Date	Quantity	Construction	Numbers	Examples of Tare weights	Notes
1383	A681	24/10/31	75	10/32-1/33	39501-75	39501 8-16-0, 39504 8-16-0	'Conflat D'. AVB, eight brake blocks
1383	A681	24/10/31	75	12/32-5/33	39576-650	39576 7-19-0, 39650 8-0-0	'Conflat C'. Provided with AVB from 1935, eight brake blocks ('Conflat D')
1382	A682	24/10/31	25	6/32-7/32	39001-25	39001 6-7-3, 39025 6-8-0	Type 1 'Conflat A'. AVB eight brake blocks
1382	A682	24/10/31	25	7/32	39026-50	39026 5-12-0, 39050 6-9-0	Type 1 'Conflat B'. Provided with AVB from 1935, four brake blocks ('Conflat A')
1382	A727	29/8/32	200	5/33-7/33	39051-250	39051 6-10-0, 39143 6-10-2	Type 1 'Conflat A'. AVB, eight brake blocks
1382A	A818	29/3/34	100	11/35	39251-350	39251 6-7-2, 39350 6-9-0	Type 2 'Conflat A'. AVB, four brake blocks. Rebuild. Later included on Diagram 1399.
1399	A917	3/4/36	50	9/38	39351-400	39351 6-10, 39400 6-10	Type 3 'Conflat A'. AVB, Morton clutch, four brake blocks
1399	A1033	14/6/38	50	7/40-9/42	39401-50	39401 6-9, 39450 6-12	Type 3 'Conflat A'. AVB, Morton clutch, four brake blocks
1399	A1193	1/5/40	50	9/42	39651-700	39651 6-12, 39700 6-12	Type 4 'Conflat A'. AVB, Morton clutch, four brake blocks
1399	A1733	1/10/41	103	9/42-10/42	39701-803	39701 6-12, 39803 6-12	Type 4 'Conflat A'. AVB, Morton clutch, four brake blocks
1399	A2519	16/4/43	102	1944	39804-905	39804 6-13, 39905 6-13	Type 4 'Conflat A'. AVB, Morton clutch, four brake blocks
1399	A3220	4/5/45	50	3/47-5/47	39906-55	39906 6-10, 39955 6-10	Type 4 'Conflat A'. AVB, Morton clutch, four brake blocks

Note: NR = No record

Below:
Plate 48 No 39248 (Diagram 1382), one of the last of the second batch of 9ft-wheelbase fitted 'Conflat B' wagons, seen here brand-new in August 1933. This and the first batch of fitted 'Conflats' have four crib-rail brackets, all the others having just three. The number 76 on the solebar was the code for Ashford Works, Lancing being 41 and Eastleigh 15; in BR days these numbers were increased by 4000. *R. Chorley collection*

Figure 21

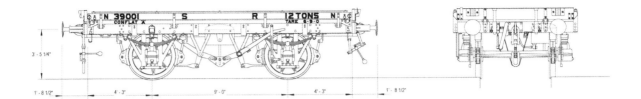

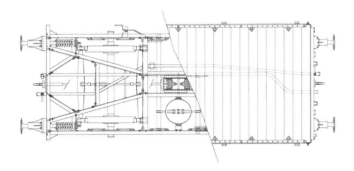

Southern Railway
12 Ton Container Truck
9 ' - 0'' Wheelbase Fitted
SR Diagram 1382

Below:
Plate 49 Another of the Diagram 1382 wagons. A useful photograph for modellers, this shows the construction of the siderail. The container is No FX563 of Diagram 3015, a 1933 rebuild of Diagram 3002. *R. Chorley collection*

Above:
Plate 50 A very nice view of No 39047, one of the Diagram 1382 wagons built without automatic brakes. This wagon is seen in Nine Elms yard, carrying insulated container No AF337 (Diagram 3014). The rope lashing is an everyday job, and as can be seen, the result is practical rather than elegant. *R. Chorley collection*

Below:
Plate 51 No 39164 (Diagram 1382), built in June 1933. The photograph was taken in October 1939 and the wagon is more or less as built, but the type designation has been altered to 'Conflat S', and the quarter weight painted out. The load is a trailer of anti-aircraft balloon gas cylinders. People from the Goods Department did not mind roping this sort of traffic, but the other companies' container wagons had spring-loaded shackles, and the lack of these made the Southern wagons unpopular for containers in their later years. *T. A. Barry collection*

Right:
Plate 52 No 39504 (Diagram 1383), seen at Ashford when brand-new in October 1932. Notice the steam-heat pipes carried by all the fitted 'Conflats' and the eye-bolt suspension; as far as Southern wagons were concerned, this was unique to 'Conflat' C and D types and the 'Pill-box' brake vans. *R. Chorley collection*

Below:
Plate 53 A nice end view showing (amongst other details) the removable end stanchions. These were a later addition, and not all the Conflats had them. *R. Chorley collection*

Above right:
Plate 54 No 39035 (Diagram 1382), built in July 1932 as an unfitted wagon and provided with vacuum brakes at some time from 1935 to 1937. It was posed for this photograph in November 1944 carrying new container No BD1224 (Diagram 3026); it has been reclassified as a 'low fit' and has lost its 'N' status, making it a 'common user' wagon. The writing generally corresponds to the 1936 style, but in this case the tare still quotes quarters. *R. Chorley collection*

Below right:
Plate 55 One of the earlier fitted wagons as repainted with '1942' writing. There is plenty of photographic evidence to show that, whilst many wagons were built during the war with unpainted woodwork, wagons given a heavy overhaul at this time were if possible given a full repaint. The container is one of 50 Diagram 3025s built for the LMS in 1944. *Authors' collection*

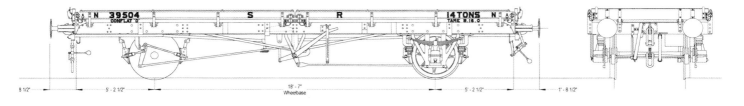

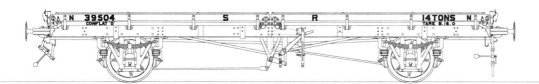

Southern Railway
14 Ton Container Truck (Long)
18 ' - 7'' Wheelbase Fitted
SR Diagram 1383

Vehicles built with 4 Lamp Irons
Righthand ones removed later.

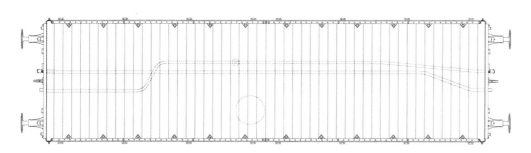

Figure 22

4 Tons
Tare 1'16'0"
723 Cu.ft.

S R
B D   1224

39035
LOWFIT   S   R   13 T
SR.
STANDARD
39035   6·6·0

Load 4 Tons
Tare 1'16'3"
Capacity 723 Cu.ft.

L M S

B   2253

39154 13T   S R
39154   6·11

Figure 23

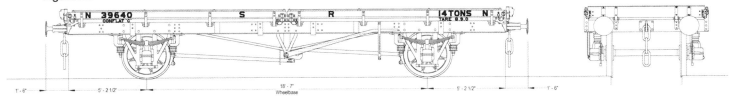

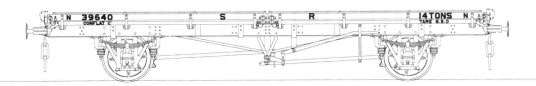

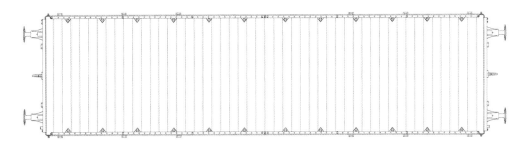

Below:
Plate 56 No 39351, the first of the 10ft-wheelbase Diagram 1399 wagons, built in September 1938 and featuring four brake blocks, Morton clutch and a single brake cylinder, and reverting to three crib-rail support brackets. All these Conflats were provided with wheel bar fixing racks, but not all had the wheel bars. This wagon is seen when only seven months old, but the letters 'XP' are possibly a later addition. The load is again gas cylinders, these being a very common sight during World War 2. *T. A. Barry collection*

Above:
Plate 57 No S39682 (Diagram 1399), a wagon built in September 1942 and known to some as a Type 4 (although how it differed from Type 3 No 39351 in the last picture is unknown). It is seen in a typical BR condition, with the designation now 'Carfit S'. 'Lowfit S' was also commonly found on these wagons in later days. *R. Chorley collection*

Below:
Plate 58 Another of the later wagons in BR days carrying a Diagram 3013 container. By this time, the wagon would have been painted in bauxite with white writing; the container was probably red. *Authors' collection*

Two basic types of container truck were built. One (Diagram 1382) used the standard 12-ton RCH 17ft 6in underframe and was intended for general duties. The other (Diagram 1383) could carry 14 tons, was 29ft long and, it would seem, was intended to replace the long LSWR 'Ruck' wagons (Diagram 1645) on the Southampton-Nine Elms services, where they carried two of the standard insulated containers closely roped back-to-back. The two types had many details in common, and both were designed as dual-purpose vehicles capable of also carrying road vehicles, for which they were fitted with wheel-bar racks, although they did not all carry the wheel bars. The first three orders were provided with lashing hooks, but the last 20 vehicles of the fourth order had these replaced with lashing rings, these being used on all subsequent wagons and later fitted to some of the earlier ones.

The short wagons were classified by the CME as Types 1 to 4; there are certainly differences between these groups, but it is not clear to which differences the types referred. The long wagons were provided with what was known as 'Guildford & Dorking' drawgear, presumed to have been specially strengthened in some way, possibly as a result of a breakaway on that heavily graded line.

Both types of wagon were originally built in fitted and unfitted versions, the latter finding work as road-vehicle trucks or runners. It was not long, however, before it was decided that all these wagons should be fitted, and in April 1935 the necessary authority was given for this work to be carried out, but it was not until 1937 that it was completed. An unusual feature of all the fitted wagons was that they were provided with steam-heat pipes. This, of course, enabled them to run on passenger-train services in the winter, or with banana vans, but exactly why this equipment was provided on these particular wagons is not known, and it is not thought to have been found on any other Southern wagons other than the banana vans and a few of the meat vans.

Both designs were well received, and, although only 150 of

the long type were built, the general-purpose version, if it may be so described, went on to total 755 wagons. This version of the design went through the usual evolutions of the standard RCH underframe, which was extended to 10ft from 1935, and the '1939'-type underframe, with non-continuous drawgear from 1940.

The container traffic continued to grow steadily, but from the war years onwards so too did the conveyance of road vehicles, and these wagons were increasingly used for this traffic; the other companies' container wagons were preferred for containers, as they were provided with screw shackles, which were much more convenient to use than the ropes required on a Southern wagon.

Mention has already been made of the various types of wagon provided for the Dover-Dunkirk train ferry service. In addition to these special vehicles, however, a number of ordinary SR wagon types were allowed to run on the Nord Railway of France by special arrangement, and these included container trucks Nos 39001-250/501-650.

Postwar, at least, Dunkirk was regarded as a normal Southern depot, and it was not unusual for ordinary British wagons to travel there. They should not have gone any further, but it is recalled that on one occasion a request was received from the SNCF for spares for a BR mineral 'stopped' at Lille; how and in what circumstances it got there is anyone's guess. In 1950 two of the long type came into the limelight when they were transferred to the passenger stock as baggage trucks for use on the 'Golden Arrow' service. These were Nos 39582/614, which became Nos S4207/8. For this duty they were repainted in the Southern Region version of the crimson red livery, later changed to Southern Region green. In 1961 the use of the baggage boxes was discontinued, and the wagons reverted to freight stock with their original numbers.

Only one of these wagons is known to be preserved, this being one of the long type, and can be found on the Bluebell Railway.

Figure 24

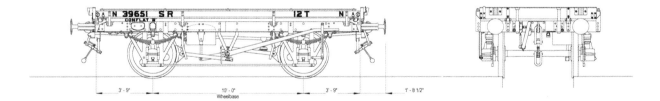

Southern Railway
13 Ton Container Truck
10 ' - 0" Wheelbase Fitted
SR Diagram 1399

Chapter 5.
Mineral Wagons

As already mentioned, coal was always the backbone of the railways' freight traffic, the Southern being no exception, but, apart from loading a comparatively small amount from coastal shipping and that produced in Kent, the greater part of this traffic came onto the Southern in private-owner wagons.

In 1923 the SR recorded a mineral-wagon fleet of 4,755 wagons, all of which were former SECR vehicles, except for 225 which came from the LBSCR. In that year, however, it was decided that many of these wagons were more accurately described as 'open goods', and in 1924 the figure was down to 2,111 — roughly 6% of the total number of traffic wagons. Almost all these wagons were standard 12-ton RCH minerals built between 1910 and 1914, so they were comparatively new.

However, the majority were destined to have quite short lives, the first being withdrawn as early as 1925. Their totals held up well enough until the years of the depression, but thereafter they were withdrawn as surplus to requirements and as a source of wheelsets for the various 'Rebuild' wagons that Ashford produced in the 1930s.

By 1933 the number of minerals was down to just 741, although to some extent this very low figure was explained by the use of large numbers of the new eight-plank open goods for coal traffic, especially in Kent. During the course of that year, however, 200 12-ton seven-plank minerals were produced, and by the end of the year these had been followed by the first of 989 20-ton eight-plank wagons.

SR Mineral Wagons

Diagram	Order	Date	Quantity	Construction	Numbers	Examples of Tare weights	Notes
1384	A639	14/4/31	200	8/33-10/33	40001-200	40001 6-3-2, 40100 6-6-0	
1386	A678	4/9/31	100	12/33-2/34	40201-300	40291 8-18-1, 40235 8-19-0	'Loco Coal'
1386	A786	25/10/33	200	6/34-3/35	41001-200	41001 8-18-0, 41200 9-0-0	
1386	A810	27/3/34	680	10/34-4/35	40301-980	40301 9-0-0, 40620 9-1-0, 40980 9-0-0	Order originally for 700 wagons, amended 13/8/34
1374	?	?	2	1934	18780, 27545	27545 5-14-1	Rebuilt from Diagram 1369
1386	A937	3/7/36	9	12/39	41201-9	41201 8-19-0, 41209 8-17-0	Order originally for six wagons only
1390	A2843	6/4/44	100	1945	41210-309	41210 7-3, 41309 7-3, 225 6-11, 41228 6-10	
1390	A3083	7/11/44	1850	1945/6	NE267100-8949	NR	No bottom doors. LNER Diagram 192

Note: NR = No record

Below:
Plate 59 No 40040 (Diagram 1384). Regrettably the official De'Ath & Condon photograph of one of these wagons seems not to have survived. This picture was taken by H. C. Casserley in March 1937, when the wagon was already four years old. Seven-plank minerals with steel underframes were a little unusual in themselves, but what is particularly interesting about this wagon is that it clearly has second-hand wheels, thus making it technically a 'Rebuild', but there was no record of this, so one must conclude that the works saved a little money on its own account.
H. C. Casserley

Figure 25

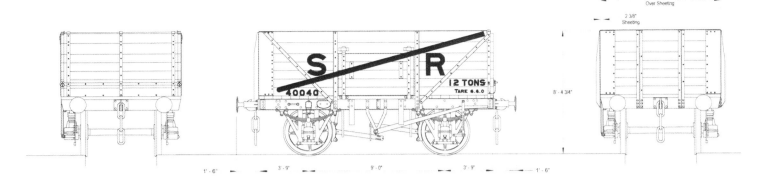

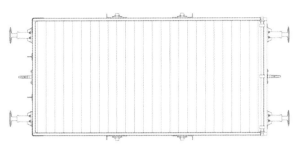

Southern Railway
12 Ton End Door Mineral Wagon
9 ' - 0" Wheelbase
SR Diagram 1384

Above:
Plate 60 No S40008 (Diagram 1384), photographed after what was probably its first (and possibly its last) full overhaul. It has the usual Bulleid modifications, but it is basically still in the condition in which it was built. These were very rare wagons, this being one of only three photographs known to exist. *National Railway Museum, York*

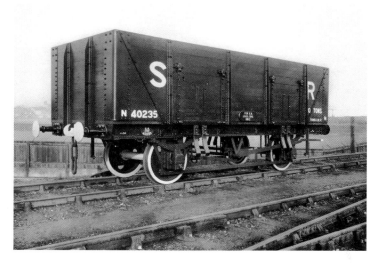

Above:

Plate 61 No 40235 (Diagram 1386), new in January 1934. The white axles, buffer heads and hooks are definitely not painted in their standard colour! Note the RCH 10 x 4½ in axleboxes standard for these wagons. Nos 40201-300 were all 'boarded' for locomotive coal only, but they were not Departmental wagons in the normal sense of the word; the livery is absolutely standard, except for the photographic finish already mentioned. As a design, these wagons were not unlike certain LNER vehicles. *R. Chorley collection*

Above:

Plate 62 No S40610 as shopped by Ashford in 1948. The wagon seems to have been entirely re-sheeted; the new planks do not quite line up with the corner plate holes, and some of the bottom corner bolts have been left out. And what, one wonders, has happened to the tops of the corner plates? *National Railway Museum, York*

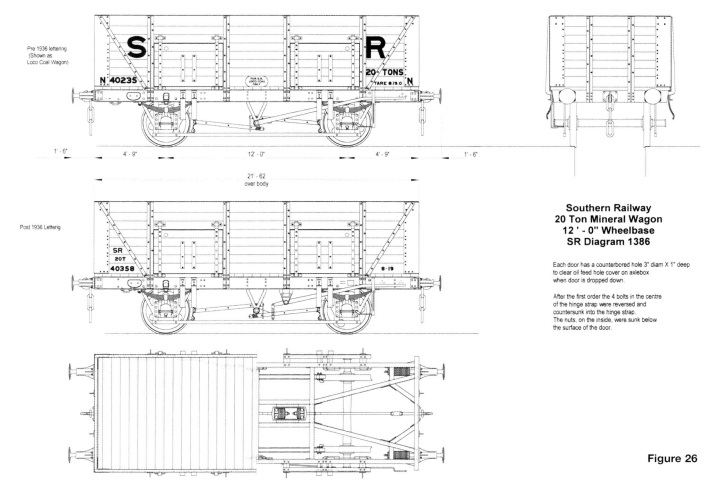

Pre 1936 lettering
(Shown as
Loco Coal Wagon)

Post 1936 Lettering

**Southern Railway
20 Ton Mineral Wagon
12 ' - 0" Wheelbase
SR Diagram 1386**

Each door has a counterbored hole 3" diam X 1" deep
to clear oil feed hole cover on axlebox
when door is dropped down.

After the first order the 4 bolts in the centre
of the hinge strap were reversed and
countersunk into the hinge strap.
The nuts, on the inside, were sunk below
the surface of the door.

Figure 26

Left:
Plate 63 No 41214 of Diagram 1390, seen as new in April 1945 and showing very well the '1942' writing applied to these and the open goods wagons of the period, all ironwork being black, except for the white diagonal strap indicating the end door. These wagons also have bottom doors, and, hoppers apart, are believed to have been the only Southern wagons to have this feature. The bottom doors were possibly requested by the RCH as a part of the national mineral-wagon balance. The only coal-drops on Southern Railway property were inside Durnsford Road power station, although one or two 'foreign' depots south of the river had them.
National Railway Museum, York

The 12-ton wagons were similar to the standard RCH design but had the wider door of the standard SR open goods wagons. They had end but no bottom doors and were built on a steel underframe. It was more usual to construct mineral wagons with a wooden underframe, but Ashford was to build them and was organised to build wagons with steel underframes. The 20-ton wagons were built on the standard RCH 21ft 6in steel underframe and had neither end nor bottom doors. For their time they were quite impressive wagons. The LNER had some of almost identical appearance. It had originally been intended to build 1,000 of these wagons, but 20 were built as open goods ferry wagons. The remaining nine used the underframes of some passenger-rated milk wagons which had proved unsatisfactory as four-wheelers due to their rough riding. Neither drawings nor photographs of these nine wagons have come to light, but it is quite likely that they varied in small details from the original build.

Mention must be made of two former Brighton five-plank open goods (Diagram 1369) that were rebuilt in 1934 as seven-plank minerals. The exact purpose of this exercise remains a mystery; one was sent to the Isle of Wight, while the other remained in obscurity on the mainland.

By 1936 the mineral fleet was back up to 1,575 wagons and, in terms of carrying-capacity, reached its peak, at 19,600 tons.

The numbers of the pre-Grouping 12-ton wagons continued to drop during the war years, and in 1945 a batch of 100 RCH 13-ton eight-plank minerals was built, this time with end and bottom doors, provided probably to make up the Southern's pool contribution. Again, they had steel underframes, but this was the norm for the eight-plank design. These wagons were followed by an order for no fewer than 1,850 similar wagons for the LNER, and one wonders if

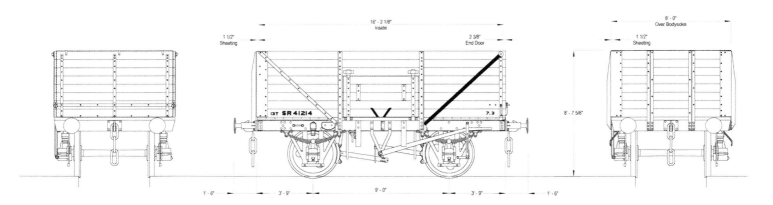

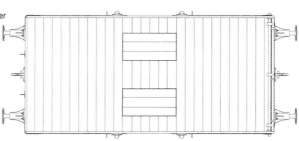

End Door. Top and Bottom 2 Planks are 2 3/8" thick the central 5 Planks are 1 1/2" with 7/8" packings under the Door Straps.

**Southern Railway
13 Ton Mineral Wagon
With End and Bottom Doors
9 ' - 0" Wheelbase
SR Diagram 1390**

Figure 27

this was not in fact a LNER design 'traced off' and given an Eastleigh drawing number.

As mentioned earlier in the book, Bulleid had an all-steel mineral wagon designed with the object of producing a wagon that was significantly lighter than the standard designs then being built. With a carrying-capacity of 17 tons and a tare of 6 tons 17cwt the wagon was undoubtedly lighter than the conventional designs, but equally there can be no doubt that it would have been an expensive wagon to build and maintain, and of course it was completely non-standard. Bulleid does not seem to have had any HO authority to build this wagon, which was probably regarded as an experiment. It was numbered 1428S and seems to have spent its entire life as an internal in Lancing Works yard.

The Southern mineral was always a rare beast; some of the 20-ton wagons were non-'common users' allocated to Kent Loco coal traffic, but even these do not seem to have wandered far. The war must have dispersed them somewhat, but even in the 1950s one would have had to travel down to the Kent Coalfield area to be sure of finding any. On 1 January 1948 they formed just 4% of the fleet inherited by BR's Southern Region.

Above:
Plate 64 It is far from certain that the Diagram 1390 wagons are an SR design. Comparison of this wagon — LNER No 268158, built at Darlington in 1945 to LNER Diagram 192 — with SR No 41214 in the previous picture reveals the only differences (apart from the axleboxes) to be thicker sides on the LNER wagon, as is apparent from the capping clips; the Southern wagon has these on the end door, but not the sides. *R. S. Carpenter Photos*

Above:
Plate 65 The Bulleid all-steel mineral, photographed at Lancing in September 1948 and destined to become No 1428S. The underframe is the same as that seen under the open wagon in Chapter 3, but the buffers have external plungers — not so unusual in mainland Europe, but believed unique in Britain. The body was claimed to have a capacity of 17 tons, but one doubts its durability, the strengthening plates being only touch-welded. Note the LNER-type axleboxes, a design much favoured by Bulleid. Did he have anything to do with the design in his LNER days? *R. Chorley collection*

Chapter 6.
Covered Goods Wagons

Covered goods wagons were the second-most numerous type of Southern wagon, and there was a considerable increase in their numbers in Southern days as they replaced the sheeted opens. In 1923 they made up just over 11% of the fleet, and this remained fairly constant until about 1931. Thereafter there was a steady rise until the outbreak of war, after which construction increased rapidly until by 1948 they made up no less than 27% of the wagon stock and as might be guessed, the vast majority were by then of standard SR design.

There was no great shortage of covered goods wagons on the Southern in 1923, but there were two outstanding orders from the LSWR, each for 100 vehicles, and one from the SECR for the conversion of six of its latest design to a 'ventilated' version.

The South Western vans were built in 1923/4 (Diagrams 1408/9), the South Eastern conversions in l923 (Diagram 1427); all carried pre-Grouping numbers.

When in 1924 a further 100 covered goods were ordered, there was no time to prepare a design based on the new '1923' standard RCH underframe, so, as Ashford was to build the vehicles, it was decided to use the latest SECR design (Diagram 1426). (Details of the LSWR designs will be found in Volume One, those of the SECR examples in Volume Three.)

The first SR design for a covered goods wagon was one for the narrow-gauge Lynton & Barnstaple line; full details of all that line's goods stock appear in Volume Two.

It was not until May 1929 that the first standard Southern Railway covered goods wagons appeared, and, if there was any doubt as to the design origins of the opens, there was certainly none where the covered design was concerned. The Lancing Drawing Office prepared the drawings, and the underframe was the now-standard '1923' RCH design, but the body was based on Lynes' SECR design, although as mentioned previously, the doors were simplified by the omission of the bottom drop-door.

The new wagons were allocated to Diagram 1428. No fewer than 450 were built in the next two years, and these were followed by a fitted version, of which 526 were built between June 1930 and July 1935. As with the opens, there were 'Rebuild' versions using second-hand wheels. First came 750 using LSWR wheels (Diagram 1429) and then a fitted batch of 300 rated at 12-tons, the wheel origins of which were not stated (Diagram 1428A). All these wagons had the standard 9ft wheelbase.

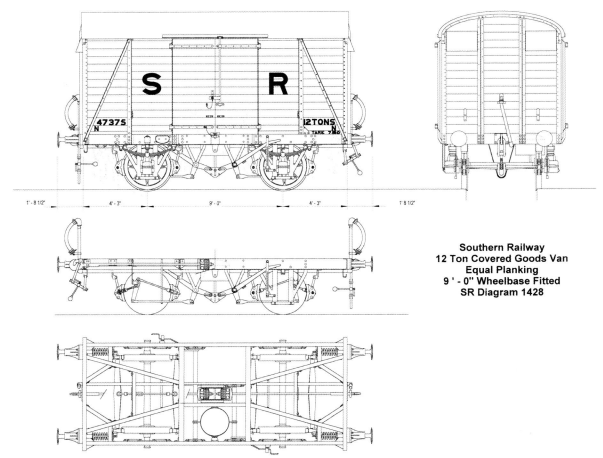

Southern Railway
12 Ton Covered Goods Van
Equal Planking
9 ' - 0" Wheelbase Fitted
SR Diagram 1428

Figure 28

Covered goods wagons built or purchased by the Southern Railway

Pre-Grouping covered goods wagons on order 1/1/1923

Diagram	Order	Date	Quantity	Construction	Numbers	Examples of Tare weights	Notes
1408	LSWR	5/21	100	1923	50 of 42233-75, 44276-325	NR (Diagram tare 7-3-1)	
1427	SECR	?	6	1918	45617-9/21-3	45621 7-0-3	Diagram 1426 converted 1923
1409	LSWR	5/22	100	1924	43326-425	NR (Diagram tare 7-3-1)	Became SR order E3

Pre-Grouping covered goods wagon design ordered by the Southern Railway

Diagram	Order	Date	Quantity	Construction	Numbers	Examples of Tare weights	Notes
1426	A26	17/03/24	100	12/25-1/26	47101-47200	NR (Diagram tare 6-17-2)	

SR standard covered goods wagon designs

Diagram	Order	Date	Quantity	Construction	Numbers	Examples of Tare weights	Notes
1458	L110	6/4/25	4	8/27	47042-5	47042 6-12-0, 47043 6-12-0	Lynton & Barnstaple line (1ft 11½in gauge)
1428	A129	26/6/25	100	5/29-6/29	45908-46007	45908 7-1-0, 46007 6-17-2	
1428	A262	20/6/27	100	6/29	46008-107	46008 6-19-1, 46105 6-17-2, 46107 6-17-2	
1428	A345	8/6/28	100	6/29-12/29	47201-300	47201 6-18-0, 47272 6-18-2, 47300 7-13-2	
1428	A470	17/5/29	100	6/30-9/30	47301-400	47301 7-1-2, 47375 7-17-2, 47400 7-17-0	AVB 1 x 18in cyl, eight brake blocks
1428	A578	16/5/30	150	8/31-9/31	47401-550	47401 7-1-0, 47550 7-1-0	
1429	A640	14/4/31	450	11/31-1/32	44427-649/51-85/7-97/9 etc	44427 6-15-0, 44718 6-17-0, 46190 6-17-2	Rebuild; LSWR wheels etc
1429	A641	14/3/41	150	1/32-3/32	46774-923	46774 7-11-0, 46923 7-10-1	Rebuild; LSWR wheels etc.
							AVB 1 x 15in cyl, eight brake blocks
1428	A738	7/10/32	225	11/33-3/34	47701-925	47701 7-14-1, 47925 7-15-2	AVB 1 x 15in cyl, eight brake blocks
							125 possibly 12-ton Rebuilds
1428	A763	9/6/33	51	3/34-4/34	47926-476	47926 7-11-2, 47976 7-12-0	AVB 1 x 15in cyl, eight brake blocks
1428A	A811	27/3/34	300	6/35-7/35	47977-48276	47977 7-16-2, 48101 7-15-0, 48276 7-14-0	1-ton Rebuilds. AVB 1 x 15in cyl, eight brake blocks
1430	E823	3/8/34	100	3/35-5/35	45918/23/5-6/9/32-3/40 etc	46100 6-19-0, 47274 6-18-0, 47301 7-1-2	Diagram 1428 converted
							AVB 1 x 18in cyl , four brake blocks, WP
1458	A866	30/4/35	500	5/36-9/36	48277-48776	48277 7-9-0, 48501 7-9-0, 48776 7-7-0	AVB 1 x 18in cyl , four brake blocks
1459	?	1936-8	100	8/36-3/38	48333-6/54/5/77/8/669 etc	NR (No tare quoted on the Diagram)	Diagram 1458 converted for H&P Ltd biscuit traffic 'PARTO' AVB 1 x 18in or 2 x 15in cyl, four brake blocks.
1458	A916	3/4/36	450	2/37-1/38	48777-49226	48777 7-14, 48981 7-11, 49226 7-14	AVB 2 x 15in cyl, four brake blocks
1460	?	?	4	11/37-6/38	48323/59/980, 49168	48323 7-13-1, 48980 8-2-0, 49168 8-2-0	Diagram 1458 converted for egg traffic. AVB: 48323/59 1 x 18in; 48980, 49168 2 x 15in, four brakeblocks
1458	A969	6/5/37	325	11/38-10/39	49227-551	49227 7-13, 49303 7-13, 49551 7-10	AVB 2 x 15in cyl, four brake blocks. '2+2' planking commenced with this order, generally from 49428
1458	A1034	14/6/38	400	5/40-12/40	49552-951	49552 7-18, 49720 7-8	AVB 1 x 18in cyl, four brake blocks. 200 completed at Eastleigh
1458	A1175	27/2/40	750	2/41-6/41	59251-60000	59251 7-15, 59735 7-9 (VP), 59773 7-13	AVB 2 x 15in cyl, four brake blocks, some built VP fitted later. 300 completed at Eastleigh
1458	A1182	1/5/40	360	7/40-1/41	64921-65280	64921 7-10 (1 x 18), 64953 7-10 (2 x 15)	AVB mixed 1 x 18in or 2 x 15in, all four brake blocks
1455	A1732	1/10/41	534	5/42-9/42	44719-82/4-835/9 etc	45103 7-4, 45321 7-4	Some of these vehicles were finished at Eastleigh, a few at Lancing
1455	A1939	9/3/42	200	6/42-1/43	65281-480	65364 7-3, 65365 7-6, 65458 7-5	Some finished at Eastleigh, some at Lancing
1455		9/3/42	150	1942	LMS 521140-289	NR	LMS Lot 1334, LMS Diagram 2078
1455	A1939	9/3/42	650	6/42-1/43	GW 144269-918	NR	GWR Lot 1430, GWR Diagram V35
1455	A2300	20/11/42	499	6/43-10/43	65481-979	65598 7-1, 65560 7-2, 65705 7-2	50 finished at Eastleigh and 70 at Lancing
1454	A2300	20/11/42	1	11/43	65980	65980 7-2	As Diagram 1455 but built with single-radius roof
1455	A2506	14/4/43	300	12/43-1/44	59101-59250, 65981-66130	65981 7-6, 65998 7-7, 66130 7-6	Some of these vehicles were finished at Lancing
1455	A2517	15/4/43	250	9/43-12/43	LMS 523290-523539	NR	LMS Lot 1373, LMS Diagram 2078
1455	A2518	16/4/43	250	9/43-12/43	54001-54250	54001 7-2, 54125 7-6, 54250 7-3	54188 noted with a BR plate 'Built Derby 1943' — almost certainly an error
1452	A2853	19/4/44	543	?/45-12/45	49952-94 50901-51000 etc	49952 7-0, 50901 7-4, 54251 7-3	A few finished at Lancing. Order includes 93 war-loss replacements
1452	A3218	4/5/45	510	3/46-7/46	56501-57010	56501 7-2, 56725 7-3, 57010 7-2	
1452	A3353	15/4/46	240	7/49-11/49	B752350-B752589	NR (Diagram tare 7-0)	BR Lot Pt 2062
1452	A3353	15/4/46	160	9/49-11/49	B752790-B752949	NR (Diagram tare 7-9)	AVB 1 x 18in cyl, four brake blocks. BR Lot Pt 2063 SR Nos 57022-181 allocated but not used
1452	A3445	1/8/47	200	8/49-12/49	B752590-B752789	NR (Diagram tare 7-0)+G24	BR Lot Pt 2062 SR Nos 57182-381 allocated but not used
1452	A3448	1/8/47	150	11/49-12/49	B752950-B753099	NR (Diagram tare 7-9)	AVB 1 x 18in cyl, four brake blocks. BR Lot Pt 2063 SR Nos 45480-555, 46191-22893-327 allocated

Note: NR = No record

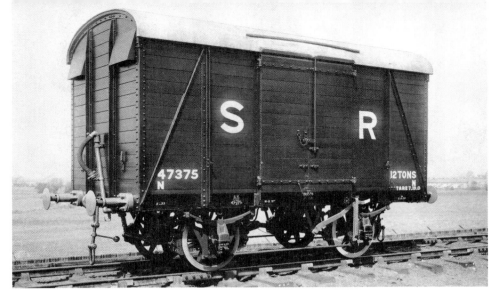

Left:
Plate 66 No 47375 (Diagram 1428), built in August 1930. This photograph, taken in May 1933, shows it in as-built condition; presumably the wagon had come into shops for some attention and was available for the 'official photograph'. Eight brake blocks and one brake cylinder were specified for all the 9ft-wheelbase covered goods wagons built with vacuum brakes. *R. Chorley collection*

Right:
Plate 67 In the absence of a photograph of a non-fitted Diagram 1428, here is No S44475, a non-fitted Diagram 1429. As a 'Rebuild' provided with LSWR wheels and axleboxes, it is rated at 10 tons, but it is otherwise very similar to an unfitted Diagram 1428. It is seen here after overhaul in 1948, but, apart from the livery, it is as built. Notice in the background the eight-plank open with 18in initials in good condition, 10 years after they officially became obsolete. *National Railway Museum, York*

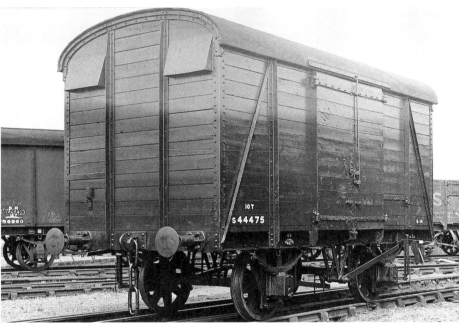

Left:
Plate 68 No S46919, a fitted example of Diagram 1429, again virtually as built. Impossible to tell from the picture is that, to accommodate the LSWR wheelsets, the solebars are two inches further apart than on those vehicles built to standard RCH dimensions. No photograph is available of a Diagram 1428A; this was the 12-ton rebuild, presumed built to standard RCH dimensions throughout, using wheels taken from SECR 12-ton RCH minerals, many of which were withdrawn at the time. *National Railway Museum, York*

Above:
Plate 69 No 46097 (Diagram 1430) ready for traffic in May 1935. This wagon has one brake cylinder and four brake blocks arranged in the manner usually used by the Southern for retro-fitting a 9ft-wheelbase wagon with vacuum brakes. At this time one would expect a white roof, but, even allowing for variations in photographic reproduction, this one seems to be dark grey. Note the tare weight in both imperial and metric units. *R. Chorley collection*

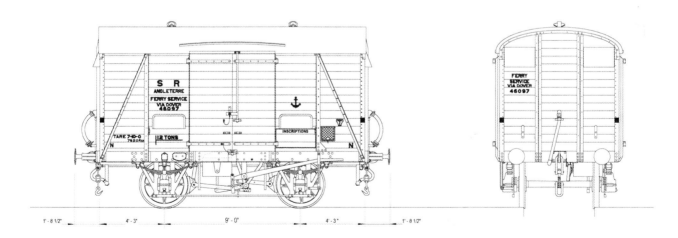

Southern Railway 10 Ton Covered Goods Van Dover Ferry Service
9' 0" Wheelbase Fitted with Vacuum Brake and Air Brake Pipe
SR Diagram 1430

Figure 29

In 1934 there arose a need for vans for the forthcoming Dover-Dunkirk train-ferry service, and it was decided to convert 100 of the Diagram 1428 type. The conversion involved the addition of Westinghouse brake pipes, safety chains, additional side ventilators and of course suitable writing. These vehicles were the first Southern wagons to lose their large (18in) Company initials in favour of 5in lettering — possibly a Union Internationale Chemins de Fer (UIC) standard.

In 1935 the wheelbase for all new 17ft 6in wagons was lengthened to 10ft in accordance with an RCH decision, and this produced the Diagram 1458, of which 2,885 were built between May 1936 and May 1941. This, however, is not the full story, for in late 1938 the '2+2' planking started to appear, and approximately 1800 of them exhibited this feature. This was

followed in July 1940 by the adoption of the '1939' RCH underframe design, this applying to the last 1,110. All the Diagram 1458s were fitted, although a few went into traffic originally as 'piped' vehicles until such time as their vacuum cylinders became available. The history of some of these vehicles is complicated. At least 67 went to the War Department as new or nearly-new vehicles, most for use in SR-constructed workshop trains. Others were used to house mobile generator sets also owned by the Government, and yet others passed in and out of Departmental use for other wartime reasons. The majority of the WD-owned vans finished up at the end of the war on various military railways, but examples have been noted in the Middle East and Continental Europe; there is even one preserved in Vienna.

Right:
Plate 70 No 48679 (Diagram 1458), an early example of the 10ft-wheelbase version of the standard Southern van. Not many of these vehicles carried the 18in Company initials, as these were about to give way to the 5in standard. In fact this photograph well illustrates the 'bastard' style that was used on a number of vehicles at this time — large initials but all other writing to the new '1936' standard. The brakes have one 18in cylinder and four brake blocks with lift-links. Notice that the 10ft-wheelbase wagons have no rain-strip over the doors. *F. Foote collection*

Below:
Plate 71 No 48977 (Diagram 1458), which differs from the wagon shown previously in that it has two 15in vacuum cylinders and a Morton clutch. This photograph shows the other side of the brake arrangement on No 48916 portrayed in Chapter 2. The writing has now settled down to the standard '1936' style. *R. Chorley collection*

Below right:
Plate 72 A nice end view of a standard covered goods wagon. It happens to be a 10ft-wheelbase wagon built on a 1923 RCH underframe; had it been built on the 1939 version there would be a vertical line of three rivets visible either side of the draw plate. *R. Chorley collection*

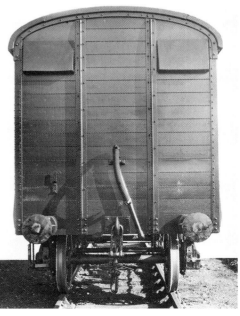

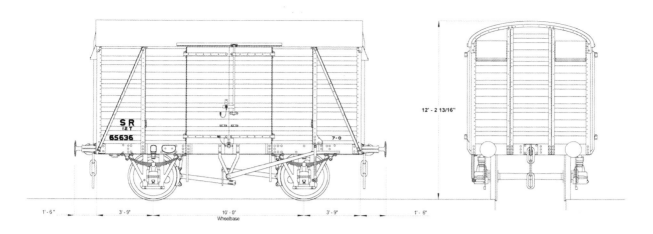

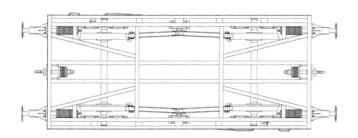

Southern Railway
12 Ton Covered Goods Van
Unequal Planking
10 ' - 0" Wheelbase
SR Diagram 1455

Figure 30

The next development produced Diagram 1455. This is best described as an 'austerity' version of the previous design — there was no vacuum equipment, and, although the bodywork featured the '2+2' arrangement of the previous design, some utilised home-grown fir, such vehicles having a second internal 'skin' of vertical planks.

Whilst on the subject of bodywork generally, it should be explained that it was Southern practice to build steel underframes complete in one shop and then shunt them round to another for the woodwork to be put on — a method that could lead to minor variations appearing between wagons with consecutive numbers. This came about because the shunters would be asked to put so many underframes into the shop; they would do this, but not necessarily in numerical order. There were a lot of minor variations in the planking of the wartime-built vans, some having normal planked doors and '2+2' sides and *vice versa*. Under the direction of the Railway Executive Committee (REC), the design was built for both the GWR and the LMS; the former had 650 and the latter 400, all being built 1942-4. These vans generally had consistent '2+2' doors and sides and were finished in their respective owners' liveries.

The shortage of suitable timber became very serious as the war progressed, and in 1944 it was decided to use plywood for the bodywork, including, in some cases, the centre section of the roof. A new diagram (1452) was issued for the plywood vans, and the first of these appeared in January 1945. The Southern already had considerable experience of plywood, as it had been using this material since 1929 for all its covered containers. Presumably this use had not previously spread to wagons on account of cost or possibly the extra thickness required. Whatever the reason, plywood soon established itself as a most suitable material for covered vans, and thereafter the Southern used nothing else.

Mention must be made of a couple of very interesting experiments carried out in 1943. The problem of the leaking roofs, already noted, was virtually cured by the adoption of plywood sides, as this stopped the 'racking' that led to the roof boards' moving. However, this was not before a van was built with a single-radius roof (No 65980, to Diagram 1454); another (No 49363) was rebuilt with a ridge roof rather like the Italian Railway vans, being also clad all over in 'Ruberoid' — a material that had by this time replaced canvas as the standard roof covering. There was also a second 'penthouse'-roofed van (No 49720) that was only partially clad in Ruberoid. As it has proved impossible to find any photographs of this wagon, it is appropriate here to include a short description of the method of its construction. A standard wagon fron Diagram 1458 was used, the only alteration to the body ironwork being the replacement of the curved roof irons with flat-sided 'V'-shaped examples. (See Fig 32 for the end profiles.) Two bodyside quarters (on opposite sides of the body) were sheeted with 2¾ x½ in horizontal boards, with the exception of the bottom 1ft 10in of the ends, which were ¾in thick. All the horizontal; boards, doors and roof were covered with Ruberoid. The joint in the ridged roof was covered by a 3½ x¹⁄₁₆ in galvanised steel strip. The lightweight door was the same as that provided on the first ridged-roof wagon (No 49363, illustrated on page 66). Bulleid clearly thought these were ideas worth trying, but there was no follow-up.

As a wartime design, the Diagram 1452 was conceived as a non-fitted wagon, but 250 were built with vacuum brakes in 1945, and BR was able to build a further batch in 1949. It should, perhaps, be explained that, whilst World War 2 had ended in 1945, the shortage of materials etc it had occasioned lasted in some cases into the 1950s. No fewer than 1,803 Diagram 1452s were built, including 750 for BR.

Left:
Plate 73 No S49186 (Diagram 1459), one of the wagons built new as a 'Parto' (partitioned) in 1938; earlier examples were converted from Diagram 1458s. It had been thought that all 100 'Partos' were always allocated to Huntley & Palmer's biscuit traffic from Reading, but this one, seen in 1952, is lettered to work between Nine Elms and Bideford. The wagon seems to be as built, with two 15in cylinders and a Morton clutch, but the wheels have almost certainly been changed from the disc type with three holes. *R. S. Carpenter Photos*

Right:
Plate 74 No 48323 (Diagram 1460), built in December 1936. This wagon was repainted in June 1938 in the livery of the Express Dairy Co. The main body colour is dark blue and the private lettering is cream-shaded light blue. Four vans were painted in this manner, but all reverted to their normal livery in February and March 1942. The blue colour was not as dark as 'Navy' blue, but considerably darker than the shade currently used by 'Express Dairy Transport'. *R. Chorley collection*

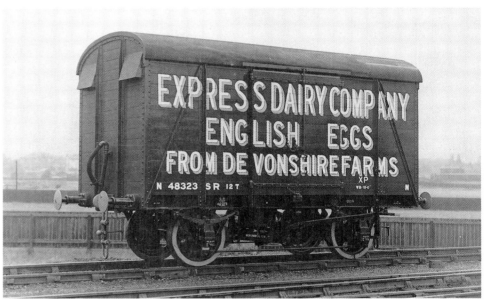

Left:
Plate 75 No S49820 of Diagram 1458. The '2+2' planking was introduced in this diagram, the first dating from January 1939. Of the 2,885 wagons built to this diagram, approximately 60% had the 2+2 planking. The 1939 version of the RCH standard underframe also appeared under these wagons, around 40% having this feature. The brakes are of the single 18in-cylinder type with lift-links. *Authors' collection*

Above:
Plate 76 No 1971S, a Diagram 1458 built in April 1941 as No 59773, and rebuilt as a mobile generator set in November 1944. The underframe of this wagon was built at Lancing, and the body at Eastleigh. The body and underframe are probably painted light grey, a colour used for various service vehicles during and after the war. Service vehicles were normally taken from older stock, but something in the order of 80 to 90 of these vans were taken new or nearly new, either as service vehicles or for conversion into workshop-train wagons for the Army. *R. Chorley collection*

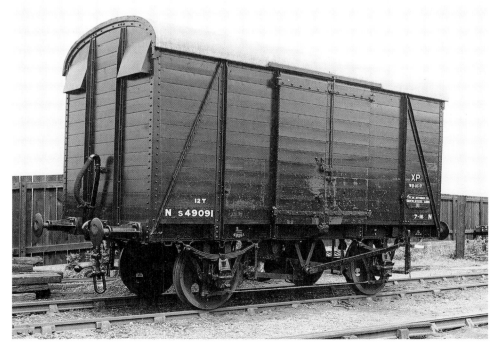

Right:
Plate 77 A fine view of one of the early Diagram 1458s — No S49091 — after overhaul at Ashford in 1948. This wagon was built in 1937 with two 15in vacuum cylinders and a Morton clutch. *National Railway Museum, York*

Above
Plate 78 GWR No 144293, one of the 650 Diagram 1455, built for the Great Western between June 1942 and January 1943. The livery is grey, but how closely it matched the owners usual shade is not known. The under gear is black, the normal GWR practice for these items was we believe grey. Note the stiffening ridge pressed into the end louvres, this was a Bulleid feature designed to give greater strength. *Ray Chorley collection*

Left:
Plate 79 This Diagram 1458 van — No S65171 — it should have had '2+2' planking. The completion of this particular order was much delayed, and this wagon seems to have been 'lost' for so long that it was finished with plywood sheeting. What occurred was that the wagons were built in skeletal form and then stored at outstations until such times as material was available for their completion. The problem was that they were not always stored where they were supposed to be, and so they became lost until a special search found them. *Authors' collection*

Left:
Plate 80 No 49363 (Diagram 1458), built in January 1939 and rebuilt with a ridged-roof body in 1943. The bodywork is of very narrow horizontal planks, covered all over in 'Ruberoid', a rubber-like material much used by the SR for standard van roofs. The boarding reads: 'This wagon to be returned loaded or empty to Bricklayers Arms and not to work off the S Rly'. The wagon is seen in damaged condition, possibly a result of enemy action at Nine Elms in May 1944. Note also the lack of a tail-lamp bracket; fitted SR wagons normally had one on the left-hand side. When this wagon was withdrawn is not known, but it was noted in traffic in 1961.
R. Chorley collection

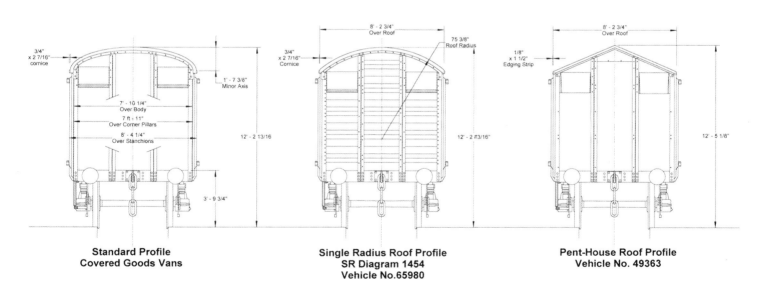

Standard Profile
Covered Goods Vans

Single Radius Roof Profile
SR Diagram 1454
Vehicle No.65980

Pent-House Roof Profile
Vehicle No. 49363

Southern Railway
Profiles Covered Goods Vans

Figure 31

Above:
Plate 81 No 54409 (Diagram 1452), seen when new at Ashford in 1945. Vans, unlike the open goods, were given fully painted bodies throughout the war. The livery is the normal brown with white lettering on black patches. The roof is light grey Ruberoid.
National Railway Museum, York

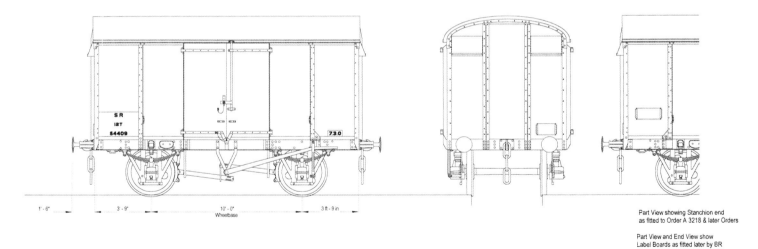

1' - 6"   3' - 9"   10' - 0"   3 ft - 9 in
Wheelbase

Part View showing Stanchion end
as fitted to Order A 3218 & later Orders

Part View and End View show
Label Boards as fitted later by BR

**Southern Railway
12 Ton Covered Goods Van
10 ' - 0" Wheelbase
SR Diagram 1452**

Figure 32

Above:
Plate 82 No 50933 (Diagram 1452). Order No A2853 had the centre portion of the roof formed of plywood, the flanks being of normal timber. The photograph shows this form of construction very well! *R. Chorley collection*

Below:
Plate 83 No B752909 (Diagram 1452), built in November 1949 and one of the last SR-designed goods wagons constructed. These later vans had the left-hand body stanchion cropped off at the solebar and a left-hand gusset plate. Of much greater interest is that this wagon is fitted with Bulleid's welded wheels; not many wagons had these, and they were not considered a success. Note also that the lift-link brake is still being used. *R. S. Carpenter Photos*

Chapter 7.
Meat and Fruit Vans

Meat vans divide into two categories: those built to carry freshly slaughtered meat and those built to carry refrigerated or frozen meat. The LSWR had lost six refrigerator vans in World War 1, but for some reason it did not order any replacements until 1922. Had there been any pressing urgency about the matter they would presumably have been built to the existing South Western design, but there was a further long delay in their construction and it was not until 1928 that they were finally built (Diagram 1476). They were designed at Eastleigh, and, whilst the general concept followed previous practice, the body design was new; they were built on the standard 1923 RCH 17ft 6in underframe. These were the only true refrigerator vans built by the Southern Railway. It had been thought that the main body colour was white with black letters, but it is now believed that they were painted in the standard SR colours for this class of vehicle, namely stone body with Venetian red letters and a brown solebar.

A design for a fresh-meat van appeared in 1931 (Diagram 1486). With its 'Lynes roof', prominent ventilators and non-standard length, this was altogether a rather unusual vehicle. It was also the only Southern design to feature a sliding door — a detail probably dictated by a high platform somewhere at one of the several rail-served abattoirs in the West of England where these vans were normally to be found. The earlier refrigerator van was fitted but had the rather basic arrangement of four brake blocks and a 'lift link'. The meat van had the Southern 'power brake' arrangement, with eight brake blocks. Seventy-five meat vans were built in 1931 and were followed by a further 25 in 1934. In the 1960s there was a decline in meat traffic, and some (if not all) ended their lives as ordinary covered goods vans.

The year 1931 also saw the introduction of an insulated van design (Diagram 1477). There seems to have been some confusion as to the exact nature of these vehicles: the Rolling

Meat and fruit vans built by the Southern Railway

Pre-Group meat-van design built by the Southern Railway

Diagram	Order	Date	Quantity	Construction	Numbers	Examples of Tare weights	Notes
1482	E107	6/4/25	25	11/26	51171-95	NR (Diagram tare 8-5-0)	LSWR design. AVB 1 x ? cyl, eight brake blocks

SR standard meat- and fruit-van designs

Diagram	Order	Date	Quantity	Construction	Numbers	Examples of Tare weights	Notes
1476	E1	25/1/22	6	9/28	50494-9	NR (Diagram tare 9-18-2)	Refrigerator van AVB 1 x 18incyl, four brake blocks
1477	E472	17/5/29	25	2/31-3/31	50500-24	50500 9-10-3, 50524 9-10-3	Insulated van AVB 1 x 18in cyl, eight brake blocks
1486	A533	17/5/29	75	1/31-2/31	51196-220/41-90	51196 9-6-0, 51220 9-5-2, 51290 9-7-0	Meat van AVB 1 x 18in cyl , eight brake blocks
1477	E580	16/5/30	50	2/31-3/31	50525-74	50525 9-10-3, 50538 9-10-3, 50574 9-10-3	Insulated van AVB 1 x 18in cyl, eight brake blocks
1486	A643	14/4/31	25	4/34-6/34	51291-315	51291 9-4-3, 51315 9-3-0	Meat van AVB 1 x 18in cyl, eight brake blocks
1478	A812	27/3/34	200	8/35-12/35	50575-774	50575 9-0-0, 50641 9-0-0, 50674 9-0-0	Banana van AVB 1 x 18 cyl, eight brake blocks
1479	A1009	22/12/37	125	4/38-7/38	50775-899	50775 9-7, 50814 9-7, 50876 9-7	Banana van AVB 1 x 18 cyl, eight brake blocks

Note: NR = No record

Left:
Plate 84 No 50496 (Diagram 1476), one of the refrigerator vans as built. Someone in the Eastleigh Drawing Office has added in red ink the letter 'R' in a circle; this suggests a proposed modification to the livery, but, if ever carried out, it cannot have lasted long. *R. Chorley collection*

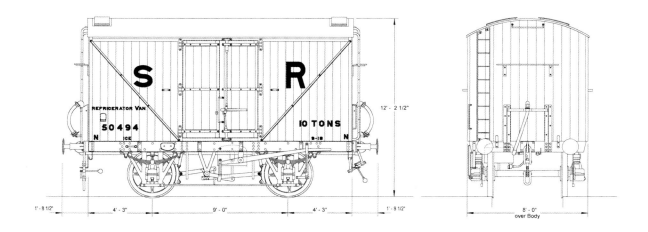

**Southern Railway
10 Ton refrigerator Van
9 ' - 0'' Wheelbase
Fitted with Vacuum Brake and Steam Heating Pipe
SR Diagram 1476**

Figure 33

Right:
Plate 85 This 1936 view of No 50494 shows well the construction of these wagons and provides another example of the '1936' writing combined with the 18in Company initials. Notice that the lamp irons are attached to the headstock and that the body is basically a separate component.
R. Chorley collection

Above:
Plate 86 No 51247 (Diagram 1486).
A note on the back of the original photograph claims 'out of date lettering', but it was very much in date when the picture was taken in 1931. *R. Chorley collection*

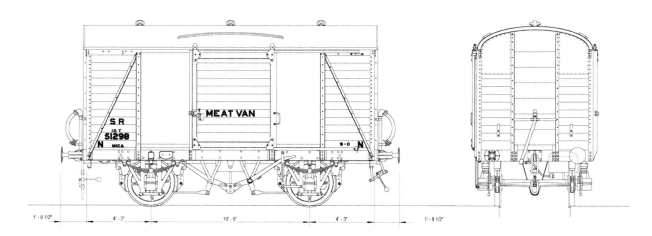

**Southern Railway
Meat Van
10' 0" Wheelbase Fitted
SR Diagram 1486**

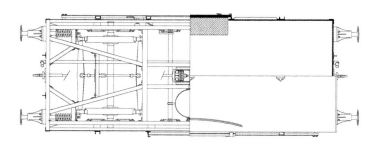

Figure 34

Right:
Plate 87 No 51298 (Diagram 1486), one of the second batch built with the '1936' writing. This wagon has SECR axleboxes, probably recovered from withdrawn 12-ton minerals. Compared to ordinary covered goods wagons, these vehicles were fairly heavy, and, although rated to carry 10 tons, did in fact have 12-ton running-gear.
R. Chorley collection

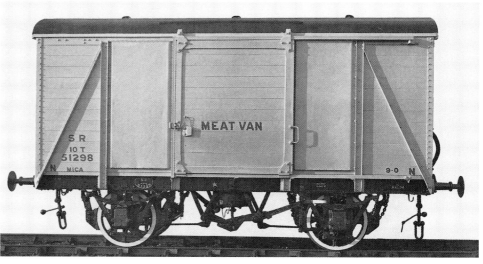

Left:
Plate 88 No S51216 in BR days but still basically as built. Some had steam-heat pipes in later years, and some finished their lives as ordinary covered goods vans. *T. A. Barry collection*

S.R. has entirely remodelled its rail services for Market Produce, Fruit, Meat, etc.

Swift Transit for Market Produce
to London, Midland and Northern Towns.

West of England to London Markets.

Express Freight Trains operate on weekdays from the West of England, arriving in London soon after midnight, ensuring meat, dairy and other market produce being delivered in time for the early morning markets. Furthermore, a special fast freight service is arranged on Sundays, as may be required, to provide for delivery of traffic into the London Markets first thing Monday.

Kent to London Markets.

With the availability of a service of express freight trains from Kent to London each weekday, growers are assured of the market produce arriving in time for delivery into the principal markets during the early hours of the morning following the day of loading.

Kent to Midlands, Wales and North of England Markets.

To enable fruit growers in Kent to take full advantage of the Markets in the Midlands, Wales and North of England, a special express freight service runs during the Season at passenger train speed to London, linking up with the North and West-bound express freight services from London the same evening, enabling the traffic to reach the principal towns, such as Liverpool, Manchester, Birmingham, Leeds, Derby, Bristol, Cardiff and other important places, the morning following that of loading at sending station.

Tamar Valley Flower and Fruit Traffic.

Express Passenger Train Services are provided during the season for the conveyance of flowers, fruit, &c., from the Tamar Valley District to London and the Midlands and North by which all the principal markets are reached early in the morning after loading.

Hampshire Fruit Traffic.

Express Passenger Train Services are provided during the Season for fruit, etc., from Stations in the producing Districts of HAMPSHIRE with the object of ensuring early arrival, in good condition, in LONDON, the MIDLANDS, WALES and NORTH OF ENGLAND, etc.

Acceptance of Traffic.

During the fruit and vegetable season, in order to meet the convenience of senders, loading stations are kept open for the acceptance of produce (by prior arrangement with the Station Master or Agent) after the recognised closing time.

Delivery in London.

Consignments are delivered to the London Markets (Borough, Covent Garden, Spitalfields) or any address within ordinary delivery radius upon request being made at the forwarding station.

Returned Empty Packages from the London Markets.

To permit of the prompt return of the empty packages to the fruit loading and other forwarding stations, services are provided which enable such packages to reach destination stations on the morning of the day following that of loading.

Train Services.

Separate publications are issued giving detailed particulars of the train services for the conveyance of fruit and vegetables from Kent, Hampshire and the West of England to London and Northern towns.

75

Left:
Plate 89 The body of wagon No 50538 (Diagram 1477) was built at Eastleigh on an underframe supplied by Ashford. Here we see the complete wagon back at Ashford for the official photograph in February or March 1931. Basically the body is identical to that of the refrigerator van except that it lacks the ice facilities.
R. Chorley collection

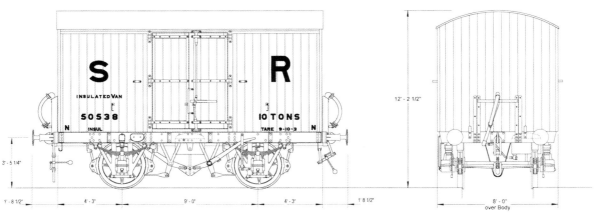

Southern Railway 10 Ton Insulated Meat Van
9 ' - 0" Wheelbase
Fitted with Vacuum Brake
SR Diagram 1477

Figure 35

Stock Committee Minutes refer to them as 'refrigerator vans', but refrigerator vans have some form of refrigeration, and these vehicles did not. The body of this new design was very similar to that of the true refrigerator van but lacked the ice tanks and their associated ladders. These vans could be used for a range of commodities, including meat or bananas and, indeed, were built just as Elders & Fyffes, the well-known banana importers, started to use Southampton Docks on a regular basis in preference to Hull, where this traffic had previously been handled. There were two orders for these vans — one for 25 and a second for 50 — built in successive batches in February and March 1931.

The banana traffic built up rapidly. The Southern possessed 99 former LSWR banana vans but these were not nearly enough, and it was necessary to hire banana vans from the LNER, which, having lost the traffic from Hull, was, no doubt,

more than happy to oblige. In 1933 there were 225 of these — 25 fitted and 200 unfitted. Their running numbers suggest they were all ex-North Eastern Railway, but by 1935 their number had grown to 325, and from photographic evidence it can be seen that there were also former Great Central and Great Eastern vehicles involved, and there may have been others. During the time that these vans were on loan to the Southern, they retained their original colours and numbers but had their owners' initials replaced by the letters 'SR'.

Giving some idea of just how heavy the banana traffic could be, it was recorded that, on one day in 1934, no fewer than 681 wagons were loaded in a period of 21 hours. To assist, some 94 (and possibly a few more) South Western refrigerator vans had their ice tanks etc removed, thus converting them into insulated vans. However, these could be used only in the warmer months, because their lack of steam heating meant that they were

Right:
Plate 90 No S50561 (Diagram 1477) after overhaul in 1948. Given that Ashford was still using SR brown at the time, it is presumed that this wagon is in SR stone with red writing. *M. King collection*

unsuitable for this traffic in the winter when the fruit had to be kept warm. One of the new insulated vans (No 50538) was provided with steam-heating equipment in October 1934, but this was removed a year later; whether this was an experiment that failed or one tried in connection with a new design is unclear.

Presumably the Southern's Directors were unsure how long the banana traffic would remain at Southampton, because it was not until March 1934 that they authorised the construction of an SR banana-van design (Diagram 1478). Two hundred were built, entering traffic between August 1935 and February 1936. They were very similar to the insulated vans, but the

Above:
Plate 91 The van on the left of this picture, known to be LNER No 25080, was one of the various LNER banana vans that were loaned to the SR from 1933 to 1937. Of North Eastern Railway design, it has vacuum brakes. The livery would be bauxite brown with white letters. The coach is a standard Maunsell (Lynes) design, complete with buck-eye coupler. *F. Foote collection*

bodies had horizontal planks (rather than vertical ones) and they were, of course, fitted with steam heating.

On 5 June 1936 a fire destroyed the shed used for banana traffic in Southampton's Old Docks. It was reported that between 60 and 70 'refrigerator vans' which were in the shed were destroyed but that some 500 other wagons were not affected and were available for banana traffic. The identity of vehicles destroyed remains a mystery: almost all the SR-owned examples can be accounted for, so presumably the fire victims were LNER vehicles.

In November 1937 there was further bad news when it was reported that the Standard Fruit Co, for which Elders & Fyffes were the British agents, had decided to berth its ships at the Royal Albert Docks in London and that consequently the LNER, which would be handling this traffic, was requesting the return of its wagons! All was not lost, however, because assurances had been given that a considerable level of banana traffic would remain at Southampton. To compensate for the impending loss of the LNER wagons, 125 additional banana vans were ordered the following month, and, in order to hasten delivery, 125 ordinary covered goods already on order were to be built as banana vans (Diagram 1479). These were not converted, so presumably it was a matter of using the materials on order; in any case, they looked very similar to ordinary vans. These first entered traffic just five months later, and they proved as satisfactory in service as the original design. In 1939 12 were fitted with 'Dukold' bunkers, turning them into dual-purpose banana/refrigerator vans; how long they retained this feature is not known, but it is believed susequently to have been removed.

The banana vans represented a very important part of the Southern's goods stock and were widely travelled, but, once again, there were not many of them. All the Southern meat and fruit vans were non-'common user', but from 1 March 1941 they were 'pooled' with the other companies' stock.

One final point of interest: shunting banana vans into the Fyffes siding at Fratton provided the only known example of normal electric stock (usually a 2-BIL or similar) being used to shunt revenue-earning goods traffic. A Brighton 'E1' tank would bring the wagons round from the 'New yard' to Fratton West, and then, to save the locomotive running round, the electric unit would complete the job.

Left:
Plate 92 No 50641 (Diagram 1478) as built in October 1935. All these meat and fruit vans had one brake cylinder, and all except the refrigerator vans had eight-clasp brake blocks. *R. Chorley collection*

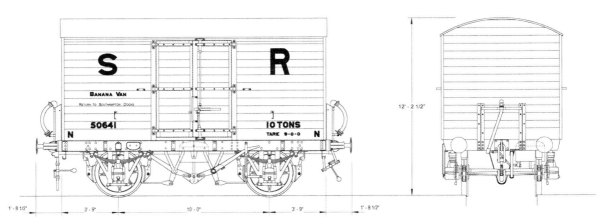

**Southern Railway 10 Ton SR Diagram 1478
Fitted with Vacuum Brake and Steam Heating**

Figure 36

Left:
Plate 93 No 50746 (Diagram 1478). This undated photograph appears to have been taken either immediately pre- or post-World War 2. (For the benefit of those who were not about at the time, there was no banana traffic in the period 1940-5, and these vans were used as ordinary insulated vans for meat traffic.) Note that 'XP' and 'WB' have been added in white. *Authors' collection*

Right:
Plate 94 No S50609, seen at Feltham in 1962. The livery is standard BR bauxite with a yellow spot, the latter indicating that this van has had additional insulation fitted (1961) and that, although it retains steam-heat pipes, it has had the internal fittings removed. Note the straw packing showing under the door; spectacular spiders, some as big as a man's hand, could be found amongst this on unloading. *A. Blackburn*

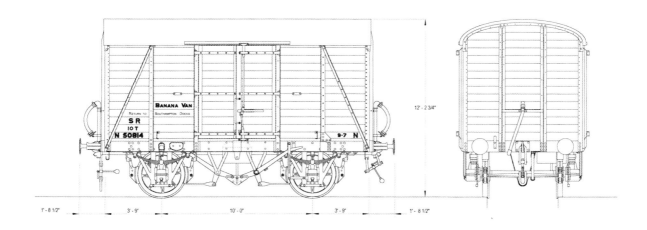

Right:
Plate 95 No 50886 (Diagram 1479), as built. These vans, based as they were on the standard goods design, looked very like their humble sisters but lacked the end ventilators, and the insulation and steam-heating equipment made them somewhat heavier. *F. Foote collection*

Southern Railway 10 Ton Banana Van SR Diagram 1479
Fitted with Vacuum Brake and Steam Heating

Figure 37

Right:
Plate 96 No S50870 at Eastleigh in 1950 in the company of two former Brighton horseboxes. These vans became 'common user' vehicles during the war and were thus no longer branded for return to Southampton, although they were still frequently found there in postwar years. The van is painted bauxite brown, and the horseboxes Southern Region version of BR red (a much brighter shade than that used by the other regions). *T. A. Barry collection*

Chapter 8.
Cattle Trucks

The carriage of cattle was the first class of traffic to be discontinued by BR. As far as the Southern was concerned, it can be seen from the wagon-stock returns that the serious decline in this class of traffic had begun as early as 1928. On 1 January that year the Southern owned 1,515 cattle wagons; by the beginning of 1947 the figure was down to 695. World War 2 and the shortage of petrol had held the figure at around 900, and by the beginning of 1948 it was back up to 879 (100 new wagons having been built the previous year), but it was clearly only a matter of time, and most railwaymen concerned with looking after the cattle in transit were glad to see the back of them.

In 1923, however, when all this was in the future, the Southern inherited two outstanding orders for cattle trucks — one from the LSWR for 25 and the other from the SECR for 50.

As cattle trucks frequently got wet, either from the cattle or from the hosing-out which followed each journey, it was generally thought better to build cattle wagons on wooden underframes. Thus it was that, when further orders were called for in 1925-7, it was decided to use the existing 1917 SECR design (Diagram 1515). This had reached a total of 389 wagons before it was superseded in 1930 by a steel-framed design (Diagram 1529). In fact, cattle wagons as a whole tended to have rather short lives, and some of the early SR-built wagons did not survive to see Nationalisation.

Cattle trucks built by the Southern Railway

Pre-group Cattle trucks on order 1/1/1923

Diagram	Order	Date	Quantity	Construction	Numbers	Examples of Tare weights	Notes
1502	LSWR	May-22	25	1923	51846-51870	NR (Diagram tare 7-14-0)	VP LSWR Nos allocated
1515	SECR	?	50	11/23-12/23	52769-52818	NR (Diagram tare 7-2-1)	VP SECR Nos allocated

Pre-Grouping cattle-truck design built by the Southern Railway

Diagram	Order	Date	Quantity	Construction	Numbers	Examples of Tare weights	Notes
1515	A25	27/05/24	100	1925	52819-81, 53391-427	NR (Diagram tare 7-2-1)	VP
1515	A106	11/05/25	100	1926/7	53428-527	53448 7-9-0, 53527 7-8-0	VP
1515	A165	08/07/26	100	9/27-6/28	53528-627	53528 7-8-2, 53627 7-9-0	VP

SR standard cattle-truck design

Diagram	Order	Date	Quantity	Construction	Numbers	Examples of Tare weights	Notes
1529	A343	06/06/28	100	4/30	53629-728	63629 8-8-1, 53632 8-10-0, 53728 8-8-1	AVB 1 x 18in cyl, eight brake blocks
1529	A471	17/05/29	100	4/30	53729-828	53729 8-8-2, 53828 8-8-0	AVB 1 x 18in cyl, eight brake blocks
1529	A579	16/05/30	49	10/31-11/31	53829-44/6-78	53829 8-8-2, 53878 8-9-0	AVB 1 x 18in cyl, eight brake blocks. 50 wagons authorised; 53845 not built
1529	A970	06/05/37	50	2/39-3/39	53879-928	53879 8-13, 53928 8-10	AVB 1 x 18in cyl, eight brake blocks
1530	A3219	04/05/45	101	10/47	52418-518	52418 8-0, 52518 8-2	VP
1530	A3354	15/04/46	150	10/47-11/47	52268-417	52268 8-4, 52417 8-2	AVB 1 x 18in cyl, eight brake blocks
1530	A3446	01/08/47	150	10/49-12/49	B891250-399	NR (Diagram tare 8-8)	AVB 1 x 18in cyl, eight brake blocks. SR Nos 52001-150 allocated but not used

Note: NR = No record

Left:
Plate 97 No 52617 (Diagram 1515) was one of the last of its type built and is seen here in the Willesden area in the 1930s. The Belgian ferry van next to it was one of the many hundreds built in Britain for the Army in World War 1. The lightly coloured wagon sheet on the right is a curiosity, wagon sheets usually being black in colour. *HMRS*

Above:
Plate 98 A Diagram 1515 seen after the war in such a dilapidated state that its number is indecipherable; it may be an SECR-built example, as it has SECR axleboxes. Some of these early SR-built wooden-framed cattle trucks did not last long enough to see Nationalisation. *R. Chorley collection*

Below:
Plate 99 It has proved almost impossible to find a decent picture of an SR freight train headed by a Brighton locomotive, so here, at least, is one shunting. The location is the headshunt of the 'Chatham' yard at Ashford, and the engine is probably ex works. Clearly visible is the lettering on the end of Diagram 1529 No 53767; although this wagon belonged to the second batch ordered, both first and second batches were in fact built consecutively in 1930. *T. A. Barry collection*

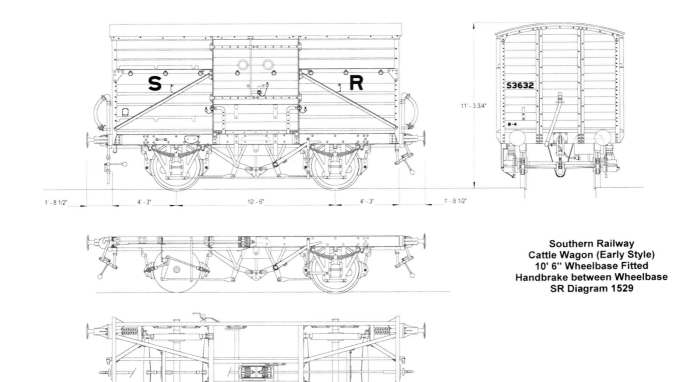

Southern Railway
Cattle Wagon (Early Style)
10' 6" Wheelbase Fitted
Handbrake between Wheelbase
SR Diagram 1529

Figure 38

Below:
Plate 100 No 53632 (Diagram 1529). Unfortunately this official photograph is somewhat damaged, but it still shows the details very clearly. Notice the 12in initials and the end radius to the floorboards. SR records refer to these cattle trucks as being of RCH design, but this can refer only to their main dimensions and details; as far as is known there was no definitive RCH cattle-truck drawing. *R. Chorley collection*

Above:
Plate 101 No 53629 after overhaul at Ashford in 1950. There are no visible changes from the original except for the writing. As far as is known, cattle trucks at this period were 'common user', but the letter 'N' on this wagon (also been observed on other Southern cattle trucks) might indicate otherwise. *National Railway Museum, York*

Below left:
Plate 102 No 53732 (Diagram 1529), seen towards the end of its life. The top doors are drooping a bit, but the wagon is still virtually as built except for the livery. Sadly no examples have survived into preservation. *Authors' collection*

Below right:
Plate 103 An end view of a Diagram 1530. Notice that the vacuum pipe is carried on the headstock; the earlier cattle trucks and, indeed, most fitted SR designs had 'high level' pipes. *A. E. West collection*

Above:
Plate 104 No 52345 (Diagram 1530). This is a nice photograph of a typical example of the Bulleid variant of the SR steel-framed cattle truck. Some of these vehicles were intended to have aluminium roofs, but the authors have seen only examples with plywood. *Kent Arts & Libraries*

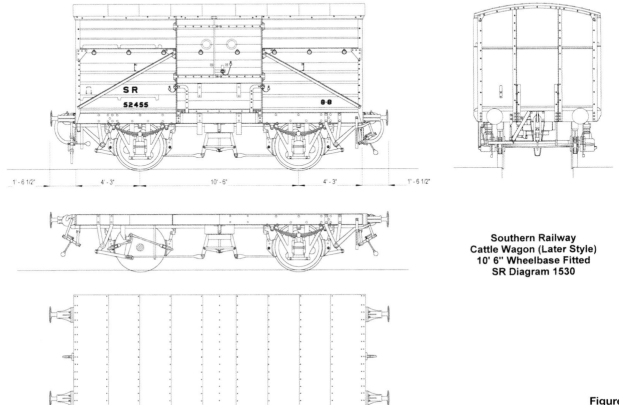

1' - 6 1/2"   4' - 3"   10' - 6"   4' - 3"   1' - 6 1/2"

**Southern Railway
Cattle Wagon (Later Style)
10' 6" Wheelbase Fitted
SR Diagram 1530**

Figure 39

The 1930 design was very much a steel-framed version of the SECR design; the end framing was different and it was fitted, but otherwise it was virtually unchanged.

The design was modified somewhat in 1947 when further vehicles were required to replace worn-out stock (Diagram 1530). The end planks were replaced by plywood, reinforced on the inside by metal left over when Bullied carriage windows were stamped out (remember the SR never wasted anything) and the roof boards by aluminium sheets. Lastly the brake-gear linkage was modified and the handbrake lever moved to the extreme end of the wagon — a move no doubt welcomed by shunters. (Readers may be surprised at how much 'splatter', in either form, could be produced by a cow!)

One could be reasonably sure of finding Southern cattle wagons around Exeter, Salisbury, Chichester or Ashford, but, again, they were not very common and never represented more than 4% of the stock, and by the beginning of 1948 just 2.6%.

Above right:
Plate 105 The brake gear of the Diagram 1530 is unique to that design; here is the brake, complete with its cross-shaft. Just discernible is the end of an LNER-type open-fronted axlebox. Many of these wagons had this component, and they may have been built with them. Note also that the buffer is of the short type, mounted on packing. By this period it was more usual to use a longer buffer on piped or fitted vehicles. *A. E. West collection*

Centre right:
Plate 106 The vacuum cylinder of a Diagram 1530, with its unique brake-work designed to give compensated and equalised brake forces on all brake blocks. *A. E. West collection*

Right:
Plate 107 No S52495 at Axminster in May 1959. Some of these trucks entered traffic with vacuum pipes only and had their vacuum cylinders fitted later. Notice that cattle trucks are 'handed' — the movable partition is at one end only and thus the fixing brackets on the sides are both at the same end. *A. E. West collection*

Chapter 9.
Goods Brake Vans

There was probably no vehicle more typical of its railway than the goods brake van (GBV), as soon as you saw one you knew at once to whom it belonged and there was certainly no mistaking a Southern example.

The standard SR goods brake design took some time to emerge, and there were one or two false starts and, one suspects, some ruffled feathers somewhere.

If one briefly considers the GBV orders outstanding in 1923, it can be seen that the LBSCR van was totally unacceptable to guards on the other two sections, on account of the outside-brake wheels, and as far as the South Western men were concerned, lack of side duckets. The LSWR van was very good in all respects but did not reflect Lynes' approach to the subject; the SECR van had a very good brake and did, and so

Goods brake vans built or purchased by the Southern Railway

Pre-Grouping goods brake vans on order 1/1/1923

Diagram	Order	Date	Quantity	Construction	Numbers	Examples of Tare weights	Notes
1547	LSWR	?	20	1922/3	20 of 55075-99	55075 24-5-0	Conversion of China-clay container flat
1576	LBSCR	21/7/22	11	1923	55917-55927	NR (Diagram tare 20-7-2)	LBSCR numbers allocated
1560	SECR	?	20	11/23-12/23	55476-55495	NR (Diagram tare 25-0-02)	SECR numbers allocated

Pre-Grouping designs built or purchased by the Southern Railway

Diagram	Order	Date	Quantity	Construction	Numbers	Examples of tare weights	Notes
1549	E44	9/7/24	20	1917/8	55100-55119	NR (Diagram tare 19-15-0)	Built MRCW Co for the WD, purchased 7/24
1560	L110	11/5/25	20	1/27-2/27	55496-55515	55496 25-0-0, 55515 25-0-0	

SR standard goods brake vans

Diagram	Order	Date	Quality	Construction	Numbers	Examples of tare weights	Notes
1578	L261	7/6/27	50	4/28-3/29	55943-92	55943 25-0-0, 55964 25-1-0	Ducket on left-hand side of body. Diagram 1560 underframe
1578	L344 Pt	23/3/28	30	6/29-10/29	55516-8 etc	55516 25-0-0, 55565 25-0-0	Ducket on left-hand side of body. Diagram 1560 underframe
1579	L344 Pt	23/3/28	20	10/29-3/30	55519-21 etc	55519 25-0-0, 55526 25-0-0	Ducket on right-hand side of body as all subsequent vans, new underframe design. 55538-9/42-5/51/3/5/7
1579	L473	17/5/29	25	5/30-8/30	55566-85	55566 25-7-0, 55585 25-0-2	officially built Brighton, probably bodies only
1579	L473	17/5/29	25	8/30-1/31	55993-56022	55993 25-1-0, 56022 25-2-2	
1579	L581	16/5/30	100	5/31-4/32	56061-160	56061 25-2-3, 56160 25-5-2	56130/2-260 underframes built Lancing, bodies Ashford.
1579	L645	14/4/31	100	12/32-5/33	56161-260	56161 25-4-0, 56260 25-2-0	Twelve authorised to be provided with AVB but this was later cancelled
1581	A746	21/12/32	50	8/34-9/34	55675-724	55710 15-8-0, 55724 15-11-0	15-ton version of standard 25-ton van
1580	E772	11/7/33	1	9/33	56263	56263 27-4-3	Bogie van converted from AC motor luggage van AVB 2 x 18in cyl, 16 brake blocks
1580	E790	24/11/33	20	3/34-1/25	56261-2/4-81	56261 27-15-0, 56274 27-17-2	Bogie van converted from AC motor luggage van AVB 2 x 18in cyl, 16 brake blocks
1550	A867	30/4/35	25	5/36-8/36	56282-306	56282 25-9-0, 56295 25-8-2	Standard bogie van, underframe built Lancing. AVB 2 x 18in cyl, 16 brake blocks. Six later WP
1579	A971	6/5/37	20	1/40-3/40	56307-326	56307 25-6, 56326 25-16	Additional window in body end. 2+2 sheeting. Order altered from 25 vans 22/09/37
1561	A997	29/9/37	3	9/38	55180-2	55180 16-8, 55181 16-8	Built on underframe of 'B2X' tenders. AVB 1 x 24in cyl, four brake blocks
1579	A1036	14/6/38	25	8/40-10/40	56327-51	56327 25-4, 56351 25-9	Some if not all built Lancing. These and all subsequently vans have 2+2 sheeting
1579	A1185	1/5/40	50	3/43-9/43	56352-401	56352 24-14, 56360 25-16	Underframes probably all Lancing, bodies by Ashford, Lancing and Eastleigh
1579	L1194	1/5/40	40	5/43-6/43	56402-41	56402 22-13, 56441 22-2	
1579	L1656	16/7/41	20	10/41	WD11002-21	NR	'Express goods brake vans' built for the MoS AVB 2 x 18in cyl and WP
1579	A1843	16/12/41	53	4/42-7/42	56442-94	56442 23-117, 56491 21-10	zome had their bodies built at Eastleigh
1579	A1852	23/12/41	20	3/42	WD11022-41	NR	Built for the MoS. AVB 2 x 18in cyl and WP
1570	RCH	?	1	4/46	56060	NR (Diagram tare 20-0)	Four built by the LMS (Lot 1352), one for each of the 'Big Four'
1582	A3222	4/5/45	54	1/48-11/48	55621-74	55621 24-2, 55674 24-18	New brake gear, no sanding and differing draw-gear. Some bodies built Lancing
1582	A3355	15/4/46	50	12/47-11/48	55121-70	55121 24-15, 55170 24-11	Some built entirely at Ashford, others had their bodies built at Lancing
1583	?	?	2	5/48, 7/48	55675/713	55675 16-1, 55713 15-0	Diagram 1583 modified for use on the Canterbury & Whitstable line

Note: NR = No record

Left:
Plate 108 No DS55490 (Diagram 1560), a 'Dance Hall'. This design was fully covered in Volume Three but is illustrated here to emphasise the vast difference in the bodywork between these vans and what followed. No DS55490 was built in 1923 and transferred to the CCE in November 1959; it was allocated to New Cross Gate, where this photograph was taken in December 1967. Livery was black body with yellow writing — standard for a Departmental in 1959. *A. Blackburn*

this was the van selected for future construction, albeit on a slightly modified underframe. In fairness to Lynes, the importance of the ducket to the South Western guards may not have been explained to him; as far as an Ashford man was concerned, duckets on goods brake vans were obsolete.

In 1924 an order was placed for 20 further South Eastern 'Dance Halls', as they were known (Diagram 1560), but before anything much could be done about this the General Manager was offered 20 virtually brand-new vans built for the War Department to an LSWR design. The price, at £110 each, was a fraction of what the Ashford vans would have cost, so SR General Manager Sir Herbert Walker lost no time in settling the matter. In 1925 20 goods brake vans were ordered, and this time a further batch of 'Dance Halls' was built, but there were to be no more. The design was criticised for having an unnecessarily large (expensive) body and for lacking duckets. It would be very interesting to know who raised this criticism, but one suspects a South Western man.

Below:
Plate 109 No 55975 (Diagram 1578) brand new in Lancing Works yard in 1928. A 'Pill-box', it features left-handed duckets, heavy footboard brackets, closed-ended sandboxes and open axlebox guides. Note that although this photograph was taken shortly before Lancing gave up wagon repair work, there are still quite a number of wagons visible in the background. *R. Chorley collection*

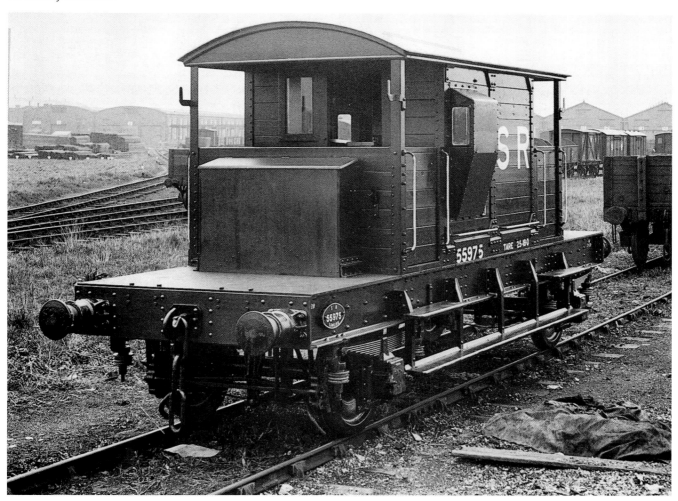

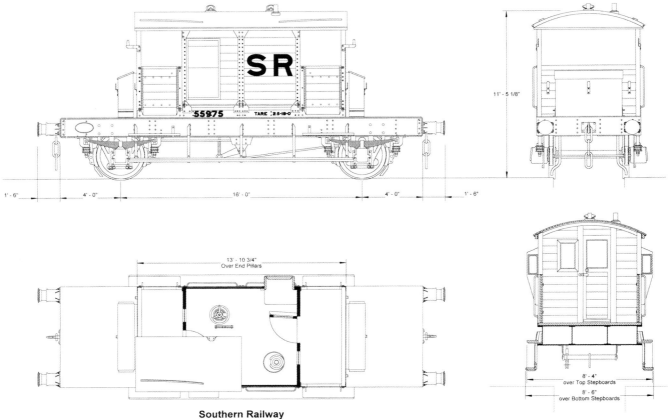

Southern Railway
25 Ton Brake Van
Orginal Design Lefthand Ducket
SR Diagram 1578

11' - 5 1/8"

13' - 10 3/4"
Over End Pillars

8' - 4"
over Top Stepboards

8' - 6"
over Bottom Stepboards

Figure 40

Left:
Plate 110 No DS55961 (Diagram 1578), built at Lancing in 1928, transferred to the CCE in April 1964 and allocated to Three Bridges Mechanised Renewal Depot. It was one of 35 'Pill-boxes' transferred to the Chief Civil Engineer at this time and is seen in typical BR condition, with an extra window at the ends and the sandboxes removed. As far as is known none of the 25-ton four-wheel vans retained its sandboxes, although some of the 15-ton vans and all of the bogie vans did. Most of the four-wheel vans acquired additional end windows. The standard Departmental livery at this time was olive-green body with white lettering and black undergear.
Authors' collection

It was against this background that, when an order was placed in 1927 for a further 50 25-ton vans, the Drawing Office at Lancing was 'asked' to prepare the design. (At the higher levels of a department it was all very gentlemanly, and one 'asked' people to do things; further down the pecking order, requests became orders.) What resulted was unlike anything that had been seen on the back of a goods train before, although the LNER was quick to follow the general idea. The underframe was the modified Ashford design that had been used under the last of the 'Dance Halls', but the small, centrally placed body was entirely new, and no one would be able to say this was too large! It was true that it normally had

to accommodate only one man, but the inside really was very cramped and rather dark, and, it was pointed out, the doors opened onto the space where the guard was likely to be sitting. This latter point was attended to, but not before 30 of the next order for 50 had been built. It would seem that all that was required was to hang the door on the opposite side, but for some reason it was decided to reverse the entire body layout, mirror-fashion (Diagram 1579). Eastleigh Drawing Office designed this modification, but Lancing built the vans. Almost everything on the Southern seems to have had a nickname, and these vans were known to the staff as 'Pill-boxes'.

Left:
Plate 111 No 56235 (Diagram 1579), at Ashford to have its photograph taken in 1933 and illustrating right-handed duckets, light footboard brackets, strengthened axlebox guides and a lamp iron added to the sandbox. The sandboxes still have closed ends, but this was the last batch of vans built with this feature. *R. Chorley collection*

Right:
Plate 112 No 55995 (Diagram 1579), built at Lancing in 1930 and seen at Wadebridge in July 1948. The sandboxes have been recently removed, but it has not yet acquired an additional end window. *Authors' collection*

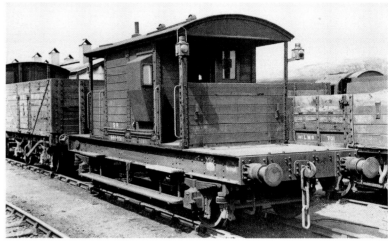

Figure 41

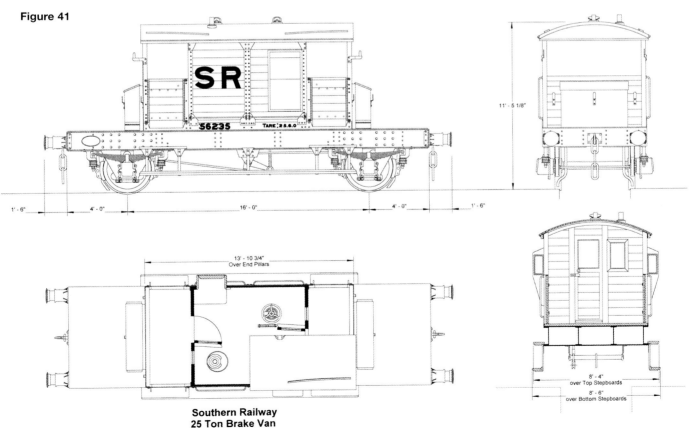

**Southern Railway
25 Ton Brake Van
Equal Planking
SR Diagram 1579**

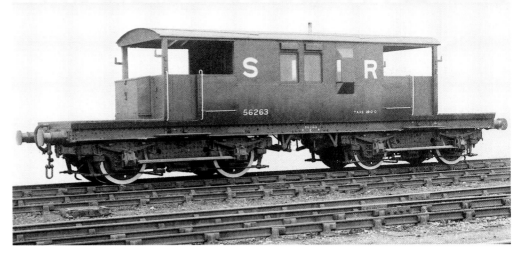

Right:
Plate 113 'Gondola' No 56263 (Diagram 1580). This is the prototype rebuild of the LBSCR-designed 'AC' motor luggage vans. This van differed from the main series in that it had closed-ended sandboxes, and one suspects there may have been one or two other minor variations. The duckets were recovered from electric suburban units that had been converted to periscope observation; as already mentioned, the Southern never wasted anything that might be put to future use. *R. Chorley collection*

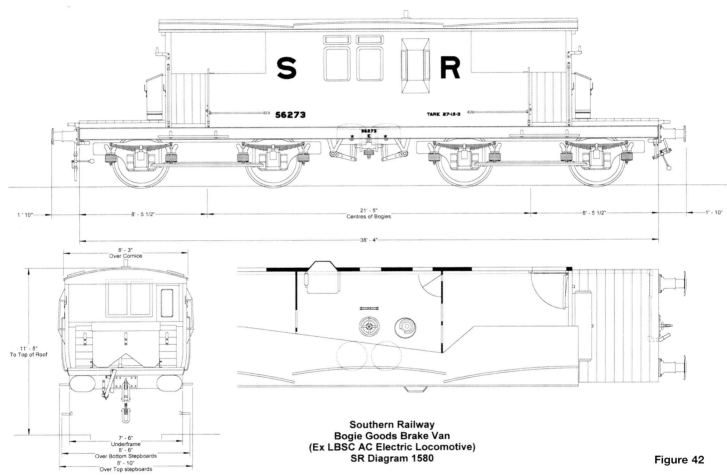

1' 10"   8' - 5 1/2"   21' - 5"
Centres of Bogies

8' - 5 1/2"   1' - 10"

38' - 4"

8' - 3"
Over Cornice

11' - 5"
To Top of Roof

7' - 6"
Underframe
8' - 6"
Over Bottom Stepboards
6' - 10"
Over Top stepboards

**Southern Railway
Bogie Goods Brake Van
(Ex LBSC AC Electric Locomotive)
SR Diagram 1580**

Figure 42

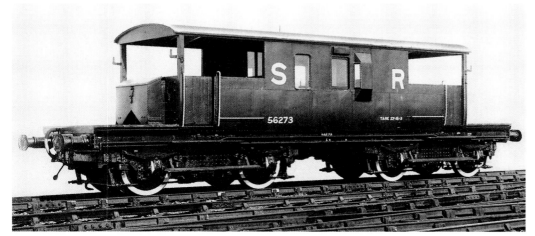

Left:
Plate 114 No 56273, one of the production series, seen newly converted at Eastleigh in August 1934. These vans were 'handed', and the spacing of the windows differed from one side to the other. The vacuum pipe ran along the solebar of the side with widely spaced windows. (Note that only one of the windows on this side has a drop-light.) These vehicles were undoubtedly the finest goods brake vans ever to run in Great Britain. *R. Chorley collection*

Towards the end of 1932 thought was being given to the fully fitted goods trains that would shortly be introduced and in particular to their brake vans. At first it was proposed to provide 12 of the standard 25-ton vans with vacuum brakes, but the underframe did not lend itself easily to the addition of brake cylinders, and, it must be admitted, they did not ride too well at speed either.

It so happened that, ever since 1929, the Southern had had 21 redundant LBSCR 'AC' motor luggage vans in store. Authority had been given to convert these into bogie bolster wagons, but little if anything had been done about this when someone realised that they might be rebuilt to better advantage as goods brake vans for the fitted trains. Authority was given in July 1933 to convert one, and just three months later No 56263 was ready for inspection (Diagram 1580). The result was without doubt the finest goods brake van that had ever been built for a railway in Britain. Authority was given two months later to proceed with rebuilding the remaining 20, and by January 1934 the job was complete. Some referred to these vehicles as the 'Gondola vans', but officially they were known as 'Bogie goods brake vans, express service'. Had they been entirely new, some might have criticised their cost, but as rebuilds they were real bargains.

The new vans made a great impression on all concerned, and just over a year later the Board authorised the construction of a further 25. These were built on a shortened version of the standard carriage underframe and had standard carriage bogies. Some of these new-build vans had light metal sheeting over their body planks; on some this covered just the van portion, on others it included the sides of the verandahs as well. It seems they were built in this way, but no explanation can be offered for this unusual feature. These vans were generally known as 'Queen Marys'. Diagram 1550 was allocated, which seems to have been a mistake as this was already allocated to three South Western Diagram 1541s modified for use on the Canterbury & Whitstable line. Possibly this was the result of a misunderstanding in the Rolling Stock Office — we shall never know.

Both bogie designs gave excellent service. One of the rebuilds and several of the new vans served with the Army, and on one occasion one of them was used to convey the Prime Minister, Sir Winston Churchill, on an inspection of the long-range guns at Martin Mill. The conversions were withdrawn in the late 1950s as non-standard, but in 1957 five were allocated to the Chief Civil Engineer at Redbridge for use with the long-welded-rail trains, and these gave a further 10 years' service. The standard vans remained as a class in general use into the 1970s; some received air-pipes, and a few are still retained today for special duties. Happily several have been preserved.

Above:
Plate 115 'Queen Mary' No 56282 (Diagram 1550), the first of the standard bogie brake vans, brand new at Ashford in July 1936. The doors on the inner ends of these vans were to one side, and, for the first time, two end windows are provided. The sandboxes on these vans stand high to provide clearance for the sand pipes over the axles. Note the letter 'A' under the number, denoting Ashford as its repair works, the AC rebuilds 'belonging' to Eastleigh. Note also the two stars indicating the position of the vacuum-cylinder release cords. *R. Chorley collection*

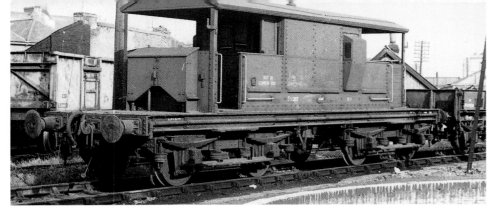

Plate 116 No 56287 in the 'Far West' at Wadebridge in July 1964. This was one of the vans finished with all the side planks sheathed in light metal sheet. No definitive explanation has been given as to why this was done, the most likely being that the timber was found to be unsuitable for a good paint finish; the Southern did not spend its shareholders' money without good reason. *Authors' collection*

Plate 117 No 56296, built in Ashford in May 1936 with part steel-sheathed sides. Photographed at Seaton Junction in May 1963, this van was one of six Diagram 1550s fitted with air brakes in June 1961 for working Continental traffic between Hither Green and Dover. Livery is standard BR brown body with white writing and black solebars and undergear. *Authors' collection*

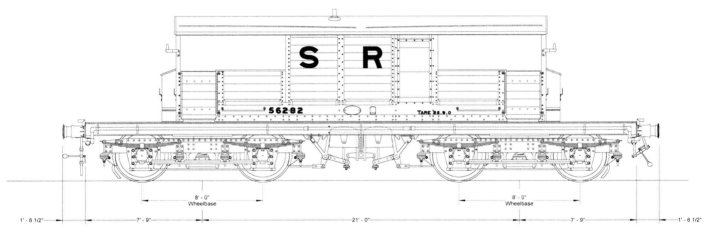

56282   TARE 24.9.0

8' - 0" Wheelbase

8' - 0" Wheelbase

1' - 8 1/2"   7' - 9"   21' - 0"   7' - 9"   1' - 6 1/2"

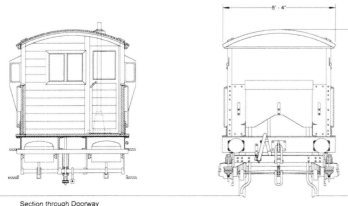

8' - 4"

11' 3 3/4"

Section through Doorway looking toward Centre of Vehicle (Bogie omitted)

**Southern Railway
25 Ton Bogie Brake Van
SR Diagram 1550**

Figure 43

Figure 44

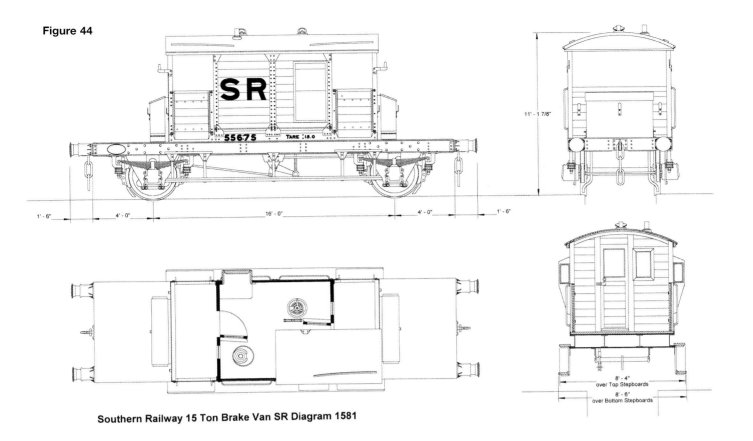

11' - 1 7/8"

1' - 6"   4' - 0"   16' - 0"   4' - 0"   1' - 6"

8' - 4"
over Top Stepboards

8' - 6"
over Bottom Stepboards

Southern Railway 15 Ton Brake Van SR Diagram 1581

Right:
Plate 118 No 55689 (Diagram 1581) brand new in August 1934. This is the 15-ton version of the standard goods brake van. The body is identical to the heavy vans, but the sandboxes now have the middle portion of sheeting cut out. The underframe is lighter, and the axleboxes are of the smaller, standard RCH divided type. The livery is standard for the period — dark brown body and solebars, light red ends, including the headstocks; just discernible under the gate is that the red colour of the internal end extends to the floor. The writing is white and all else black, including on this van the buffer casings; these could vary, and on some goods brake vans they were red. *R. Chorley collection*

Left:
Plate 119 No 55687, seen at Wareham in typical BR condition, with sandboxes removed, an additional window in the end and the tail lamp iron relocated. Livery is light grey body with white writing on black patches, undergear and solebars being black. *T. A. Barry collection*

93

As the new heavy vans came into traffic, work was found for the lighter vans on the many minor branches or on local 'trip' workings. To some extent the South Western 'Road vans' (Diagram 1541) became almost a standard class for these jobs, but by the 1930s many of the lighter vans (10-12 tons) were reaching the end of their lives, and it was decided to build a lightweight version of the standard van to replace them. These new vans (Diagram 1581) had an identical body to that of the 25-ton vans but had a lighter underframe design and were rated at 15 tons. Most were allocated to specific duties, and many spent their entire lives so employed. In 1948 two had their roofs modified for use on the Canterbury &

Whitstable line (Nos 55675/713); a year laster two were provided with large toolboxes and transferred to Departmental stock for use with the weed-killing train (55711/9, later DS456/7), and in 1971 two were sent to the Isle of Wight (55710/24), where one happily survives today (2002) on the Isle of Wight Steam Railway.

The next new design was a replacement for four old South Eastern Railway vans that were used on the Folkestone branch. Some would describe these as 'Incline brakes', but both they and their three successors were classified as ordinary goods brakes (Diagram 1561). What was very unusual about these vans was that they had an open goods

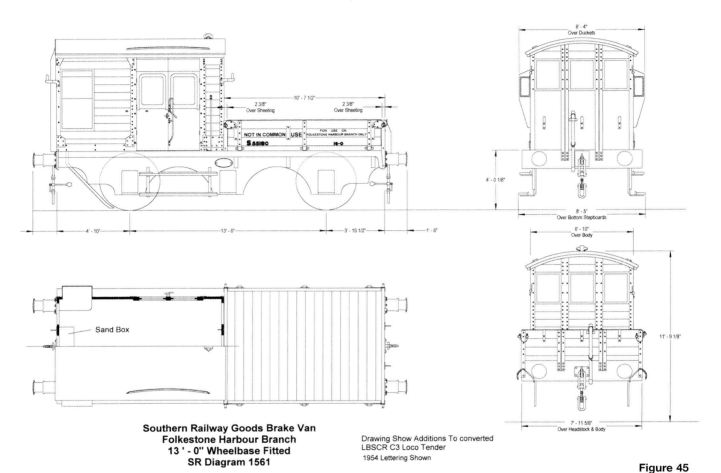

**Southern Railway Goods Brake Van
Folkestone Harbour Branch
13 ' - 0'' Wheelbase Fitted
SR Diagram 1561**

Drawing Show Additions To converted
LBSCR C3 Loco Tender
1954 Lettering Shown

Figure 45

Left:
Plate 120 No 55180 (Diagram 1561), seen at Folkestone Junction in July 1954. Why the middle axle was removed is a mystery, as by all accounts these vans could have done with the extra weight. According to the C&W records, the frames of these vehicles came from LBSCR Class B2X engine tenders, but that was only half of the story, because they were built originally for the 'C3' class. *Authors' collection*

Above:
Plate 121 No 56365, new in June 1942, illustrating the final development of Diagram 1579. The last five orders all had '2+2' planking and a second window in the body end. The livery is to the 1937 standard. As mentioned previously, it was not unknown for the wheel rims to be picked out in white on normal production, but in this case such enhancements were the result of wartime pride. *R. Chorley collection*

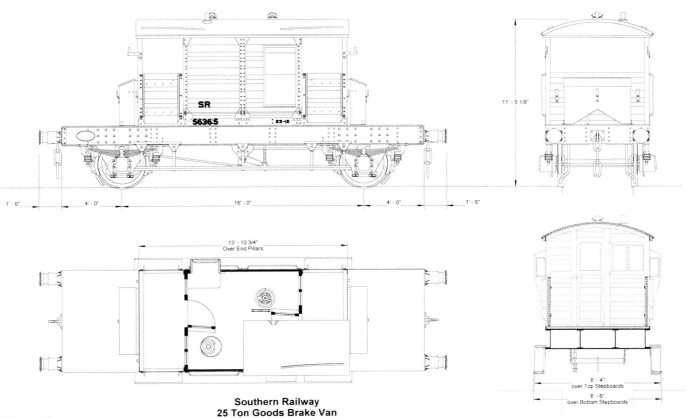

Figure 46

Southern Railway
25 Ton Goods Brake Van
2+2 Planking Style wth Sanding Gear
SR Diagram 1579

compartment at one end, making them a sort of road van. The purpose of this compartment initially presented the authors with something of a mystery; there is nothing in the Divisional Appendix relevant to the Folkestone Harbour line, but at this time there was no road access to Folkestone Warren, and there is mention 'in connection with the saving of life at sea' that, when necessary, trains would stop in this area to convey the Coast Guard's life-saving equipment, and this, presumably, was the reason for the open compartment. The Southern vans were constructed on the underframes of LBSCR tenders and as such had much in common with two shunting trucks built at the same time for Bournemouth West; apart from this they were more-or-less an assemblage of standard body parts. They entered service in September 1938 but within two years were on loan to the Martin Mill Military Railway, where they spent most of the war. Thereafter they seemed to spend most of their time standing together in a siding at Folkestone Junction, but they must have had some use, because a local goods guard remembered them as having poor brakes — one wonders why the middle axle was removed. At Ashford they were remembered because, when they came in for overhaul, they went first to the locomotive shops to have their running-gear attended to and were then transferred to the wagon shops for body work and painting.

Meanwhile construction of the standard van (Diagram 1579) had continued, but in 1940 the design was revised to provide for a much-needed additional window in the end and '2+2' planking. There were also some changes made to the drawgear at about this time.

In 1941 the Southern was called upon to provide the War Department with what were described as 'Express goods brake vans'. These were of the current design but were provided with air-brake pipes and two vacuum cylinders, the latter mounted in the only practicable position, on top of the underframe end. This order was followed by a second, for a further 20, and these were supplied in 1942. Why these vans were required is not clear, but 16 of the first batch went to the Middle East, whilst the remainder finished up on various military railways in the UK. In 1949 two came into BR stock via the Shropshire & Montgomeryshire Railway and were given the numbers M360327/8. The former was noted in Feltham Yard one day in the 1960s bearing the inscription 'The original rough bastard'; no one could ever pretend the 'Pill-boxes' were comfortable to ride in, but in the opinion of many they did have a very good brake, and that is what they were built for.

In 1947 the design was further revised, and this was recognised by the issue of Diagram 1582. The brake gear was modified to give equal forces on each brake block, the drawgear was further modified and — very welcome to the guards — yet another end window was added. Lastly the sanding gear was removed. Sanding gear was a very good thing, provided it worked, but it did demand a supply of sharp dry sand and maintenance. In the conditions prevailing at the time this was no longer possible, and, in the years to come, the sanding gear was removed from the four-wheeled vans as they passed through shops. The bogie vans retained their sandboxes unused as they were less trouble to leave on than take off.

Above:
Plate 122 No S56371, built at Lancing in 1943 and seen in August 1949 at Winchester in early BR Southern Region livery — SR brown body with red ends. *A. E. West collection*

Above:
Plate 123 No 55170 (Diagram 1582), illustrating the final development of the 'Pill-box' design, altered brake gear and lack of sandboxes being the most obvious differences. This photograph was taken in September 1948, when No 55170 was just eight months old. In theory (and possibly in fact) it was the last SR goods brake van built. *Authors' collection*

Figure 47

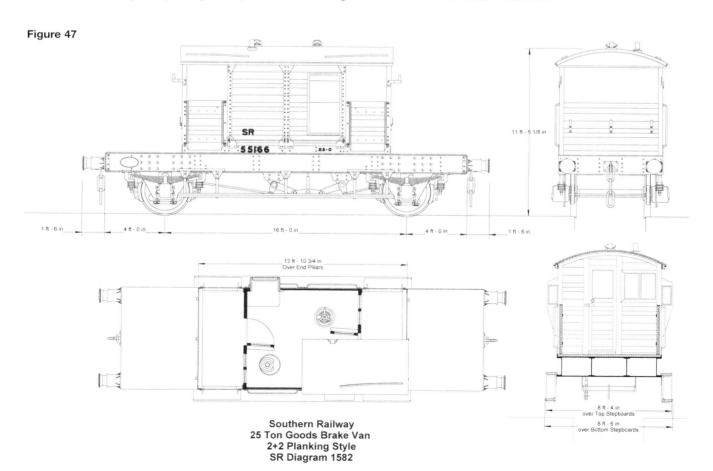

Southern Railway
25 Ton Goods Brake Van
2+2 Planking Style
SR Diagram 1582

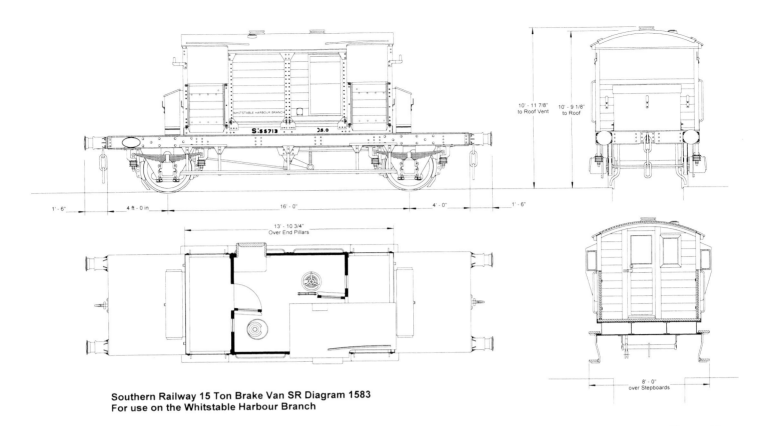

Southern Railway 15 Ton Brake Van SR Diagram 1583
For use on the Whitstable Harbour Branch

Figure 48

Above:
Plate 124 No S55713 (Diagram 1583), one of the two 15-ton vans cut down in 1948 to work on the Canterbury & Whitstable line, seen here at Canterbury. Note that the stepboard brackets have also been set back. *D. Cullum*

The last type of goods brake van to be noted was a design prepared by the RCH in conjunction with the trade unions. In 1942 all the country's goods brakes had been 'pooled', and this had led to some unfavourable comparisons being made! The result was a new van designed by the LMS in an attempt to produce something that would please most (if not all), and the LMS built one for each of the main-line companies. The Southern allocated Diagram 1570 to its example, and no further reference to it appears in SR records. According to those goods guards — all Southern men — who have volunteered an opinion, the GWR van rode well but was disliked to the point of refusal on account of its having an outside brake (not funny if the verandah was leading and all the muck was blowing back off the train). The LNER and the very similar BR vans had pleasant accommodation but did not ride well; the Southern four-wheel vans had poor accommodation, rode badly but had the best brake. The various LMS designs were neither one thing nor the other, but some (like the GWR vans) had long lockers in them that were good for sleeping on when necessary! That left the SR bogie vans, which, with their comfortable ride, decent bodywork and powerful brakes, were in a class of their own.

SOUTHERN RAILWAY

Detailed Information will gladly be given on any of the subjects contained in this booklet by the following :

RAIL RATES, STORAGE, etc.

A. H. LINGARD, Commercial Assistant,
London Bridge Station, S.E.I

Phone—(Goods Train Rates) : Hop 5100, Ext. 2421/2
,, (Passenger Train Rates) : Hop 5100, Ext. 2413
,, (Lighterage, Wharf Rates) : Hop 5100, Ext. 2418

RAIL SERVICES, ROAD RATES AND SERVICES

F. BUSHROD, Superintendent of Operation,
Waterloo Station, S.E.I

Phone—(Freight Train Section) : Hop 5100. Ext. 2186/7
,, (Road Transport Section) : Hop 5100, Ext. 2451/2
,, (Container Section) : Hop 5100, Ext. 2188

CHANNEL ISLANDS AND CONTINENTAL TRAFFIC, RATES AND SERVICES

C COOPER, Continental Assistant,
Victoria Station, S.W. I

Phone—Hop 5100, Ext. 2483 or 2487

or any of the

S.R. DIVISIONAL SUPERINTENDENTS

at the following Addresses :

W. A. BROWN, London District Freight Division (all London Goods Depots, Wharves, etc.), London Bridge Station. Hop 5100, Ext. 2468
C. J. C. LATHAM, London (Central Division) (approximately old L.B.S.C.R. area), London Bridge Station. Hop 5100, Ext. 2439
A. WHITE, London (East Division) (approximately old S.E.C.R. area), London Bridge Station. Hop 5100, Ext. 2148
J. E. SHARPE, London (West Division) (London-Portsmouth-Reading-Southampton, etc.), Waterloo Station. Hop 5100, Ext. 2327
E. HIGHT, Southern Division (Bournemouth-Weymouth-Salisbury, etc.), Southampton West Station. Southampton 4241, Ext. 690 or 642.
P. NUNN, Western Division (West of Salisbury), Exeter (Central Station). Exeter 4194, Ext. 34
G. H. HARE-DEAN, South Coast Representative, Brighton Station. Brighton 3186, Ext. 23
or at any Station or Goods Depot on the Southern Railway system

SOUTHAMPTON DOCKS

Owned, Managed and Developed by the Southern Railway.

Excellent express freight train facilities are in operation each weekday with Southampton Docks, to and from London and Northern Towns for the conveyance of important merchandise such as fruit, meat, eggs, etc., and also for all other classes of traffic passing to and from this country and the Colonies, North and South America, and other foreign countries, as well as market produce from the Channel Islands.

Prompt despatch and delivery in London is assured, whilst traffic going to Northern Towns is afforded a speedy transit.

To enable Colonial and overseas produce loaded in the morning at Southampton Docks to be delivered into the London Markets during the afternoon of the same day, a fastly timed train runs, as may be necessary, at 12.25 p.m., and in order to facilitate prompt clearance and delivery in London, it has been arranged for the Agent at Nine Elms Depot to advise (about 2.0 p.m.) each of the consignees as to the quantity of traffic on their account forwarded by this special service.

The Company will undertake to effect delivery in London the same day by prior arrangement.

Further information as to service times, etc., will be gladly furnished on application to the Docks and Marine Manager, Southampton Docks (Telephone: Southampton 4241, Extension 404), or to the Traffic Manager (Operating Dept.), Waterloo Station, S.E.1. (Telephone : Hop 5100, Extension 2188).

Above:
Plate 125 No 56060 seen at Feltham in 1961. As built except that the fixed side lamps originally provided have been removed and for some reason a second label clip has been provided below the original one. *Author's collection*

Chapter 10.
Bogie Bolster Wagons

It is interesting that, although the LMS and LNER built large numbers of single- and double-bolster wagons over the years, the Southern and the Great Western did not build any. As far as the latter was concerned it was a matter of policy, and the Great Western preferred to build bogie bolsters. One could say the same of the Southern, but in truth it had little need of any kind of bolster wagon. The traditional timber traffic had all but disappeared, and, whilst on the other railways this was to some extent balanced by an increase in steel traffic, this did not exist on the Southern. In the south, the story of the single- and double-bolster wagon was one of continuous decline. There was still a quantity of batten traffic, but this was now usually carried in square-ended open goods wagons with the load of one overlapping the next, the last load having an empty runner to protect it.

In 1923 there was an order outstanding for 20 LSWR bogie bolster wagons, and these were built in 1923/4 (Diagram 1597). As a pre-Grouping design, these were described fully in Volume One but merit inclusion here as their construction was continued by the Southern. These wagons were not conventional bogie bolsters, as they had been designed to the limit of the loading gauge in order that they could be used without their bolsters to carry military equipment. They were very useful in this role, and a further 30 were built in 1926, bringing the class total to 100. They were also a part of the small group of ordinary non-ferry Southern vehicles authorised to run on the Nord Railway of France. They rarely carried timber but were much used to carry new rails from Bridgwater, on the Somerset & Dorset (S&D) to Redbridge Works.

It was the increase in the length of rails from the previous

SR-built bogie bolster wagons

Pre-Grouping bogie bolster wagons on order 1/1/1923

Diagram	Order	Date	Quantity	Construction	Numbers	Examples of tare weights	Notes
1597	LSWR	1921	20	1923/4	57833-52	NR (Diagram tare 18-9-1)	LSWR Nos allocated. Five built in 1923, 15 in 1924

Pre-Group bogie bolster design ordered by the Southern Railway

Diagram	Order	Date	Quantity	Construction	Numbers	Examples of tare weights	Notes
1597	E108	11/5/25	30	4/26-9/26	57853-82	NR (Diagram tare 18-9-1)	LSWR design. Total Diagram 1597 built 100

SR standard bogie bolster designs

Diagram	Order	Date	Quantity	Construction	Numbers	Examples of tare weights	Notes
1598	L873	24/5/35	25	1/37	57883-907	57883 21-2-0, 57896 21-3-0	57898-900 altered for Robel cranes 5/37. Renumbered 64622-46 in 1945
1598	L1282	8/8/41	30	7/43-9/43	57908-37	57908 21-5, 57937 21-5	Fabricated buffer guides
1598	A2503	13/5/43	50	1945	57938-87	57938 21-8, 57987 21-6	Self-contained buffers, as per all subsequent orders
1599	A3221	4/5/45	52	6/46-10/46	57988-58039	57988 20-9, 58039 20-9	AAR cast steel bogies, as per all subsequent orders
1599	A3302	10/4/45	11	6/46-7/46	64738-48	64738 22-0, 64748 22-0	Also found on Diagram 1787. Provision for Robel cranes
1599	A3356	15/4/46	6	1/48	64749-54	64749 21-3, 64754 21-3	

Note: NR = No record

Left:
Plate 126 Diagram 1597 No 57606 at Eastleigh in September 1942, loaded with a Naval motor boat built in the locomotive works. The wagon was actually built by the LSWR, but the SR-built versions are believed to have been identical, apart from the number plates and initials on the axleboxes.
Authors' collection

Plate 126 One of the 30 or more Diagram 1597s used in postwar years for conveying the Bertram Mills Circus, seen here at Feltham in 1963 with the C&W repair shop in the background. Notice the holes that have been drilled in the siderail to accommodate the shackles used to secure the circus vehicles; several 'Bertram Mills bogies' had this feature. The livery was grey with white lettering on black patches.
A. Blackburn

Plate 128 Bertram Mills gave up using BR *c*1965, and, after a short period in store most of the vehicles concerned were transferred to the CCE. They were too short for track panels or rail, but ideal for carrying switches and crossings. Here we see DS57840 in Engineer's olive green livery. Still in as-built condition, the wagon has been downrated to 30 tons on account of its age.
Authors' collection

standard length of 45ft to 60ft that led to the design of the Southern's one and only bogie bolster design, known to all as the 'Borail'. The Southern had started to use 60ft rails in the 1920s, but it was not until 1936 that it was decided to adopt this length as standard. From photographs it would seem that, in the past, 60ft rails were carried on the South Western bogies, with a runner at both ends, but rails are easily crippled if not handled with care, and the general introduction of 60ft rails made the provision of a more suitable wagon essential.

The new design (Diagram 1598) was 64ft over headstocks. Eight bolsters were provided, but the stanchions were normally fitted only in the middle six. The first batch of 25 wagons was delivered in January 1937; although these carried traffic-wagon numbers, they were lettered 'ED', so there seems little doubt as to the traffic they were intended for, and in 1945 they were renumbered into the Engineer's fleet. The design proved to be exactly what was wanted, and there were five repeat orders, although each new batch had some detail variation.

Bulleid's touch can be seen in the fabricated buffer guides of the second batch, something that was not repeated; his greatest contribution to the design was the introduction in 1946 of the American-designed three-part cast-steel bogie. In a sense, this bogie was wasted under the 'Borails', as the old diamond design was adequate for the low speeds at which they normally ran, but it was the new standard SR design, and there is no doubt that it was a very fine and reliable bogie.

There is not a lot to be said of the traffic 'Borails', except to note that they also spent a great deal of their time delivering rails, which now reached the Southern from such places as Scunthorpe or Workington, having come all the way by rail. No more did they come across the Bristol Channel from South

Wales to Bridgwater by S&D steamer. Otherwise, 'Borails' might be found carrying new traffic, such as long reinforcing bars or rolled steel joints.

It will be noted that the last batch were built to carry 'Robel' rail cranes. Robel was a German company specialising in the production of permanent-way tools etc. These cranes could be mounted two-to-a-wagon and were used to load or unload rails. They were first used for this purpose in England to handle the Southern's first 'Long Welded Rails' which were installed in the Brighton-line tunnels in 1937. In theory these cranes threatened to over-stress the wagon solebars, so small gusset plates were welded into the solebars at the crane mounting-points to prevent this. However, this fine point was frequently overlooked, and it was not unusual for the cranes to be used on wagons which lacked this feature. A modern form of these cranes is still used today on specially modified 'Salmon' wagons.

The floors of the 'Borail' wagon were made of steel chequer plate, and in later years some of these plates started to wear rather thin. To avoid the need to replace the entire floor, recourse was made to strengthening with ¾in tongue-and-groove boards, which gave the impression that these wagons had conventional wooden floors.

These wagons gave outstanding service, especially in the 1960s and '70s, when they were used very intensively despite approaching the end of their lives. They were perhaps a little lightly built for their size and, when rough-shunted empty, had a tendency to 'whip', whereupon a great cloud of dust and general muck would be flung into the air, to the accompaniment of a loud bang! One or two finished their lives as crane runners, but most served as rail wagons into the 1970s and several still see further service on heritage railways.

Above:
Plate 129 No 57896 (Diagram 1598) brand new at Ashford in January 1937. Although the wagon has a traffic number, the letters 'ED' denote an Engineer's wagon, so the colour is probably red oxide, of the rather 'orange' shade used by many private owners. The headstock appears very light in colour, but it is facing west directly into the sun. This first batch of these wagons had LSWR diamond-framed bogies and SECR self-contained buffers with round heads. *R. Chorley collection*

Below:
Plate 130 No 57994 (Diagram 1598), a traffic wagon seen when brand new in 1945. This was one of the third order for these wagons, with American-designed bogies and Bulleid's self-contained buffers with oval heads. One of the two skeletal vans in the background appears to have diagonal bracing intended for planked construction; it will almost certainly be finished with plywood. *Kent Arts & Libraries*

Figure 49

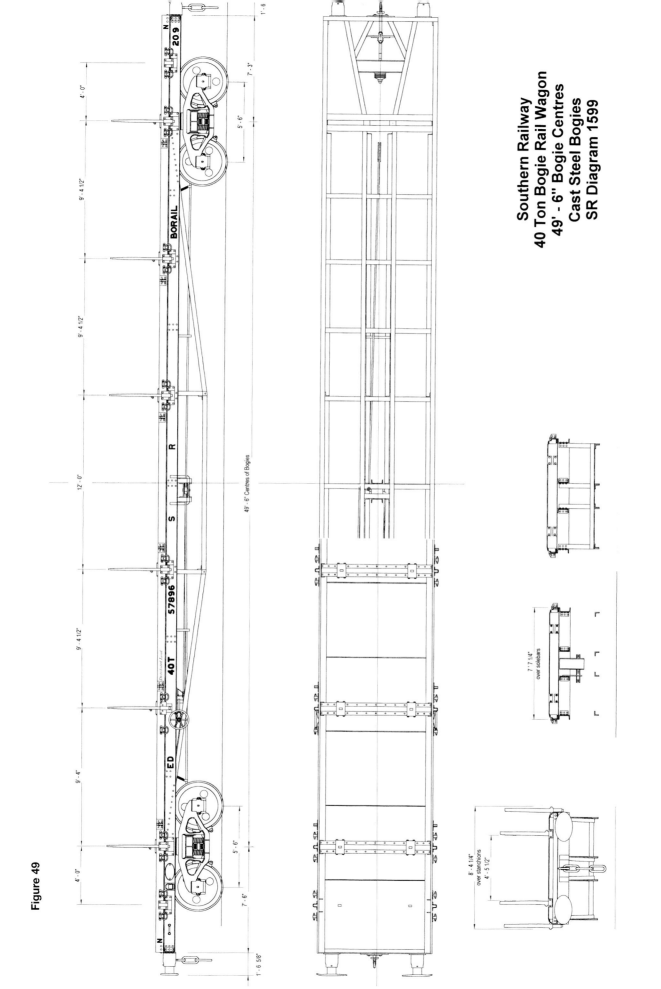

Southern Railway
40 Ton Bogie Rail Wagon
49' - 6" Bogie Centres
Cast Steel Bogies
SR Diagram 1599

Plate 131 Seen in 1946 is No 64741 of Diagram 1599 and, later, Diagram 1787; the latter describes these wagons as 40-ton bogie rail wagons for 'Robel' cranes. The purpose of the high stanchions is unknown, but they certainly had nothing to do with 'Robel' cranes. In May 1959 this particular wagon had low triangular brackets mounted on the floor over the bogies, to enable it to carry concrete footbridge sections; the changes visible here may have been the result of some earlier modification for this traffic. *Kent Arts & Libraries*

Plate 132 No DS64629, built as No 57890 in 1937 and seen here loaded with track panels at Hoo, some time in the late 1960s/ early 1970s. Note that this wagon has acquired the later self-contained buffers with oval heads.
T. A. Barry collection

Plate 133 No 57908 at Ashford in August 1949. One of the second order built in 1943, it has Bulleid's fabricated buffer guides with buffer springs behind the headstock; this feature was not perpetuated in later orders. The wagon is lettered 'Borail', but this was a traffic wagon, and the livery would have been SR brown.
F. Foote collection

Plate 134 A close-up view of the Bulleid fabricated buffer guide. Note that the wagon has been provided with an 'Instanter' coupling — a BR modification. *A. Blackburn*

Plate 135 A close-up view of the Bulleid self-contained buffer. Notice how the outer edge of the oval buffer is curved round as a precaution against buffer-locking. A sliding lug prevents the head from rotating. *A. Blackburn*

Chapter 11.
Machinery & Well Trucks

It is perhaps only when considering the more specialised vehicles that one becomes fully aware of the scale of the difference between the Southern and the other three companies serving the more industrial areas. It is impossible to show pages of special, exotic heavy-duty wagons, because, with just two exceptions, the Southern did not own any. When the occasional need did arise for such a wagon, it was a simple matter to hire one, normally from the line to which the load was consigned; it was rare indeed for such a load to pass between two Southern stations. One might think of the traffic passing between the Naval Dockyards, perhaps, but the larger items were often more conveniently taken by sea.

One of the rare exceptions to this picture was the regular traffic of steam-rollers and the like coming out of Messrs Aveling & Porter's works at Strood. The SECR had a small fleet of well trucks used largely for this traffic, and in 1923 there was an outstanding order for 12 more to replace some of the older wagons. Lynes had prepared a drawing for these while he was still at Ashford, but it was not until October 1923 that it was possible to build them (Diagram 1681). They are believed to have been the first new wagons built with SR numbers. They were a good, straightforward example of this class of wagon, and further batches were built in 1928 and 1942. They carried 20 tons, increased to 21 tons in 1942. In Southern days they were lettered 'WELL B', although the records had them as 'Mac B'; in BR days they were 'Lowmack SD'.

Like all the machinery and well trucks they were non-'common user', Nos 61048-59/86-98 being among that group of Southern wagons that could by special arrangement run on the Nord Railway of France.

The Southern Railway staff magazine liked to feature unusual loads, and naturally enough these wagons were often the type to be found carrying them. Examples noted included a very large (but not out-of-gauge) German container (one of a number consigned to East Grinstead), 65 lions (!) in special road trailers belonging to the Swiss circus Knie (Southampton Docks to Olympia) and cable drums 10ft 8in in diameter (Eastleigh to Southampton Docks; these were originally intended to go by road, but the first lorry loaded overturned). Excavators, road-making machines and such like were the more normal loads.

In 1942 three (Nos 61055/7/9) were sold to the Government and loaded with emergency mobile rectifier sub-stations. They seem not to have left the Southern, however, and in 1951 they returned to railway ownership still carrying their rectifiers.

As a class, these wagons lasted well, although one was lost to enemy action in 1941. In the 1960s quite a number passed into departmental use, most being used by the Civil Engineer to carry gantries for re-laying single-line track. These wagons were without doubt one of Lynes' best and most useful designs, and several survive in preservation.

One well wagon that was not standard stock deserves special mention — No 387S, a bogie well purchased in 1926 specially to move transformers from Peckham Rye to Gloucester Road. It was a most unusual vehicle, having been built towards the end of World War 1 as a rail gun mounting. As might be expected, it was of very heavy construction, its tare weight of 39 tons being only one ton less than its carrying capacity. It cost just £267, which was probably cheaper than hiring a suitable vehicle from one of the other companies. Unfortunately no drawing or photograph is available, but according to the diagram it had a length over headstocks of 41ft 3in, a width of 8ft 5in and a central well 16ft 0in long. Following its initial use, this wagon seems to have languished on the buffers somewhere, and it might more usefully have joined the others of its type which had been retained by the military and which emerged in 1940 carrying heavy guns for Beach Defence duties. As it was, it was broken up for scrap.

Machinery and well wagons built or purchased by the Southern Railway

Pre-Grouping machinery wagons on order 1/1/1923

Diagram	Order	Date	Quantity	Construction	Numbers	Examples of tare weights	Notes
1681	SECR	?	12	10/23	61048-59	NR (Diagram tare 8-14-0)	'Mac B', uprated from 20 to 21 tons 7/42

Pre-Grouping machinery wagon design ordered by the Southern Railway

Diagram	Order	Date	Quantity	Construction	Numbers	Examples of tare weights	Notes
1681	E109	11/5/25	13	1928	61086-98	NR (Diagram tare 8-14-0)	'Mac B', uprated from 20 to 21 tons 7/42
1681	A1096	16/5/39	22	6/42-7/42	61151-72	61151 9-7, 61172 9-5	'Mac B', uprated from 20 to 21 tons 8/42-11/43

War Department bogie well wagon purchased by the Southern Railway (former gun mounting)

Diagram	Order	Date	Quantity	Construction	Numbers	Examples of tare weights	Notes
1850	?	1926?	1	MCW&F 1918	387S	39-2-0	Length over heasdstocks 41ft 3in, length of well 16ft, width 8ft 3in, bogie centreline 25ft. The body of this unusual vehicle could be lowered to the track

SR standard well wagon designs

Diagram	Order	Date	Quantity	Construction	Numbers	Examples of tare weights	Notes
1690	C Rob	4/6/25	2	11/27	61099, 61100	61099 26-13-1	'Crocodile wagon'
1682	L1887	23/10/42	11	1/44-6/45	61101-10, 64600	61101 12-17, 61110 13-3	'Flatrol' No 61110 built to carry an excavator / drag line

Note: NR = No record

Plate 136 No 61057 (Diagram 1681) was one of the first built in 1923 to the order of the SECR and is seen here in March 1927 loaded with a former LBSCR steam-roller. Note that the wagon is lettered 'Well B', despite the records' referring to these wagons as 'Mac B'. *National Railway Museum, York*

Figure 50

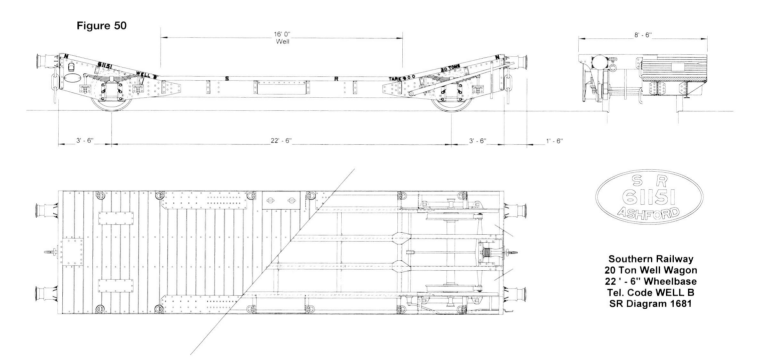

16' 0"
Well

8' - 6"

3' - 6"   22' - 6"   3' - 6"   1' - 6"

S R
61151
ASHFORD

**Southern Railway
20 Ton Well Wagon
22 ' - 6" Wheelbase
Tel. Code WELL B
SR Diagram 1681**

Plate 137 No 61090 (also Diagram 1681) was one of the second order. The buffers and couplings seem to have been specially painted for the photograph; normally they were black, although the buffer castings were frequently brown. If, as believed, the plate frame followed brake van practice, this too would have been brown. *National Railway Museum, York*

Left:
Plate 138 One of the three 'Well Bs' (Nos 61055/7/9) sold to the Government in October 1942 and fitted with a mobile rectifier. They returned to railway ownership in January 1952, still carrying rectifiers, and this one is seen in Southampton Docks sometime in the 1950s in the ownership of the Docks & Inland Waterways Executive. Livery is light grey all over with white writing; 'X' is on a black patch. *Authors' collection*

Right:
Plate 139 No S61056 after overhaul at Ashford in April 1948. Except for No 61058, destroyed by enemy action in April 1941, all these wagons were uprated to 21 tons during the war. *National Railway Museum, York*

Right:
Plate 140 No 61153 at Eastleigh in October 1949. This was one of the 1942-built wagons, construction of which was allocated to Ashford, but all of which are believed to have been built at Lancing. Note the load is roped over its springs to stop it bouncing. *T. A. Barry collection*

Right:
Plate 141 These wagons have always been found useful for departmental purposes, and as early as July 1942 Nos 61166 and 61168 were lettered to work between Eastleigh, Brighton and Ashford Works only. In 1963 at least four went into internal use with the CM&EE, and a little later the CCE took 10 as portable plant wagons. In 1966 seven were left in traffic, 10 were with the CCE and one was with the CME as a wheel wagon. No DS61091, photographed at New Cross Gate in 1970, illustrates the correct way of securing the binding chains when not in use. (The chain lockers were getting thin by this time.) The livery is grey with black underframe, with white letters on black patches. *A. Blackburn*

Figure 51

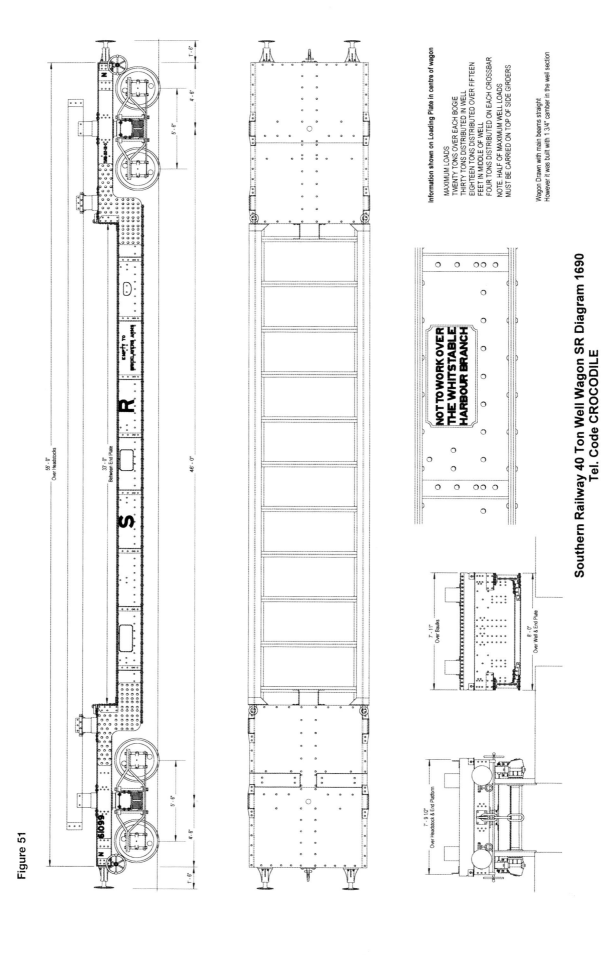

Information shown on Loading Plate in centre of wagon

MAXIMUM LOADS
TWENTY TONS OVER EACH BOGIE
THIRTY TONS DISTRIBUTED IN WELL
EIGHTEEN TONS DISTRIBUTED OVER FIFTEEN
FEET IN MIDDLE OF WELL
FOUR TONS DISTRIBUTED ON EACH CROSSBAR
NOTE. HALF OF MAXIMUM WELL LOADS
MUST BE CARRIED ON TOP OF SIDE GIRDERS

Wagon Drawn with main beams straight
However it was built with 1 3/4" camber in the well section

NOT TO WORK OVER
THE WHITSTABLE
HARBOUR BRANCH

Southern Railway 40 Ton Well Wagon SR Diagram 1690
Tel. Code CROCODILE

Left:
Plate 142 No 61099 (Diagram 1690), built by Charles Roberts in 1927 and seen in that works' yard at Horbury Junction, near Wakefield. One wonders to what extent the Southern actually designed these wagons; it seems probable that a specification was written and the detail left to the builders, as they were very similar to some 'crocodile' wagons owned by the other companies. *R. Chorley collection*

Below:
Plate 143 No 61099 again, and now equipped with the loading baulks manufactured at Eastleigh. Notice the camber in the underframe and how, when the wagon is empty, this has the effect of lifting the baulks off the outer bolsters. No 61100 was allocated to Nine Elms when new, moving to Feltham in 1939. BR coded these wagons as 'Weltrol SA'. *R. Chorley collection*

The two special wagons mentioned at the start of this Chapter were 40-ton bogie well wagons built in 1927 (Diagram 1690). These were the sort of orders the Southern found more cost effective to put out to contract. Five firms tendered, and the order went to Charles Roberts & Co at a cost of £700 each, which at that time was about the price of a good semi-detached house in Surrey. The Southern was very proud of these wagons and a full description appeared in the technical press, together with a very good drawing. This showed a dimension that is normally absent from such things, namely the degree of camber built into the underframe of a bogie vehicle, which in this case was $1\frac{3}{4}$in over a length of 35ft. They could carry a maximum load of 40 tons — 20 tons over each bogie, 30 tons distributed over the well, or 18 tons over 15ft about the centre of the well. As is normal with this type of wagon, there was no floor as such; instead there were 11 movable cross-bars, to allow the load to be dropped between them if a few extra inches were required. In addition, two removable timber baulks were provided to support unstable loads, and these could be adjusted in width as required. The loads envisaged were ships' propellers, armour plate, gun mountings and engines, all of which points towards traffic in and out of the Naval Dockyards or Southampton Docks. One of the wagons was allocated to Nine Elms, the other to Bricklayers Arms. They could travel over the whole of the SR except the Whitstable branch, and, bearing in mind the very sharp curves that could be found in the dockyards, they were designed to negotiate a curve of 132ft radius. As already stated, the SR staff magazine rarely lost the chance to record a special load, but there was never any mention of these wagons, which leads to speculation they may not have had as much use as had been hoped for. On the other hand, if they were carrying Naval traffic, then photography might not have been encouraged; one was certainly not allowed to take a camera into the Dockyards in those days. They had long lives, and No 61099 was noted at Feltham in 1962 as a departmental 'Machinery truck', for which purpose it had been provided with a wooden floor.

Below:
Plate 144 No S61099 passed to the CCE in 1962, and in 1963 S61100 went to the Shipping & Continental Department at Newhaven, where it was broken up a year later. No DS61099 is seen in 1963, not long before it too was scrapped. *Authors' collection*

The war created a need for all sorts of strange and bulky pieces of equipment, requiring suitable wagons to carry them. The two just described were very versatile but were rather high over their side girders. Even the other companies had never had many of what was now required, and a new design was called for. The result was Bulleid at his best: a 20-ton-capacity four-wheeled well wagon (Diagram 1682). The well was 21ft long by 8ft 6in wide, and, again, movable cross-bars were provided. A load of 4 tons could be carried by each cross-bar or 15 tons about the centre line of the wagon, half of which had to be carried on the 'main girders'. As a point of interest, the camber in the side members in this case was 7/8in over 21ft. Provision was again made for side baulks, but only two sets were made for the 11 wagons ordered — 10 for the Traffic Department and one for the Engineer.

The LNER had a number of similar wagons, and Bulleid would have been familiar with these, but they were rather heavy, and (as always) Bulleid was determined to save weight. To achieve this, he based the new design upon a number of steel castings welded together, the largest of these — the main side-frame castings — believed at the time to have been the longest items ever cast. The design was unique. Nothing like it had ever been attempted before, and, once again, these wagons received a lot of coverage in the technical press. The result was really quite elegant, although the design allowed for a large part of the casting work to be left unfinished in order to save unnecessary

work. The springing was also unusual, and used vertical volute springs instead of the more normal leaf arrangement; this saved 2-3ft in length, as well as considerable weight. The general arrangement was not unlike the 'McCords' springs used at the turn of the century by both the LSWR and the SECR, but was much stronger. The castings were made by the English Steel Corporation at Sheffield, and the wagons were assembled at Lancing between April 1944 and June 1945.

The minimum-radius curve that could be traversed by the new wagons was 198ft — quite sufficient for any normal yard — but they were restricted from working between Andover Junction and Romsey and on the Lymington and Whitstable branches by reason of their width at low level. Bulleid had estimated that his design would save one ton in weight over a similar wagon of conventional construction. It is thus interesting to note that, when, in 1958, Lancing built 10 of the 'Flatrol SB' design (Nos B900027-36; BR Diagrams 2/525 and 2/533) to the same dimensions, the resulting wagons were more than two tons heavier than the original design.

Both the SR and BR designs gave good service, and, as is usual with these useful wagons, several finished their lives as departmentals. One (DS 61103) carried what is thought to have been the largest and heaviest cable-drum load ever moved by BR, from Eastleigh to Poole in November 1966. Happily one of these most interesting wagons, No 61107, survives with the Bluebell Railway.

Above:
Plate 145 No 61102 (Diagram 1682), a Bulleid cast steel 'Flatrol', complete with loading baulks. Basically, the body of the wagon consists of just four castings — two headstocks and two sidebeams — welded together, not unlike a white-metal kit! The photograph is dated 24 May 1944. *R. Chorley collection*

Left:
Plate 146 A detail of No 64600. The use of the volute spring saved at least 2ft of unproductive length, weight and money. The route restrictions were due to the presence of bridge girders on the lines concerned, combined with the wagons' width. *R. Chorley collection*

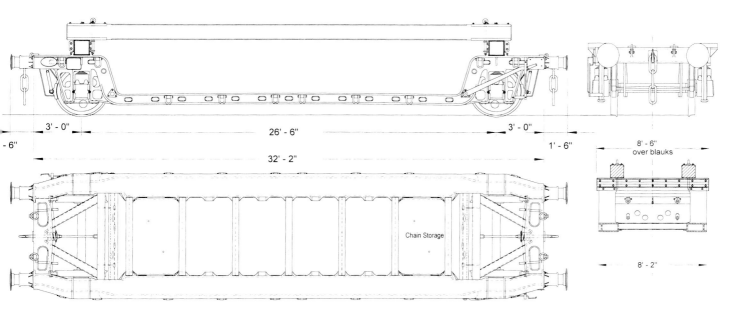

**Southern Railway 20 Ton Well Wagon SR Diagram1682
Cast Steel Underframe**

3' - 0"   26' - 6"   3' - 0"
- 6"   32' - 2"   1' - 6"

8' - 6"
over blauks

8' - 2"

Chain Storage

Figure 52

Above:
Plate 147 A nice three-quarter view, showing the brake gear and the securing-points on the headstocks. *R. Chorley collection*

Right:
Plate 148 A useful view of No 64600 showing the movable cross-bars and their casting locations. The livery of this wagon is uncertain; in theory it should be red oxide, but it may be grey all over. (Some of Ray's old colleagues at Lancing remember building wagons that were painted grey, and this may be one of them.) *R. Chorley collection*

111

Above:
Plate 149 Another detail of No 64600. Note the standard SR label clip, a little lower than the later BR one. The numberplate seems to lack a lip round the edge. Note too the comparatively rough finish to the castings; this was a design feature, only essential surfaces being machined. *R. Chorley collection*

Below:
Plate 150 These unusual wagons were successful but they tended to crack their side members at the bottom of the swan-neck, so small gusset plates were welded in to strengthen them at this point, as can be seen here on DS61107. Like the 'Well Bs', these wagons were much sought-after by the Engineering Department. No 61103 became a cable wagon, 61107/8 went to the CCE (the latter to work between Nine Elms and the Bank!), 61109 went to the Road Motor Engineer and 64600 finished up as an internal somewhere. Most (if not all) of the departmentals acquired a solid floor of one sort or another. Happily No 61107 survives on the Bluebell Railway. *T. A. Barry collection*

Above:
Plate 151 Lastly, a photograph of DB998006, seen at Feltham in March 1968. This is one of the conventionally constructed wagons built to the same dimensions as the Diagram 1682s. As is apparent, they were very similar, but on average they were nearly 2 tons heavier. *Authors' collection*

S.R. HAS ESTABLISHED EXCELLENT MODERN DOCK AND WHARF FACILITIES

The Southern Railway has carried out a thorough re-organisation of its Thames Wharf arrangements.

These Wharves, particulars of which are given below, are situated at various points along the river, and are all connected directly with the railway.

A system of control is exercised by which traffic is expedited and barge demurrage minimised.

Traders interested in Riverside traffic can, with confidence, consign it "Via Southern Railway."

The revised arrangements have now been in operation long enough to show that traders keenly appreciate the greatly increased efficiency which has resulted.

For barge traffic, all collection orders, released Bills of Lading and Customs papers should be sent previous to the vessel's arrival in Port direct to the Company's Lighterage Agents, Messrs. The Thames Steam Tug & Lighterage Company, Ltd., 6, Lloyds Avenue, London, E.C.3.—Telephone No. Royal 1830.

Blackfriars, Nine Elms and Battersea have accommodation for barges only, while Angerstein and Deptford can accommodate both seagoing vessels and barges. In the case of Deptford Wharf vessels must not exceed 240 feet in length and 40 feet beam, and at Angerstein Wharf vessels must not draw more than 18 feet normal Spring Tides and 14 feet normal Neap Tides.

ACCOMMODATION.

Wharf.	Depth of Water.		Cranes.			
	Spring Tides.	Neap Tides.	Steam.	Hy-draulic.	Electric.	Greatest Lift.
	Feet.	Feet.				Tons.
Angerstein ..	18	14	5	—	1	5
Deptford ..	18	14	—	9	18	30
Blackfriars ..	9	5	—	4	—	1¾
Nine Elms ..	9	5	2	8	—	20
Battersea ..	11	7	3	—	—	3

FURTHER WHARF AND DOCK FACILITIES ARE AVAILABLE AS UNDER :—

Wharf.	Depth of Water.		Cranes.			
	Spring Tides.	Neap Tides.	Steam.	Hy-draulic.	Electric.	Greatest Lift.
	Feet.	Feet.				Tons.
Newhaven ...	29	24	17	—	10	15
Kingston (Shoreham)	19	15	1	—	—	4
Littlehampton ...	16	12	3	—	—	7
Strood	16	13	3	—	2	5
Queenborough ...	30	23	—	—	4	3
Whitstable ...	13½	11	—	—	2	3
Stonehouse Pool...	30	26	2	—	—	3
Fremington ...	16 to 20	7 to 10	5	—	—	6
Wadebridge ...	13	2	—	1 (hand)	—	5
Padstow	17	10	—	—	—	—
Medina (I. of W.)	22	18	—	—	2	3
St. Helens (I. of W.)	10	8	2 / —	— / 1 (hand)	— / —	4 / 10

Chapter 12.
Miscellaneous Vehicles

This really is a catch-all chapter detailing a wide spread of vehicles, both revenue-earning (stone trucks and gunpowder vans) and departmental (snow ploughs and shunting trucks).

SR-built miscellaneous vehicles

Diagram	Order	Date	Quantity	Construction	Numbers	Examples of tare weights	Notes
1317	E105	11/5/25	2	11/26	61029/30	NR (Diagram tare 7-1-0)	Stone truck (LSWR design)
1691	437	4/3/29	2	1929	S1, S2	'Light 10-7-0, loaded 18 tons'	Snowplough
1317	E646	14/4/31	15	8/33-9/33	61121-35	61121 7-1-0, 61128 7-2-1	Stone truck (LSWR design)
1712	E610	6/1/31	2	6/31	61322/3	61322 9-9-0, 61323 9-9-0	Shunting truck for Clapham Junction. LSWR tender underframe. VP later AVB 1 x 21in cyl (?), four brake blocks
1714	E827	5/9/34	2	7/35	61324/5	NR (No tare on Diagram)	Shunting truck for Dover train ferry. LBSCR carriage underframe. AVB 2 x 8in cyl, 16 brake blocks. WP
1715	A998	29/9/37	2	1/39	61326/7	61326 25-0, 61327 25-0	Shunting truck for Bournemouth West. LBSCR tender underframe. AVB 1 x 21in? cyl, six brake blocks. Steam heat
1717	?	?	2	11/47	61328/9	61328 19-6, 61329 19-13	Replacements for 61324/5 above, SR carriage underframe. AVB 2 x 18in cyl, 16 brake blocks, WP
1691	?	1948?	2	12/48	S3, S4	'Light 10-7-0, loaded 18 tons'	Snowplough

Note: NR = No record

Stone trucks

Stone traffic, primarily from Portland to Nine Elms, initially held up very well, as the early motor lorries were really not up to this sort of thing. The LSWR had evolved a very satisfactory 15-ton four-plank dropside design, and this was used for two new wagons required as replacements in 1925 and for a further 15 in 1931. Apart from using the standard Ashford-designed self-contained buffer on the second order, nothing else was changed — even the wheelsets remained at the old South Western standard of 6ft 8in. As a pre-Grouping design, these wagons are more fully described in Volume One. They were very strongly constructed, and most are thought to have survived until the Portland branch closed in 1965.

Left:
Plate 152 No 61131 (Diagram 1317), one of the Eastleigh-built, LSWR-designed block stone trucks, seen when brand new in August 1933. Notice that Eastleigh (in true South Western tradition) has chamfered off the top edges of the planks; Ashford did not do this. These were the last SR wagons to be built with a wooden underframe. *R. Chorley collection*

Above:

Plate 153 No S61132 of Diagram 1317, seen at Ashford in 1948. This very normal-looking dropside open has an underframe built like one of Nelson's battleships; underneath, it has what can best be described as a second pair of solebars set between the normal ones and the internal longitudinals, making this an unusually strong wagon.

Gunpowder vans

The Southern did not find it necessary to build any gunpowder vans and had only 38 in October 1937, at which time it was stated that, as a result of the Government's re-armament programme, a further 100 would be required. It was reported that the GWR had a number of 'iron-panelled' covered goods wagons available that could be converted at a cost of £50 each, and it was recommended that 100 of these be obtained in exchange for a like number of covered goods wagons, these to be returned at the end of the re-armament programme. The wagons were 'Iron minks', and some (at least) had been similarly converted during World War 1. Just how many of these wagons eventually came to the Southern and how long they stayed is not known, but they were lettered 'SR' and carried temporary SR numbers. No reference to them is made in copies of the Wagon Registers seen by the authors, but the wagon in the photograph carries No 59061, from which one deduces the most likely number range to have been 59001-100. In appearance they were almost identical with the LSWR gunpowder vans (Diagram 1701).

Above:

Plate 154 One of the GWR 'Iron Minks' loaned to the SR as an 'Improvised Gun Powder Van'. Livery is all-over black; the letters 'G.P.V.' and the cross on the doors are red, the remainder of the writing white. The painting of the roof is not recorded, but it looks almost white, possibly to reflect the sun? *R. Chorley collection*

Snow ploughs

These were not really wagons, it must be admitted, but they were painted wagon brown! The South of England rarely has much snow, generally speaking, but the West Country and (perhaps surprisingly) Kent have had their share over the years. As far as is known, none of the Southern's constituent companies had any independent snow ploughs, although they almost certainly had some that could be attached to locomotive buffer-beams.

It must be assumed that the winter of 1928/9 was unusually severe, as two four-wheeled snow ploughs were ordered in March 1929, both being delivered later in the year at a cost of just £30 each. The drawing and photograph show their general construction and it only remains to note that they tared 10 tons 7cwt 'light' and 18 tons 'heavy', so they must have carried some form of ballast. The winter of 1947/8 was one of the worst in living memory. Where these rather basic snow ploughs were at that time is not known,

Above:
Plate 155 SR Snow Plough No 1. As can be seen, it is a double-ended vehicle; the beam on top was used to lower or raise the headstock and could be swung around as required. The right-hand headstock is raised for propelling, and the left-hand one lowered for ploughing. The livery is wagon brown with white lettering. *R. Chorley collection*

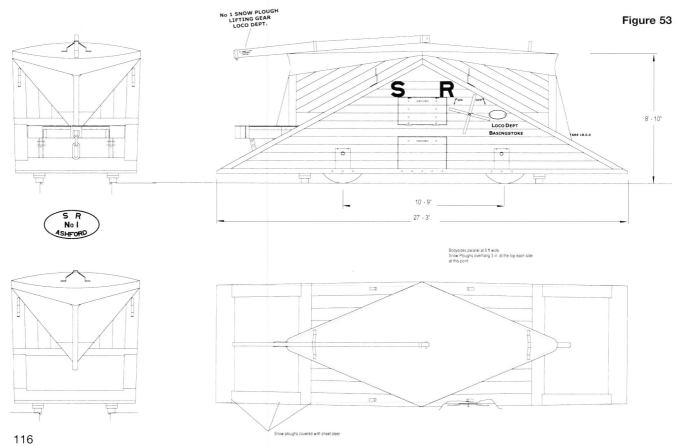

Figure 53

Southern Railway 18 Ton Snow Plough SR Diagram 1691

but they must have proved satisfactory, as in 1948 two more were ordered. They seem to have been allocated to various locations over the years, including Ashford, Basingstoke, Eastleigh and Exeter. They were numbered in their own series, S1 to S4.

Above:
Plate 156 Snow Plough No 4 at Ashford when virtually brand-new in May 1949. Both headstocks are raised, as is believed to have been normal practice when the ploughs were not in use. The only discernible difference from the earlier models is that the position of the numberplate has been altered. The general appearance of the prow suggests a turn-of-the-century battleship rather than a railway vehicle. These strange 'wagons' are presumed to have been withdrawn when the 'Schools' class tender conversions came into use in 1964. *J. H. Aston*

Shunting trucks

The Southern did not generally favour the use of shunting trucks, and the few it inherited in 1923 were not replaced. That said, it was not so unusual for those who liked the idea to place a 'Pill-box' next to the engine to ride on, rather than hang on the side of the engine, but that is to digress.

One location where the Southern did consider it necessary to employ shunters' trucks was Clapham Yard, where much of the passenger-stock shunting took place in close proximity to the running lines. In the late 1920s at least one former SECR shunters' truck was in use there, and in 1931 two Adams tender frames were used to make replacements for this or others. These were Nos 61322/3. These trucks always had a vacuum pipe, but according to the records they were 'fitted' in 1950, which seems a little odd. No details of their livery are available, but they are presumed to have had black underframes and white handrails. These two trucks were a familiar sight at Clapham over the years, but with the advent of diesel shunting engines in the 1950s they dropped out of use, and in the early 1960s one was languishing in Exmouth Junction yard; whether it was ever used there is unknown.

In 1935 two shunting trucks of an altogether different nature were supplied to Dover Train Ferry Dock for use as reach wagons. These were numbered 61324/5 and were constructed on LBSCR bogie-carriage underframes. They were vacuum-braked and also had Westinghouse air pipes so that the air brakes of Continental ferry wagons could be released by the shunting engine, Dover having an allocation of two air-braked Brighton 'E2' tanks for this purpose. The livery was standard wagon brown. In 1947 the pair went into Ashford Works as internal flats and were replaced by two Maunsell carriage underframes numbered 61328/9; these inherited their

Left:
Plate 157 No 61323 (Diagram 1712), one of the two Clapham Junction shunting trucks, converted from Adams 'A12' class engine tenders. Dimensions were as follows: length over buffer-beams 19ft 11½in; wheelbase 13ft; width within the guard rails 6ft 0½in, over footboards 7ft 6in; height to steel deck 4ft 2in, to top of hand-rail 7ft 4in; internal length of shunter's balcony 9ft 10in. *R. Chorley collection*

Right:
Plate 158 No S61322 at Exmouth Junction in March 1961. What it was doing there is a mystery; possibly it had been sent down for use on the heavily graded Topsham Harbour branch, but, if so, it must have been in the area for several years, as the branch closed in 1957. *A. E. West collection*

predecessors' 'caboose' bodies and were also provided with vacuum brakes and air pipes. Photographs dating from the 1950s show the shunting engines working onto the ferries, so presumably the reach wagons were no longer used latterly, though no withdrawal dates are to hand.

In 1937 four trucks were built to replace those provided to carry the weights used to test the goods-yard cranes. Nos 1085-8S had standard RCH 17ft 6in underframes and three-plank bodies without doors. They could carry 13 tons, made up of 12½ tons of test weights (short lengths of rail) and 5cwt of special slings, and were allocated (in numerical order) to Nine Elms, Eastleigh, Brighton and Bricklayers Arms. Their livery is believed to have been mid-grey with white lettering.

The last two SR shunting trucks were provided for use at Bournemouth West, where, according to the records, they were required 'for the brake control of coaching stock berthed in the Bournemouth West sidings'. There was a gradient of 1 in 90 between the sidings and the station, and it was the practice there to shunt stock gravitationally from the sidings into the station. Nos 61326/7 were built in 1939 and were similar in appearance to the Clapham trucks, but they were built on former LBSCR tender underframes and so had much in common with the Folkestone Harbour goods brake vans which were built at about the same time.

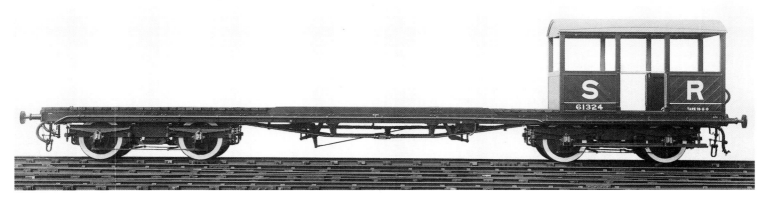

Top:
Plate 159 No 61324 (Diagram 1714), one of the two Dover shunting trucks, seen when new in 1935. The diagonal boarding is rather unusual. This truck was built on the underframe of composite carriage No 6133, a former LBSCR vehicle constructed originally in 1909. No 61325 was based on a similar vehicle (No 6150). *R. Chorley collection*

Above:
Plate 160 A side view of No 61324. Note the flitch plate riveted to the solebars about the centre line. *D. Cullum*

Left:
Plate 161 No 1088S, one of the four crane test weight trucks built in 1937, seen at Stewarts Lane, where the Outdoor Machinery Department (ODM) had its main workshops. The livery was light grey with white letters. Note the narrow-gauge locomotive on the left. *Authors' collection*

Southern Railway
Dover Ferry Shunting Truck
Fitted
SR Diagram 1714

Built on LBSC carriage Underframe

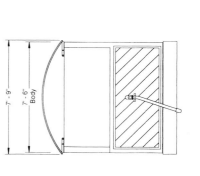

Figure 54

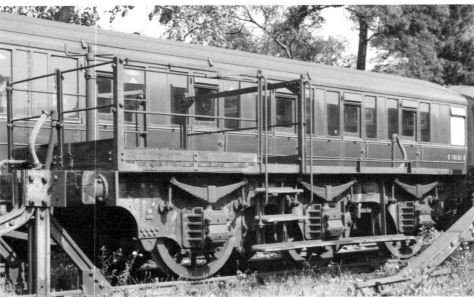

Left:
Plate 163 No 61327 (Diagram 1715), one of the two shunting trucks converted from 'C2' class locomotive tender for use at Bournemouth West. Dimensions: length over buffer beams 21ft 11/2in; wheelbase 13ft; width over side rails and bottom step boards 8ft 3in; height rail to top of wood floor 4ft 5in, to top of hand-rail stanchions 8ft 2¾in. *A. E. West collection*

Above:
Plate 164 No 61328 (Diagram 1717). In 1947 the Dover shunting trucks were given new underframes taken from withdrawn Maunsell carriages. This wagon has the underframe of Third-class carriage No 1145. (No 61329 had the underframe from No 4877.) Notice that one or two changes have been made: there is now a balcony outside the caboose, and the greater part of the truck has no floor. The minerals in the background are former Ministry of War Transport wagons on the way back from use in France, hence the French lettering. *D. Cullum*

Chapter 13.
Ballast Wagons, Ballast Brakes and Plough Vans

On 1 January 1923 there were 60 SECR 12-ton two-plank ballast wagons on order (Diagram I744), and these were built in July and August 1923, bringing the type total to 120. As might be expected, they spent their early years on the old South Eastern & Chatham section, where they seem to have often run as complete trains. Later, as still modern and useful wagons, they were to be found all over the Southern. They had long lives and one or two lasted into the 1970s.

The Southern did not build any brand-new ballast brake vans, but in 1928/9 seven quite new LBSCR 20-ton goods brakes were rebuilt as ballast brakes. There were 10 more in 1937 and very similar conversions of 10 SECR 'Dance Halls' in 1953. As pre-Grouping designs, these vehicles will be found in Volumes Two and Three respectively.

SR-built ballast wagons, ballast brakes and plough vans

Pre-group Ballast wagons on order 1/1/1923

Diagram	Order	Date	Quantity	Construction	Numbers	Examples of tare weights	Notes
1744	SECR	?	60	7/23-8/23	62427-62486	62427 5-11-2, 62486 5-11-2	SECR Nos allocated

Pre-Grouping ballast plough vans ordered by the Southern Railway

Diagram	Order	Date	Quantity	Construction	Numbers	Examples of tare weights	Notes
1748	C Rob	?	3	1932	62030-2	62030 20-5-0, 62031 20-7-2	SECR design (minor modifications) AVB 1 x 15in cyl, eight brake blocks
1749	A3301	10/8/45	8	1/49-4/49	62857-64	62857 20-24, 62864 4/49	SECR design (minor modifications) AVB 1 x 15in cyl, eight brake blocks

SR standard ballast wagon designs

Diagram	Order	Date	Quantity	Construction	Numbers	Examples of tare weights	Notes
1771	BRCW	25/01/28	60	6/28-10/28	61945-62004	61975 8-17-3, 62004 8-18-2	20-ton five-plank all-dropside. AVB 1 x 18in cyl, four brake blocks
1772	MetCW	23/03/28	25	10/28-2/29	62005-29	62005 19-4-0, 62007 19-5-2	Bogie all-steel hopper. AVB 2 x 18in cyl, eight brake blocks. Door controls one end. Diamond frame bogies
1773	A872	24/05/35	50	2/37-4/37	63001-50	63001 8-11, 63050 8-11	15-ton four-plank all-dropside. Several had their sides removed c1946 to carry concrete p/way huts
1774	MetroC	21/11/35	22	12/36-1/37	62033-54	62033 20-10-0, 62047 20-9-0	Bogie all-steel hopper. AVB 2 x 18in cyl, eight brake blocks. Door controls divided. Diamond-frame bogies
1775	A3327	21/11/45	20	5/47-9/47	62055-74	62055 19-10, 62074 19-10	Bogie all-steel hopper. AVB 2 x 18in cyl, eight brake blocks. Door controls divided. AAR cast-steel bogies
BR1/570	A3303	10/08/45	21	1951	DB991000-20	NR (Diagram tare 10-7)	20-ton steel-sided all-dropside. AVB 1 x 18in cyl, four brake blocks. BR Lot 2065 (SR Nos 63051-71 allocated but not used)
BR1/570	A3303	10/08/45	20	1951	DB991301-20	NR (Diagram tare 10-5)	20-ton steel-sided all-dropside. BR Lot 2102 (SR Nos 63072-91 allocated but not used)
BR1/570	?	?	160	1951/2	DB991141-300	NR (Diagram tare 10-6)	20-ton steel-sided all-dropside. BR Lot 2241 DB991141-240 allocated to Eastern and North Eastern Regions, DB 991141-300 to Southern Region

SR Ballast brake vans

Diagram	Order	Date	Quantity	Construction	Numbers	Examples of tare weights	Notes
1760	L341	06/06/28	5	8/28-1/29	62840-4	62841 20-0-0, 62842 25-3-0	Diagram 1576 LBSCR-design 20-ton on goods brake van rebuilt. AVB 1 x 18in cyl, eight brake blocks
1760	L382	24/08/28	2	1/29	62845/6	62845 19-17-0, 62846 20-10-0	Diagram 1576 LBSCR-design 20-ton on goods brake van rebuilt. AVB 1 x 18in cyl, eight brake blocks
1760	A941	24/09/36	10	3/37-12/37	62847-56	62848 19-4, 62851 19-4	Diagram 1576 LBSCR-design 20-ton on goods brake van rebuilt. AVB 1 x 18in cyl, eight brake blocks
1761	?	?	10	11/53	55476 etc	55508 25-0	Diagram 1560 SECR-design 25-ton on goods brake van rebuilt. AVB 1 x 18in cyl, eight brake blocks

BR ballast hoppers developed from SR designs

Diagram	Capacity	Built	Quantity	Numbers	Average tare weight	Notes
BR1/585	40 tons	1954	50	DB992481-530	20-9	'Walrus'. As SR Diagram 1775 but BR plate-frame bogie are and modified 'four-foot' doors. BR Lot 2411
BR1/589	50 tons	1966/7	90	DB982350-439	23-10	'Whale'. Developed from BR1/585 AAB. BR Lot 3591
BR1/590	40 tons	1970	100	DB982440-539	21-14	'Sealion'. Developed from SR1775 AAB and AVB. "Gloucester" cast-steel bogie. BR Lot 3723
BR1/591	40 tons	1971	28	DB982540-67	21-0	'Seacow'. As BR1/590 but AAB and VP. BR Lots 3724 and 3777
BR1/590	40 tons	1972-4	360	DB982568-927	21-14	'Sealion'. French-designed cast-steel bogies. BR Lot 3802
BR1/591	40 tons	1981/2	251	DB980000-250	21-2	'Seacow'. French-designed cast-steel bogies. BR Lots 3966 and 4010

Note: NR = No record

Right:
Plate 165 In every book of this nature there have to be decisions as to what to include and what to leave out. Four ballast brakes, Nos 62524-7, came into this category, as, despite their description, they were not wagon stock, all four having been converted from former LCDR carriages. Two, Nos 62524/6, were former 26ft Brake Thirds, and the other two were former 25ft Thirds. They were withdrawn as carriages in December 1925 and taken into the Engineer's fleet shortly afterwards. They had long lives and were not finally withdrawn until 1950. *Authors' collection*

Left:
Plate 166 Ballast brake No 62845 (Diagram 1760), rebuilt from goods brake No 55905 (Diagram 1576) in January 1929; it is here seen in August 1934. The two planks around the window line were replaced by steel plates when the van was rebuilt, thus bringing the side lights within the Hastings-line loading gauge while still being visible to enginemen. Note the oil lamps in the roof. *H. C. Casserley*

Right:
Plate 167 No 62844, built in 1923 as No 55924 and rebuilt in September 1928. Notice the steel plate along the bottom of the sides; all the later examples of Diagram 1576 (Nos 62841-4/6/9/50/3/6) seem to have had this feature from new. *Authors' collection*

The Southern's first ballast wagon design was a 20-ton five-plank wagon with divided doors, built on the standard 21ft 6in RCH underframe. They were 60 in number, and the Birmingham Railway Carriage & Wagon Co built them in 1928 for £189 each — at the time, not much more than the cost of a standard open. For many years they were unique as the only non-hoppered fully fitted ballast wagons in the country.

There is no doubt that these vehicles were ordered as a follow-up to the Sevenoaks accident, primarily for use as stone wagons. However, for a period, at least, allocation was split equally between Redbridge Works (Nos 61945-64), Meldon Quarry (61965-84) and Angestein Wharf (61985-62004) and was denoted by white enamelled plates with 1¼

in red lettering affixed to the solebars — 'TO BE RETURNED TO [then, on a second line] REDBRIDGE WORKS' etc. These wagons were very useful, and it was said they were sometimes attached to passenger trains when it was necessary to deliver some urgently needed replacement item from Redbridge or Angestein Works. They had very long lives and, indeed, were never withdrawn as a life-expired design; when vacuum-braked stock was withdrawn from the Southern Region in the 1970s, they were transferred to the Western to serve Swindon Stores, and only when that closed in the 1990s were the survivors generally withdrawn, by which time they were the oldest wagons running on BR. Happily at least one survives in preservation, on the Bluebell.

Left:
Plate 168 No DS62855, one of the second order built in the first half of 1922 as LBSCR No 375 and rebuilt in December 1937. This shows the rebuilt end and the footsteps provided to gain access to the oil lamps, which, by the time this photograph was taken (1970), had been removed. The livery is olive green. *A. Blackburn*

Below:
Plate 169 No DS55582 (Diagram 1761), one of 10 rebuilt from Diagram 1560 goods brakes in 1953, seen at New Cross Gate in 1967. The livery is again olive green. In SR days these 'Dance Halls' were prohibited from working over the Hastings line via Battle, but this restriction was removed when they were rebuilt, even though no alterations were made to reduce any of the dimensions. *Authors' collection*

Left:
Plate 170 There was probably a nice official BRC&W photograph taken of these wagons when they were new, but it does not seem to have survived; this broadside view of No 61972 (Diagram 1771) was taken by Frank Foote. The second 'plank' down is in fact a steel channel, which made these doors very heavy. *F. Foote collection*

Figure 55

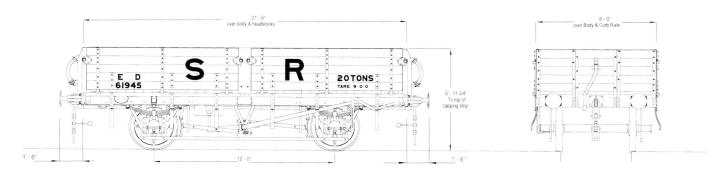

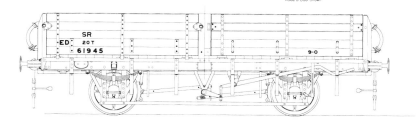

**Southern Railway
20 Ton Ballast Wagon
SR Diagram 1771**

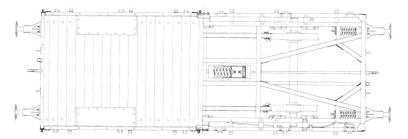

Left:
Plate 171 No DS61996 seen in July 1969 but still very much as built. An unusual feature of all Southern fitted ballast wagons was that they had a buffer length of 18in rather than the 20½in normal for fitted stock. The livery is black with white writing. The 'triangle' is light green and has been applied in error; these were painted on former open goods wagons to denote that they had been transferred to the CCE's fleet. *T. A. Barry collection*

As already mentioned, the 20-ton opens were very useful, but the bulk of the post-Sevenoaks improvements would be provided by 25 all-steel fully fitted 40-ton bogie hopper wagons. The order for these also went out to tender, and this time the Metropolitan Carriage, Wagon & Finance Co obtained the contract. The first of these wagons was delivered in October 1928, the remainder following three months later. As a basic design these wagons can be seen as a strengthened development of the LSWR hoppers of 1903, with the important difference that the door controls were now operated from a balcony on the end of the wagon. The dimensions of the two designs were not exactly the same, but they differed only

where the detail of the new design dictated otherwise. The diamond-framed bogie was identical and had been adopted by the LSWR and the Southern as a standard design. This design of wagon was destined to become something of a classic, with not only several SR and BR developments but also various export versions.

The next development was the ordering in 1932 of three ballast plough brakes to work with the hoppers referred to above. These were a detailed improvement of the Lynes SECR design, of which only one example had thus far been built. (These vans are described fully in Volume Three, as they are really a pre-Grouping design. With regard to the picture on

Right:
Plate 172 No 62014 (Diagram 1772), one of the first order for ballast hoppers, with door controls at one end only and short ballast shutes. The solebars have been painted black; this was not SR practice and seems to have been done for the photograph. The remainder are believed to have been painted in the standard livery of red oxide all over, except, of course, for the bogies, which were black. *R. Chorley collection*

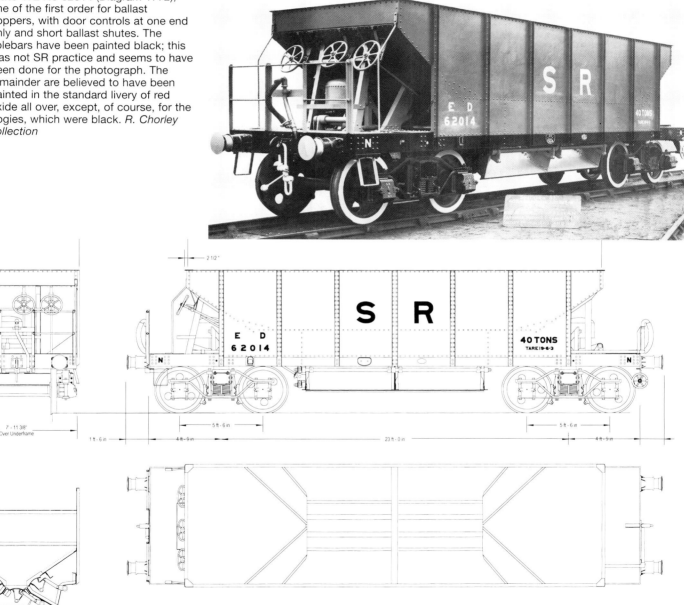

Section through Body
Showing Central Diaphragm Plate

Southern Railway 40 Ton Bogie Ballast Hopper Wagon SR Diagram 1772

Figure 56

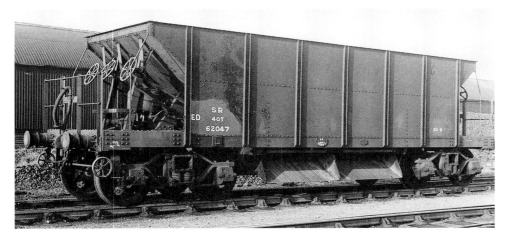

Left:
Plate 173 No 62047 (Diagram 1774). This was one of the second order, and experience with the earlier wagons had called for one or two changes. All these hoppers had their bodies divided by a central bulkhead, and the opportunity was taken to divide the doors, half being controlled from each end. The side shutes have also been lengthened, as the original design dropped the stone between the running and conductor rails. These wagons were delivered in late 1936 and early 1937, so the writing as seen here is probably original or at least repainted in the original style. *R. Chorley collection*

page 151 showing No 62030 with very strange angular lettering, it is now known that these letters were drafted by the Lancing Drawing Office but rejected in favour of the more traditional form that was ultimately adopted; it would seem this drawing was sent out to the builders, Messrs Charles Roberts, in error.) For the benefit of readers wondering how the ballast was being spread before these vans arrived, it should be explained that they were not essential to the task of discharging a hopper train; provided the doors were not opened too far, the job could be done quite well without a plough, and many permanent-way personnel actually preferred not to use them (and, of course, ploughs could not be used in the electrified area, as they fouled the conductor rail).

In 1935 it was decided to order 22 more hoppers, and these were delivered in 1936/7 by the Metropolitan-Cammell Carriage & Wagon Co (successor to the aforementioned Metropolitan Carriage, Wagon & Finance Co). In the light of experience, these differed from the earlier design in three respects. The door controls were split so that each side of the hopper — it had a transverse centre partition — could be discharged independently. This not only provided extra flexibility as to how the ballast was used but also made the task of controlling the doors much easier. The doors were so designed that (in theory) they could be closed against the flow of stone when necessary. Opening (and, to a lesser extent, closing) the doors was very heavy work, especially so on the first batch, as, when they were loaded, the body tended to bear down on the middle door bearing, making the job almost impossible. The second modification was simply to extend the side discharge shoots by a few inches so as to prevent the

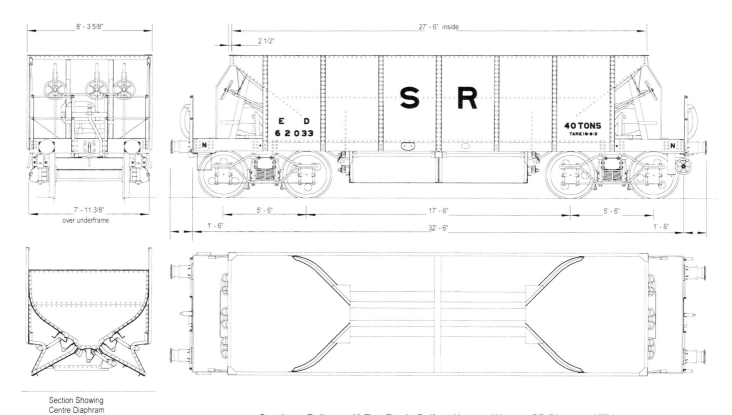

Section Showing
Centre Diaphram

Figure 57

Southern Railway 40 Ton Bogie Ballast Hopper Wagon SR Diagram 1774

Right:
Plate 174 Diagram 1773, exemplified by No 63005 brand new at Ashford in 1937, was very much a four-plank version of Diagram 1771. The second 'plank' is again a steel channel. The disc wheels are worthy of note, as they were only then coming into general use on Southern wagons.
R. Chorley collection

Right:
Plate 175 A broadside view of No 63005. This shows that the brake gear was of a type normally associated with a fitted wagon, so one may conclude from this that it was either decided to leave the vacuum equipment off for some reason or that provision was made for fitting it later. This picture also shows very nicely the 'ED' version of the '1936' writing.
R. Chorley collection

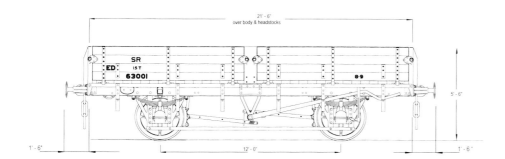

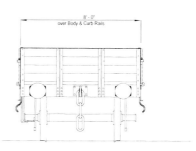

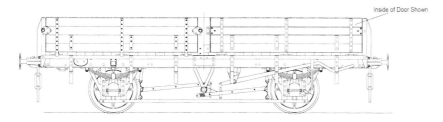

**Southern Railway
15 Ton Ballast Wagon
SR Diagram 1773**

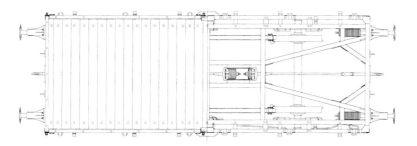

Figure 58

stone from falling onto the conductor rail. The third was more interesting and involved increasing the angle of the hopper slope from 35° to 38°. This was not as the result of any design error but reflected the changing nature of the stone that was being produced and its readiness to slide. Meldon was rather proud of the varying grades of stone and fossils encountered over the years and maintained a collection of examples for those who were interested.

The next new design to appear was a 15-ton version of the earlier 20-ton wagon, and this appeared in 1937. Why it was altered is a mystery but, with the benefit of hindsight, seems most unfortunate. The five-plank sides of the earlier design were certainly very heavy, but that could have been eased by the provision of door springs. Why the vacuum brakes were omitted is very hard to understand, and one can only guess that perhaps the earlier wagons were not being used as intensively as they should have been. In the mid to late 1940s a number of these 15-ton wagons had their sides removed in order to carry the concrete permanent-way huts that were then being produced in large numbers by Exmouth Junction Concrete Works. Each wagon could carry the accommodation hut and its associated tool hut. At least two of these wagons survive in their original condition at the time of writing.

It was not until May 1947 that it was possible to build any more ballast wagons but in that year 20 more 40-ton hoppers were produced. As already noted, all previous hopper wagons were built by contractors, but this time the latter were all busy with export work, so the railway had to build the hoppers itself. What might be described as non-standard wagon work was normally handled by Lancing, but, possibly because heavy rollers would be required to shape the internal plates, it was decided to build these wagons at Ashford. The works was very proud of them, and rightly so, for they were not the easiest of wagons to build. Another 3° was added to the end slope of the hopper, but the most important development was undoubtedly the fitting of the AAR cast-steel bogie. The original bogies had, in the absence of anything better, served quite well, but the design was not really suited to the prolonged high-speed running that was required of these wagons, and there had always been a lot of bolster coil-spring failures leading to solebar fractures. The new design did not cure the problem completely, but it produced a massive improvement.

In 1945 no fewer than eight more ballast brake ploughs were ordered, but, due to the shortage of materials and pressure on the workshops, it was not until January 1949 that it was possible to deliver them. What prompted this order is not

known, but at least they released eight ordinary Goods Brake Vans for revenue-earning duties.

Also in 1945, 41 15-ton ballast wagons were ordered, the odd one being to make good a war loss. These vehicles were not delivered until 1951, by which time they had become 20-ton wagons built on second-hand underframes. The records are silent as to how this came about, but, with Bulleid involved, anything seems to have been possible. What emerged was a wagon with steel sides and part-removable, part-drop steel ends. It was capable of carrying 8ft 6in-wide concrete sleepers, and the design allowed for a small road crane to pass through a train of these wagons, progressively unloading it. Used in this way, there seems to have been no reason why they should not have given every satisfaction; however, it was inevitable that, sooner or later, these wagons would be used for general purposes, and in this role they soon became very unpopular. The problem was that, even with the door springs provided, their sides were so heavy that they required a crane to lift them. This on its own would have been bad enough, but they arrived on the scene at much the same time as Bulleid's similarly afflicted five-plank drop-side wagons, which were foisted on to the Civil Engineer when the Traffic Department refused to accept them.

When 60 further general-purpose ballast wagons were required in 1950, the Chief Civil Engineer requested a wagon of the current London Midland Region type; what he got was a further batch of Bulleids, on the grounds that they were an existing Southern Region type. It is interesting to note that the bulk of the third batch went to former LNER territory, and one cannot but wonder if there was a Bulleid connection in this. In their later years they were used almost exclusively for stone or spoil traffic, where there was generally some form of plant to handle the doors. This in turn led to excessive damage, and, as a result, most of them were rebuilt with fixed sides in the early 1970s. As far as is known there are no survivors, and they are certainly not missed, but it should be remembered that they pre-dated the BR 'Grampus' design and that, at the time they were built, they were exactly what was required.

In 1954 BR built a further batch of the 40-ton hoppers, which by this time were called 'Walrus'. Unfortunately it was decided to make changes that were not for the better. The centre doors were changed from a rotating design that allowed control of the flow of stone to a drop flap which, once opened, committed the operator to using the lot. Worse, the fine American bogie was changed for the then standard BR plate design, presumably in the interests of standardisation. What those responsible did not apparently know was that the

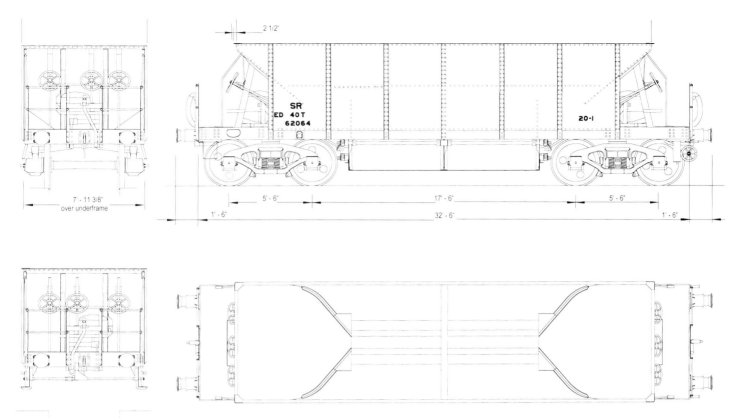

Southern Railway 40 Ton Bogie Ballast Hopper Wagon SR Diagram 1775

Figure 59

Above:
Plate 177 No DS62058 (Diagram 1775), one of the Ashford-built hoppers provided with the AAR cast-steel bogie. Each successive order had a slight increase in the angle of the end slope to the hopper, because Meldon was slowly working back through differing qualities of stone, and the later production did not slide as freely as that quarried earlier. The wagon was painted red-oxide when built but is seen here in black; the writing should be yellow but may well be white. *Authors' collection*

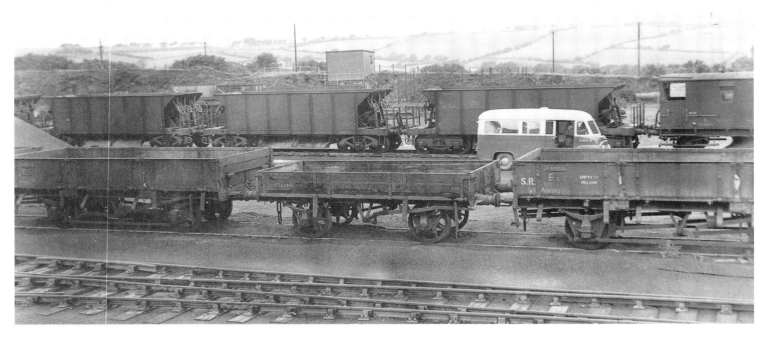

Above:
Plate 178 A nice view of Meldon yard. In the foreground is one of the SECR-designed Diagram 1744s, flanked by two BR 'Grampus' wagons; note the SR branding on one. In the background are two of the 1947 Ashford-built 'Walruses' and, next to the right, a BR-built version; they may look similar, but those on the American bogies averaged nine journeys before being 'carded' for repairs, whilst those on the BR/GWR bogies could not manage one! There is another doubtful asset on the extreme right — one of the never very useful plough brakes. The scenery is pleasing, however, and the canteen served a wonderful breakfast!
Authors' collection

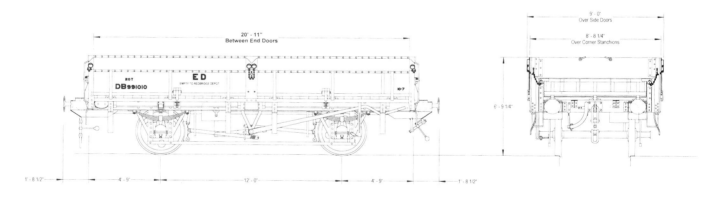

**Southern Railway 20 Ton Ballast Wagon
Bulleid Design
BR Diagram 1/570 Tel Code Lamprey**

Figure 60

Left:
Plate 179 No DB991010, seen here brand new in Lancing Works yard. This is one of the fitted wagons; the livery is black and the writing would have been yellow. Later these wagons were given the codename 'Lamprey', but one presumes this had not been advised by the time this wagon was painted. Today (2002) at least one of these wagons survives in its original condition on the Paignton & dartmouth Steam Railway.
National Railway Museum, York

Above:

Plate 180 The failings of the BR version of the 'Walrus' were well known to those on the ground, but not, it would seem, to the hierarchy, and a 50-ton version was built, called the 'Whale'. Suffice it to say that they had a very troubled early life and that those troubles were in no way the fault of the man who designed the wagon; he was badly let down by others who should have known better. All 90 of these wagons were allocated to the Southern Region, but they could not stand the speed required on Southern services and eventually (after a lot of money had been spent) settled down to a less hectic life elsewhere. *A. Blackburn*

Below:

Plate 181 No DB982556, a 'Seacow' built in 1970 and seen at Woking in 1971. At last, what was wanted — a modern version of the 1947 Ashford design, with excellent bogies, reasonable doors and footsteps long enough for a man to climb from a deep cess. Perfect? Not quite. Power operation of the doors, floodlighting and fall plates had been asked for; the first two were rejected because it was said that only the Class 33 locomotives could provide for it, the latter because 'it was not British practice'! All was not lost, however, and lighting was later provided by wagon-mounted generator sets. *A. Blackburn*

wagons destined for the Southern would be required to run at far higher speeds than was normal for any other bogie wagon on BR at that time. The result, as far as the Southern was concerned, was little short of a disaster. In 1967 the Southern Region CCE's wagon-turnaround statistics revealed that wagons of this batch were, on average, unable to complete a single round trip without being 'red carded', usually for a broken bolster coil, if not worse. Sadly, despite complaints, nothing was done about this, and, even worse, the same totally unsuitable bogie and door design was used in the 1966 'Whale' type, due to a failure of internal communication. BR was a very professionally run railway, but

it was a large organisation, and internal communication, especially between departments, was not its strongest point. Fortunately this sad story has a happy ending, and the 1972 'Sealions' and 'Seacows' have both rotating doors and excellent bogies — possibly due to the fact one of the authors was senior enough to assist with the writing of their specification, whilst another prepared the drawings!

The newer hoppers referred to are, of course, still hard at work, but some of the older ones are also still soldiering on in various hands, including some that have recently seen service in Ireland, for which purpose they have been mounted on some very strange bogies.

Left:
Plate 182 Three new ballast plough vans were ordered from Charles Roberts in 1932 to augment the original one built by the SECR in 1914. These have already been described in Volume Three, but this fine builder's photograph is included to show both ploughs lowered — something one would never see in actual use. The unusual company initials are as portrayed on a Lancing drawing; this form of lettering was not, however, accepted, so presumably the drawing was sent to Charles Roberts in error. The handbrake gear on the end is very similar to that used on SECR 'Birdcage' carriage stock.
R. Chorley collection

Left:
Plate 183 No (D)S62862, one of the eight ploughs built by Ashford in 1949. The only significant difference between these and the earlier vehicles was that they lacked oil lamps in the roof. The livery is probably black with yellow writing. Plough vans were and are very useful, but you could not use them where the 'third rail' was present and that was an ever increasing proportion of the Southern's track. A number of these vans had their ploughs modified in later years in an attempt to cope with this problem but the idea was at best only partially successful.
Kent Arts & Libraries

Chapter 14.
Containers

Although credit for the railway container as we know it must go to the LMS, the type's origins go back much further — to 1830 and the Liverpool & Manchester Railway, no less, in the case of the open version, and it was noted in Volume One that the LSWR used a 'modern' form of these for a few years. The predecessor of the covered type was the 'Lift van', and these also have a long history; recorded in Volume Two is the Isle of Wight Railway's use of these in conjunction with Messrs Chaplin's cross-Solent traffic. For the uninitiated, the difference between a lift van and a railway container was that the latter was designed to withstand constant trans-shipping and was thus much more strongly built.

As far as the Southern is concerned, the container arrived just in time to save the Southampton-London meat traffic, which in 1927/8 was being seriously eroded by road competition. The railway was handling this traffic with a mixture of fitted refrigerator vans and road-van trucks carrying open-sheeted horse carts (Volume One, page 72). Sometime prior to January 1928 — it is not clear exactly when — a number of these horse carts were rebuilt into open containers and given the numbers DM1-50. They were not modern containers as we know them, but they served their purpose. When diagrams

were allocated they became Diagram 3003. A further 30 followed in May 1929 as Nos DM51-80. One list in the authors' possession suggests there may have been 20 more, but other evidence contradicts this, and it is not thought the numbers DM81-100 were used.

Early in 1928, orders were placed for 100 purpose-built insulated containers — 50 to be built by Eastleigh and 50 by the Midland RC&W; these (Diagram 3001) were given numbers BN101-200. At this time the Southern was the only railway to own insulated containers and can thus claim to have pioneered the type; the insulation was provided by 2in slabs of cork sheet. These were followed by a slightly larger version (Diagram 3002), and these, it is believed, were the first containers to be built with plywood sheeting — a material which was to prove very suitable for container and covered goods vehicles and which was to remain a feature of all Southern-designed covered containers. They were again classified 'BN', but most do not seem to have carried this prefix. They were numbered 201-50, and 125 more were built later as Nos 301-25 and 490-589.

The insulated containers were used not only for meat traffic but also for butter, paper and bananas, the last-named

Above:
Plate 184 This is a picture of a diverted Waterloo-Southampton train entering Alton in November 1936, but over in the yard can be seen a string of Diagram 3003 containers on SR 'Conflats'; these 'containers' were converted from horse-drawn road vehicles. Dimensions: length 12ft 6in, width 6ft 6in, height of sides 3ft 6in. *T. A. Barry collection*

Basic details of Southern Railway containers

SR Diagram No	Description	Class	Capacity (tons)	Average Tare	Building Period	Traffic Numbers	Total Built	Notes/Page
3001	Large Covered Insulated	BN	3-10	1-1-2	5/28-7/28	BN101-50	50	Built by Midland RC&W Co
					5/28-10/28	BN151-200	50	Later F
3002	Large Covered Insulated	BN	3-10	1-5-2	5/29-7/29	201-50	50	Most later F or FX
					1931	301-25	25	Built Birmingham RC&W Co
					9/31-11/31	490-589	100	Most later F or FX
3003	Large Open Sheeted Meat traffic	DM	3	17-0	1928/9	DM1-50	50	Rebuilt from open, sheeted horse carts. 57 Later D
					5/28-3/29	DM51-80	30	
3004	Large Covered	B	4	1-8-2	6/30-8/30	B251-300	50	45 later BD
3005	Small Covered	A	2-10	16-2-11	5/31	A328-37	10	Nos 337-9 later to Diagram 3014
3006	Small Open	C	2-10	10-0	4/31	C340-79	40	Built Birmingham RC&W Co
3007	Small Covered Pressed Steel	A	2-10	14-1	5/31	A338-39	2	Built Birmingham RC&W Co Later AF
3008	Large Covered Insultated	BN	3-10	1-8-3	2/31	BN326/7	2	Built Butterly Co. Later F
3009	Small Open Pressed Steel	C	4	10-1-7	4/31	C380-9	10	Built Butterly Co
3010	Small Open Steel	C	4	12-0-7	8/31-10/31	C390-489	100	Built Metropolitan-Cammell CW&F Co
3011	Large Covered	K	4	1-10-3	6/32-7/32	K590-639	50	Built Gloucester RC&W Co K604/13 later BK
3012	Large Covered Fresh Meat traffic	M	3	2-5-1	10/32-1/33	M640-59	20	Later BM
					1/39	M991-1000	10	Later BM
					4/41	BM1051-60	10	
					10/43-11/43	BM1106-15	10	
3013	Large Covered Insulated	F	3-10	1-17-2	6/33	F660-83	24	
					7/33-6/34	F685-784	100	Some material supplied by
					10/36-3/37	F916-65	50	Metropolitan-Cammell CW&F Co
					5/39-8/39	F1001-50	50	
3014	Small Covered Insulated	AF	2-10	1-15-0	1933	AF337-9	3	Rebuilt from Diagram 3005
3015	Large Covered Insulated	FX	3-5	1-14-1	1933	FX510/20/4/8/48, FX551/4/63/8/9	10	Rebuilt from Diagram 3002
3016	Large Covered Insulated	F	3-10	2-4-0	7/33	F684	1	Diagram 3013 with 'Drikold' bunkers
3017	Large Covered Strawberry traffic	BS	4	2-7-2	6/34	BS785-90	6	Later BD
3018	Large Covered	BK	4	1-11-3	3/36-5/36	BK793-815	23	Later K
					6/37-7/37	BK966-90	25	24 later K
					3/43-5/43	BK1116-42	27	Later K
3019	Large Covered Bicycle traffic	BC	4	NS	4/36	BC791/2	2	Later K
3020	Small Covered	A	2-10	16-2	3/36-4/36	A841-55	15	
					9/37	A856-65	10	
3021	Large Covered	B	4	NS	4/36-6/36	B816-40	25	24 later BD
					4/37-6/37	BD866-90	25	22 later BD
					11/42-12/42	B1143-67	25	12 later BD
3022	Large Covered Egg traffic	B	NS	2-3-3	1938	Not known	2	To Diagram 3021 1942
3023	Large Open RCH Type	D	4	1-0-2	7/37-8/37	D891-915	25	
					6/42-7/42	D1081-1105	25	
3024	Large Open RCH Type	D	4	NS	7/40	D1061-80	20	'D Modified'
3025	Large Covered	BK	4	1-10-2	2/44-4/44	BK1168-1217	50	
					11/44	B2238-87	50	Built for the LMS
3026	Large Covered	BD	4	1-16-0	11/44-2/45	BD1218-31	14	
					6/45	B2941-76	36	Built for the LMS
					?/45-11/46	BD1235-1313	79	
3027	Small Covered	A	3	11-3	2/45	A1232-4	3	Built by the LMS (Pt Lot 1395)
					6/46-10/46	A1339-1413	75	
3028	Large Covered	BK	4	1-10-2	4/47-10/47	BK1314-38	25	
3029 (BR3/375)	Large Covered Insulated	F	3-10	1-15-0	1948/9	F12000B-251B	252	BR Lot 2067
BR3/550 (3024)	Large Open	D	4		1948	D21000-49B	50	BR Lot 2066

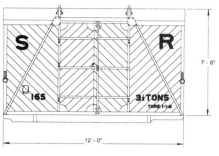

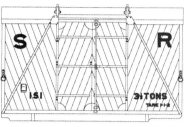

Alternative Style of Planking

**Southern Railway
Insulated Meat Container
SR Diagram 3001**

Figure 61

Below:
Plate 185 Container No BN217 (Diagram 3002, built 1929) being trans-shipped to a Chaplins horse cart at Portsmouth Town Goods on 15 February 1932. The livery would be stone with red writing, the Chaplins cart was navy blue with white lettering. The traces of straw hanging from the container suggest it may be carrying bananas. Dimensions: length 13ft, width 6ft, height 7ft. There were no cattle facilities at Portsmouth Town, so the cattle truck on the left must have been in use for some other traffic — possibly empty boxes. *Authors' collection*

passing in the late 'Twenties from London Docks to Le Havre via Southampton. They were also used for egg traffic from Boulogne to London. It was, however, for chilled or frozen meat from Southampton Docks to Smithfield Market via Nine Elms that they were chiefly employed, there being two part-fitted meat trains a day in the evening, and a third 'as required' in the early hours of the morning. It was essential that the meat arrive in time for the morning market, and a special electrically operated travelling gantry crane was built at Nine Elms to ensure that trans-shipment was effected as quickly as possible.

It was not until January 1930 that the Southern placed an order for a non-insulated container, this being for 50 large covered boxes with side and end doors, Nos B251-300 (Diagram 3004). These containers were again a little larger than their predecessors but still only 14ft long and 6ft wide. One presumes the 'Big Four' had agreed these dimensions with the RCH, but there was as yet no such thing as a standard design. The most basic requirements at this time

would seem to have been that it could be lifted when loaded by a 5-ton crane and that it would fit into most types of open goods wagon or (preferably) something with lower sides, like a road-van truck.

In 1931 no fewer than six orders were placed with contractors for various types, including two new designs for which the General Manager said there was now a requirement; there were also two experimental designs. Clearly the Company was proceeding in this area with some caution.

Dealing with the new types, first there were 10 small covered containers similar to the large Diagram 3004 design; these were Nos A328-37, allocated to Diagram 3005. The second new type was a small open, intended for brick and tile traffic, and there were three designs of these. First there was a basically wooden design and these were Nos C340-79, allocated to Diagram 3006. Second was a steel design, of which 100 were built — Nos C390-489 — to Diagram 3010. Third was another steel design patented by the Butterly Co, these being Nos C380-9 of Diagram 3009.

Right:
Plate 186 Container No B259 (Diagram 3004) built in 1930. These were the first covered containers built to what might be called the SR '1930 era' standard dimensions etc, as per the drawing of the Diagram 3021. The livery is wagon brown with white writing. The wagon is one of the Diagram 1382s originally built as an unfitted vehicle.
Authors' collection

Right:
Plate 187 The official BRC&W view of No A337, a Diagram 3005 built in 1931; this was a smaller version of Diagram 3004. Dimensions: length 7ft 3in, width 6ft 9in, height 7ft 4⅜in. Three of these containers were converted into insulated containers, there being no external change except that the doors were simplified to two full-depth doors of the standard type. *Authors' collection*

Of the experimental types ordered in 1931, the first was a small, covered pressed-steel design, of which only two were built, by BRC&W, these being Nos A338/9 (Diagram 3007). The second was another all-steel design from the Butterly Co, this time for a large insulated box, and again only two were purchased, these being numbered BN326/7 (Diagram 3008). The covered steel containers were found to suffer from condensation, so much so that some customers refused to use them and no more were built.

In 1932 an order was placed with the Gloucester RC&W Co for 50 large covered containers for furniture traffic. These containers were built as the Southern contribution to a nationwide bid by the railways for a share of the house-removal business. Their numbers were K590-639 (Diagram 3011). A contemporary account of these containers is worth quoting as it is a good general description of a container's construction. 'The floor bearings and floor framing, as well as the corner pillars, are constructed of English oak, whilst the door framing, floor and roof boards are made of ash, and white and red deal. All bolt heads and nuts are counter-sunk so that there are no projections whatever to damage the articles in transit, and, in order to allow packages to be secured, slats are provided on each side of the interior. The containers are faced on the outside with armoured plywood and are constructed to carry a load of 4 tons.' These were the last complete containers to be built by contractors for the Southern, although in 1933 there

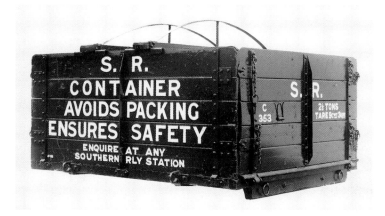

Above left:
Plate 188 Another official BRC&W photograph, this time of C353 (Diagram 3006). The sheet hoops could be moved about as required. The livery is brown with white writing.
National Railway Museum, York

Left:
Plate 189 One of the two experimental steel insulated containers built by the Butterly Co in February 1931. They were classed 'BN' but the prefix is not carried; later they were reclassified 'F'. The livery is stone with red writing. Dimensions: length 13ft, width 6ft, height at side 6ft 3in. The cart would have been painted in an approximation of carriage green, with red wheels and undergear. *Authors' collection*

Left:
Plate 190 This open container is also a Butterly design, the Southern taking delivery of 10 of these in 1931. They seem to have been a standard design and have been pictured elsewhere in other companies' liveries. Dimensions: length 7ft, width 6ft 1¾in, height 3ft. *Authors' collection*

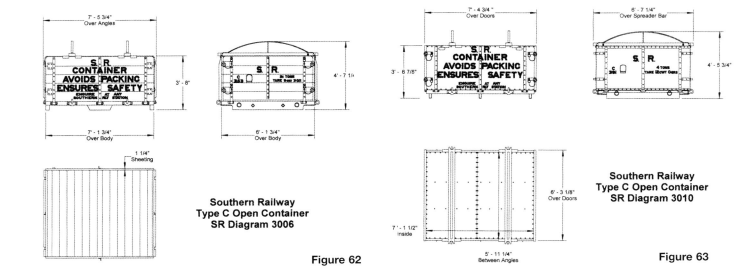

Southern Railway
Type C Open Container
SR Diagram 3006

1 1/4"
Sheeting

7' - 5 3/4"
Over Angles

3' - 8"

7' - 1 3/4"
Over Body

4' - 7 1/4

6' - 1 3/4"
Over Body

Figure 62

7' - 4 3/4"
Over Doors

3' - 6 7/8"

6' - 7 1/4"
Over Spreader Bar

4' - 5 3/4"

Southern Railway
Type C Open Container
SR Diagram 3010

6' - 3 1/8"
Over Doors

7' - 1 1/2"
Inside

5' - 11 1/4"
Between Angles

Figure 63

Below:
Plate 191 This picture will be recognisable to older readers as that used in carriage-compartment viewframes to advertise the household-removal service, and shows two 'K'-type containers — Nos 590/4 of Diagram 3011, built in June 1932. The livery was light green with a darker green zig-zag; the writing was noted as yellow. The container on the left looks to be in a much lighter colour, but other contemporary views of this particular box suggest this is merely a trick of the light. The length of these containers was 15ft 3in; otherwise their dimensions and details were very much as the Diagram 3021 drawn.
Authors' collection

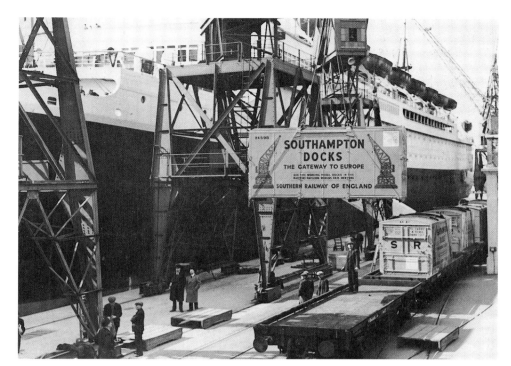

Left:
Plate 192 This interesting picture shows one of a number of containers of various types that were specially painted in connection with the World's Fair held in New York in 1939. No BK598 (Diagram 3011) is in the air, with BK811 (Diagram 3018) on the 'Conflat'. The colours of these vehicles are unknown but are presumed to have been various shades of green. The lettering in the box reads: 'SEE THE WORKING MODEL DOCKS IN THE MARITIME PAVILION, WORLD'S FAIR, NEW YORK'. *Authors' collection*

was a serious fire in the sawmill at Eastleigh, and as a result Metro-Cammell assisted with the woodwork for some Diagram 3014 vehicles then being built. For the future, Eastleigh would build the majority of all the new containers, with occasional help from Ashford and (on one occasion) Lancing.

Also new in 1932 was the first of a new design for the conveyance of fresh meat direct from the local farm or slaughter-house. Physically these containers were much larger than their predecessors, being no less than 18in higher than the earlier closed types. Structurally they differed in that they were designed to carry their load hanging from the roof, rather than lying on the floor. Twenty were built in 1932 — Nos M640-59 (Diagram 3012). Three later batches of 10 were built in 1939, 1941 and 1943 — Nos M991-1000, BM1051-60 and BM1106-15 respectively. The prefix letters changed with the latter two batches, as they did with several other types; these alterations are believed to date from 1940

but took some years to complete. From 1942 the carrying-capacity of these containers was increased from 2½ to 3 tons.

In 1933 there appeared another insulated design, Diagram 3013; this was a development of D3004, the main difference being that it lacked the end door drop flap of the earlier design. Officially, the first of this type were ordered for fish traffic from Southampton, but there is no evidence of their being used as such, and in practice they seem to have worked alongside the other insulated types, usually carrying chilled meat. In all, 224 were built — 24 in 1933 (Nos F660-83), 100 in 1933/4 (F685-784), 50 in 1936/7 (F916-65) and finally a further 50 in 1938/9 (F1001-50) — making this the most numerous design of container owned by the Southern. (There would later be 252 Diagram 3029s, but they were built for BR.)

Also in 1933, new Diagrams 3014, 3015 and 3016 were issued to cover minor modifications for special traffic requiring

Left:
Plate 193 The new electric gantry at Nine Elms, seen trans-shipping meat containers destined for Smithfield Market in the early hours of the morning. The containers (Diagram 3012) are silver with green writing, and would be modelled very attractively in litho by Hornby. *Authors' collection*

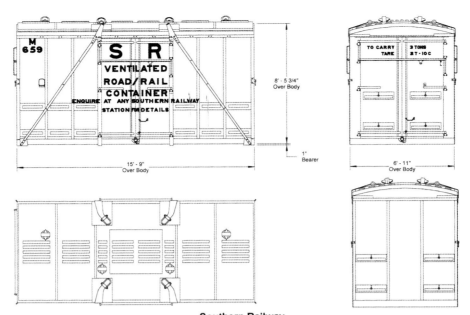

Figure 64

Southern Railway
Type BM Ventilated Container for Fresh Meat
SR Diagram 3012

Ray Chorley © 2001

Right:
Plate 194 Four Diagram 3013s posed new in October 1933 on two unfitted 'Conflat Cs'. They normally travelled in pairs as seen here; it did not matter which way round they were, the end doors not being required until they reached their ultimate destination, by which time they had been transshipped onto a road vehicle and could if necessary be turned around. The livery of these insulated containers was originally 'sea green' with red writing, but during the war this was changed to red oxide with yellow writing.
Authors' collection

Left:
Plate 195 This immaculate turn-out was a part of an exhibition held at Euston station and includes insulated container F684. This was the only one of its type, adapted from a standard Diagram 3013, the only visible difference being in the roof hatches (one at each corner); otherwise it was a standard prewar SR container, with dimensions as per the drawing of Diagram 3021. The roping was obviously done by a master; whilst it might show how the job should be done, it was not in any way typical of the everyday efforts of normal mortals!
Authors' collection

Figure 65

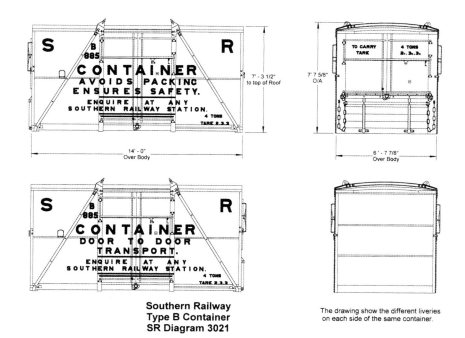

Southern Railway
Type B Container
SR Diagram 3021

The drawing show the different liveries
on each side of the same container.

increased insulation — ice cream and salmon (see the Table). Similarly, the following year six new containers were built specially for strawberry traffic; numbered B5785-90, these were allocated to Diagram 3017 and were noteworthy in being ventilated.

It was not until 1936 that further batches of general-purpose types were built. Firstly, Diagram 3018 was issued for an updated version of the 1932 Diagram 3011; these were Nos K793-815 (further batches appearing in 1937 and 1943). Then there were two bicycle-carrying versions, Nos BC791/2 (Diagram 3019). These were followed by Diagram 3020, which was an updated version of the 1931 Diagram 3005; these were numbered A841-55, with a further batch joining them in 1937 as Nos A856-65. The last new design of 1936 was rather odd, in that, although it was classed as Type B like the Diagram 3018, it had the smaller external dimensions and side doors of the current insulated design. Diagram 3021 was issued and the numbers were B816-40. There were further batches in 1937 and 1942, numbered respectively B866-90 and BD1143-67; again, note the change in prefix.

A few words on the subject of dimensions generally might be of interest here. In 1934 the RCH quoted the following external dimensions for containers: (see table below).

All the Southern types were within these dimensions, so one is left to conclude that this list was for general guidance only. What did matter, as far as the Southern was concerned, was that it needed to get two of its insulated types on the 29ft-long 'Conflat C'- and 'D'-type wagons which were specially built to carry them. This limited their maximum length to a little under 14ft 6in. The insulated type also had to have side doors for loading at Southampton and end doors for unloading at Smithfield.

In 1936 the first standard RCH-designed containers appeared, and in the following year the Southern built a series of large opens to RCH drawings. Diagram 3023 was issued and the numbers were D891-915. A further batch followed in

1942, Nos D1081-105. (For those readers wondering what happened to Diagram 3022, this was allocated to two Diagram 3021s modified to carry eggs in 1937/8; their identities are unknown, and both had reverted to their original state by 1942.)

It would seem that by the late 1930s the Southern was building containers on the basis of its share of the originating traffic, rather than on its own particular requirements as had been the case previously. The onset of war caused something of a hiatus in the construction of containers. A batch of open 'Ds' was ordered in October 1939, but these were not built until the following July. Differing from the 1937 batch in that they lacked side doors, they were numbered D1061-80 and allocated Diagram 3024.

It was not until 1944 that another new design appeared — new, that is, to the Southern, for they were constructed to a 1941 RCH design that was built by all the 'Big Four' companies. They were the first covered RCH containers to be built by the Southern and featured narrow horizontal boarding. The Southern allocated these to Diagram 3025. Fifty were built for the SR (Nos BK1168-217) and 50 for the LMS (B2238-87). There was no external difference between a 'B' and a 'BK' container, but internally the 'BK' type had a framework to which the contents could be secured. These were immediately followed by a new standard RCH design, this time of the more familiar plywood construction. Allocated Diagram 3026, 93 were built for the SR (Nos BD1218-31/5-1313) and 36 for the LMS (B2941-76). Whilst the Southern was building containers for the LMS, that company built three for the Southern as a part of a large order for all four companies. These were a small version of the previous design, and the Southern allocated it Diagram 3027; numbers were A1232-4. In 1946 the Southern built a further 75 (Nos A1339-413), and in 1947 came a further batch of BKs (BK1314-38) to Diagram 3028, these differing from the 1944-built examples in being built to a 1945 RCH design, again with plywood sheeting.

Type	Capacity	Body	Length	Width	Height at Cantrail
A	3-ton	Closed	7ft 6in	7ft	7ft 4in
B	4-ton	Closed	16ft	7ft	7ft 4in
C	3-ton	Open	7ft 6in	7ft	3ft 6in
D	4-ton	Open	16ft	7ft	3ft 6in

In 1946 the Southern ordered its last batch of insulated containers. These were generally to the dimensions of the 1932 Diagram 3011 but differed considerably in detail and had a corrugated metal end. They were originally allocated SR Diagram 3029, but later they were on BR 3/375; SR numbers were allocated originally, but they appeared in 1948/9 as F12000B-251B. The final Southern order for containers was for a batch of 50 Diagram 3024s; these were Nos D21000-49B, allocated Diagram BR 3/550.

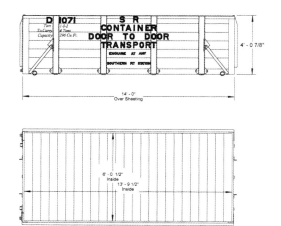

Figure 66

Southern Railway
Type D Open Container (Modified)
SR Diagram 3024

Above:
Plate 196 A Diagram 3023 open 'D' container introduced in July 1937. These were the first containers built by the SR to a standard RCH design. Notice the French wording on the end of the insulated container on the next wagon, provided on account of these containers' frequent trips to France and the Channel Islands. *Authors' collection*

Above:
Plate 197 An official view of a Diagram 3024 — another RCH type introduced to the Southern in 1940. The livery of all the open containers was brown with white writing.
Authors' collection

Figure 67

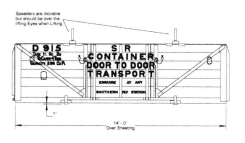

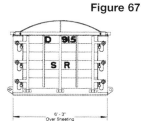
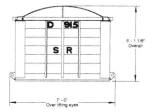

Southern Railway Type D Container SR Diagram 3023

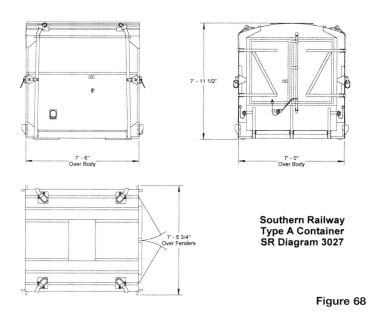

**Southern Railway
Type A Container
SR Diagram 3027**

Figure 68

Above:

Plate 198 Apart from 50 Diagram 3025s, all the SR covered containers built to RCH drawings featured plywood construction. This is a Diagram 3027, No A1362S, built in 1946, and back in Eastleigh for repainting in BR livery in September 1949; notice that it is due for examination in exactly one year's time. *National Railway Museum, York*

Left:

Plate 199 No BK1328XS of Diagram 3028. Were it not for the additional suffix letter to the number, one would never know who had originally owned this container. Built in 1947, it is seen in 1949. Notice the two LSWR vans in the background; Eastleigh was still overhauling these old vehicles at this time, but would not be for much longer: times were changing, and pre-Grouping wagons would soon become rare in traffic use. *National Railway Museum, York*

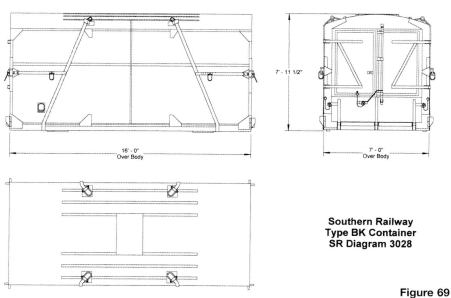

**Southern Railway
Type BK Container
SR Diagram 3028**

Figure 69

Chapter 15.
Commercial Department Travelling Cranes

Travelling cranes, by their very nature, tend to be long-lived items; they are strongly constructed in the first place and, although essential to the conduct of the railway's business, saw comparatively little use. If looked after, which they were, they would last almost for ever. They might be rendered obsolete but then they certainly did not wear out, although their wire ropes did. Thus the Southern did not need to purchase any travelling cranes until 1930, when it bought two.

Before considering the Southern's normal travelling cranes it is necessary to look at three cranes mounted on 600mm-gauge underframes. These were offered to the General Manager by George Cohen at £135 each and were purchased in 1926 for use as static yard cranes 'to be used at various points on the Company's system'. These cranes had been built in Britain for the French Government and they were mounted on the French Army's standard Decaville bogies. At the price offered they were very cheap for a crane, but it would seem that, with a maximum lift of only 4½ tons, their use was somewhat limited, and so it was that two of them finished up on the Lynton & Barnstaple line, along with the underframe of the third, converted by

Lancing into a match truck. What became of the third crane is a mystery, but the match truck cost £65 more than the cranes, suggesting that it was written off. Crane match trucks were known on the Southern as Skillet Match trucks (SM), and in SR days these always carried the same number as the crane; later, BR gave them separate numbers in the 'DS' series.

So to the normal standard-gauge cranes. Hardly anything that might be considered standard Brighton practice found favour with the Southern Railway, so it is refreshing to find that the Southern followed the LBSCR in favouring the travelling-crane designs of Messrs Booth Bros of Rodley in Leeds. The jib construction of the SR cranes was a little different, being more modern, and the underframes were a little longer, but the only other difference was the use of standard SR running-gear and drawgear, as might be expected. Cranes — even hand cranes — were not cheap. A 12-ton crane, No 119S, cost £1,650 in 1930; its runner cost £172. By 1943 inflation had taken the price of a 12-ton crane to over £4,000.

The greater part of the cranes' traditional work was the loading of long timber, and this was carried out by special

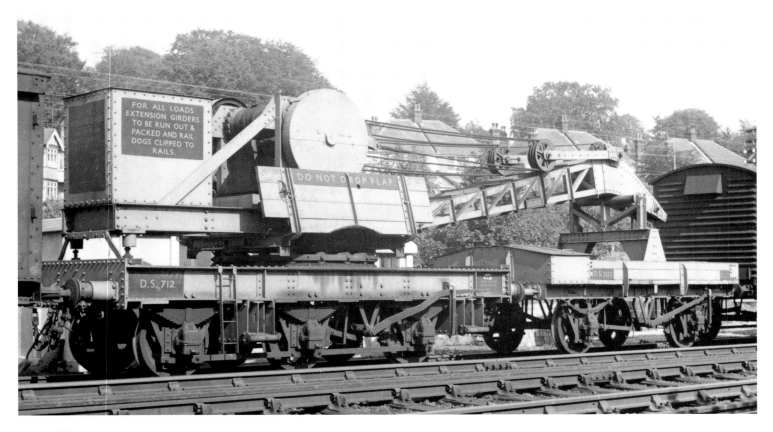

Above:
Plate 200 No DS712, a 12-ton travelling crane built in January 1941 by Booth Bros and seen here in 1958. The three four-wheeled 6-ton cranes were very similar but were a little shorter and had a considerable overhang. All the purpose-built runners or 'Skillets', as the Southern called them, were the same except that the earlier ones had a 9ft wheelbase. The livery is medium-to-light grey with white writing on black patches. *Authors' collection*

Left:
Plate 201 No 1582S, built in 1945 by Cowan & Sheldon. There were eight of these cranes allocated to the SR — four of 10-ton capacity and four 6½-ton. They were built to an REC order, and some (if not all) of the other 'Big Four' companies had similar examples. No 1582S was a 10-ton version and was just three years old when this photograph was taken at Sidmouth. The livery is light grey with white stencilled lettering. *Authors' collection*

teams of men known as 'Timber Gangs' (a title still in use in the 1960s, although by then the only thing they normally loaded was armoured fighting vehicles). As already seen in connection with the bolster wagons, the timber traffic declined rapidly, and the use of travelling cranes might have practically ceased in the 1940s had it not been for the war. This saw an upsurge in traffic, with quite a lot passing through various minor country stations that did not have a crane. As is apparent from the table, this led to a number of cranes' being ordered. During the war a number of cranes, both steam and hand, were supplied

Below:
Plate 202 DS3132, formerly double bolster No 57462 (Diagram 1595) built by the LSWR in 1888 and converted to a runner in October 1948. This wagon worked with crane DS1582. The livery is black with yellow writing. *A. E. West collection*

Left:
Plate 203 No DS1856, one of the 6½-ton cranes. These looked like the 10-ton version, so presumably the difference was in the strength of the ropes. The match wagon is a converted LBSCR batten truck, formerly No 58780, later SM1856 and finally, as seen at Feltham in 1963, DS3130. *A. Blackburn*

to the railways by the Ministry of War Transport; they carried railway running-numbers but were actually owned by the Government, which eventually sold them to BR in 1951. Booth crane No 1748S was one of these.

Cowan & Sheldon cranes, as ordered by the REC on behalf of the railway companies, were probably not what the Southern would have purchased in more normal times. They were based on their builder's static design, with the crane itself carried on what might be described as a well wagon. The crane supported its jib on a rest, and the match was needed only to provide clearance. As with so many things associated with the war, they seem to have arrived rather too late to have been of much use in their intended role, but they were a modern design and their arrival allowed for the withdrawal of some of the older cranes.

The Southern had purchased its first mobile road crane in 1926, and in many respects these were more versatile than the rail-mounted cranes, although the latter could often handle a heavier load. In the 1940s and early '50s the use of mobile road

cranes increased rapidly, but the rail-mounted travelling cranes continued to find occasional work in the country areas until the middle 1950s, by which time many of the stations they served had been closed or the traffic lost. Thereafter they simply stood around awaiting a decision to withdraw them. There are several of these 'modern' cranes in preservation, and some are actually used.

Cranes, except those belonging to the CME, were the responsibility of the Outdoor Machinery Engineer, who in SR days came under the Civil Engineer. The ODM painted all its equipment in a light-to-mid-grey colour, and in later years, at least, this included the travelling cranes; in prewar days they appear from photographs to have been painted a darker colour, possibly a darker grey or black; lettering was white.

Unfortunately no drawings of cranes are available, but readers who model in 4mm scale may like to know that Hornby makes quite an accurate model of the Cowan & Sheldon crane.

Southern Railway Commercial Department Travelling Cranes

Running Number	Capacity (max lift)	Manufacturer	Date Built	Number of wheels	Skillet Match details
441S	4½-ton	Chambers Scott & Co	c1918	8	1ft 11½in gauge L&B line. Underframe provided by the unnumbered 4½-ton crane
442S	4½-ton	Chambers Scott & Co	c1918	8	None (crane used statically at Lynton)
(None)	4½-ton	Chambers Scott & Co	c1918	8	1ft 11½in gauge L&B line. Not used as a railway travelling crane; underframe became 441 SM.
118S	6-ton	Booth Bros	1930	4	Purpose-built 17ft 6in underframe, 9ft 0in wheelbase
119S	12-ton	Booth Bros	1930	6	Purpose-built 17ft 6in underframe, 9ft 0in wheelbase
712S	12-ton	Booth Bros	1/41	6	Purpose-built 17ft 6in underframe, 10ft 0in wheelbase
1746S	6-ton	Booth Bros	10/43	4	Purpose-built 17ft 6in underframe, 10ft 0in wheelbase
1747S	6-ton	Booth Bros	10/43	4	Purpose-built 17ft 6in underframe, 10ft 0in wheelbase
1748S	12-ton	Booth Bros	10/43	6	Purpose-built 17ft 6in underframe, 10ft 0in wheelbase
1749S	12-ton	Booth Bros	10/43	6	Purpose-built 17ft 6in underframe, 10ft 0in wheelbase
1750S	12-ton	Booth Bros	10/43	6	Purpose-built 17ft 6in underframe, 10ft 0in wheelbase
1584S	6½-ton	Cowan & Sheldon	1945	4	Former LBSCR batten truck ex 58698 Diagram 1618
1585S	6½-ton	Cowan & Sheldon	1945	4	Former LBSCR batten truck ex 58455 Diagram 1618
1856S	6½-ton	Cowan & Sheldon	1945	4	Former LBSCR batten truck ex 58780 Diagram 1618
1857S	6½-ton	Cowan & Sheldon	1945	4	Former LBSCR batten truck ex 58662 Diagram 1618
1582S	10-ton	Cowan & Sheldon	1945	4	Former LBSCR batten truck ex 58737 Diagram 1618
1583S	10-ton	Cowan & Sheldon	1945	4	Former LBSCR batten truck ex 58686 Diagram 1618
1854S	10-ton	Cowan & Sheldon	1945	4	Former LBSCR batten truck ex 58728 Diagram 1618
1855S	10-ton	Cowan & Sheldon	1945	4	Former LBSCR batten truck ex 58761 Diagram 1618

Note: BR renumbered all the skillet match trucks and in some cases replaced the LBSCR wagons with similar LSWR examples.

Chapter 16.

Wagons built by the Southern Railway for the Government and other Railways, 1940-1949

The Southern supplied quite a large number of wagons to other parties, and these are included here for the sake of completeness.

Some time late in 1939 or early 1940 the Southern Railway received an order for two Mobile Workshop Trains for use with the British Expeditionary Force in France. The purpose of these trains was to give the Royal Engineers' railway-operating troops some basic locomotive and rolling-stock maintenance facility 'in the field' and to avoid lengthy journeys to base depots. Each train consisted of a machine-tool wagon converted from a standard SR 'Utility van', as well as a generator van and a stores van, both converted from standard SR covered goods vans. These two trains were completed by Ashford towards the end of March 1940 and received a full write-up at the time in the technical press.

Both the original trains were lost shortly afterwards in France, but further 21 were ordered in the years 1940-3. These later trains were very similar to the original two but included an additional 12-ton box van containing welding equipment. It is thought that the earlier of these trains went to the Middle East in 1941/2 whilst the later ones went to Europe in 1944/5. The vehicles concerned were a mix of nearly new and currently built as convenient, the goods vans all being the Diagram 1459 type.

In May 1940 the REC placed orders with the SR for the building of 890 covered goods vans for the LMS and 750 for the LNER. Both orders were built to the designs of the customers, 494 of the LMS vans being to that railway's Diagram 2070 (all-wooden body), and the remaining 396 to D2039 (corrugated steel ends). The LNER vans also had corrugated ends. All were built at Ashford except for 150 of the LNER vans, construction of which was allocated to Eastleigh. Ordered at the same time were 75 tank ramp wagons for the Army. Basically this design was a heavily constructed 'flat' with a removable wheelset which, when taken out, allowed that end to be dropped down to form a ramp. The design of these wagons has been credited to

Below:
Plate 204 Mobile workshop train No 1, seen at Ashford on 28 March 1940; in just four months' time it would be lost to the Wehrmacht. From the left are the stores and office wagon, the workshop wagon and the generator wagon. Train No 2 was identical, but all the later trains included a third covered goods wagon with welding equipment in it. The livery is probably Army khaki brown. The train is equipped with air and vacuum pipes, but the vacuum-brake cylinders have been removed. *R. Chorley collection*

Left:

Plate 205 WD fighting-vehicle ramp No 1, one of 75 built by Ashford in 1940/1, seen here in the old workshop yard. The left-hand wheel works the brakes, which apply to the wheels at that end of the wagon only. The right-hand wheel lowers a jack which when in position allows the right-hand wheelset (complete with axleboxes etc) to be moved away; the buffers swing sideways and the wagon can then be lowered to form a ramp. One of these wagons was marshalled at each end of a 'Warflat' train, thus allowing tanks to entrain or de-train wherever required, without the need for end loading docks. Dimensions: length over headstocks 17ft 6in, width over sides 8ft 10in, wheelbase 12ft. The buffers and drawgear are to French standards.
Kent Art & Libraries

Centre left:

Plate 206 No photograph is available of one of the Lancing-built tank cars when new, but this view shows one at Woking in May 1974. The four tank cradles are a little unusual in that they are of welded construction, with gusset plates.
Authors' collection

Below:

Plate 207 No WD11030, one of the second batch of brake vans built for the Army, seen on the Shropshire & Montgomeryshire Military Railway in June 1947. These vans were very similar to the later Diagram 1579 type, except for the brakes and the lack of any beading on the cantrail. The former GER van on the left is very similar to some of the banana vans loaned to the SR by the LNER in the 1930s. *H. C. Casserley*

Ashford, but at least one drawing had Brighton on it. Ashford had a continuing connection with these wagons; after the war, the works converted them into twin bolsters but later, as the Cold War developed, converted them back for their original role as tank ramp wagons.

Just 10 weeks after the vans and ramp wagons were ordered, the Southern received a further order, this time for 100 tank cars for the Air Ministry. Lancing built these between November 1940 and March 1941, with tanks supplied by a sub-contractor.

In January 1941 225 iron-ore hoppers were ordered from the Southern by the Ministry of War Transport, but two months later these were cancelled as no longer required.

In March 1941 the REC ordered all four main-line railways to prepare a number of wagons for the conveyance of aeroplane propellers. The Southern's share of this work resulted in the conversion of 50 Diagram 1369s, and these are described in Volume Two (page 14).

Twenty express-goods brake vans were ordered for the Army in July 1941 and a further 20 five months later. These are described in Chapter 9.

On 11 September 1941 an order for 1,000 open goods (small bodies) was placed with Ashford for use (it was subsequently stated) in Persia. All four railways assisted in this order, which was produced as sets of parts. The first consignment of 50 left the works just two weeks later, and the entire order was completed in exactly 10 weeks. After a gap of just over three weeks, work commenced on a further 600, and these were completed in exactly four weeks.

In March 1942 came a Railway Executive order for 1,000 covered goods vans for the LMS, GWR and SR; all these wagons were built to SR drawings and are described in Chapter 6. This was followed in April by an order for a further 250 covered goods for the LMS, and 400 opens for the LNER, and again SR drawings were used. Just over three weeks later a further 375 opens were ordered for the LNER and 465 for the LMS, details of which will be found in Chapter 3.

In May 1943 Lancing was called upon to build 25 bogie 'Warwells'. These were a standard War Department design and were amongst the strongest and most heavily built wagons ever constructed in Britain. Possibly due to a shortage of materials, the first of them was not ready until February 1944, the last in July.

Also in May 1943 came orders for Ashford to build a further 465 open goods for the LMS and 375 for the LNER, again to SR design (see Chapter 3).

In July 1943 Eastleigh was called upon to build 50 large RCH Type B containers, and these were built from July to November 1944. It will be noticed that orders judged to be of critical importance to the war effort were tackled first — sometimes within days — whilst those less so had to wait their turn.

In the months leading up to D-Day Eastleigh Works, both C&W and Locomotive, carried out a vast amount of work preparing equipment of all descriptions, much of it American, for the invasion, the main point of departure for this being Southampton. Unfortunately, although much of this interesting work did involve rolling stock, it falls outside the scope of this book.

In March 1944 Eastleigh received orders for 36 Type BD containers for the LMS; it was November before work could start on these, but all were built by February 1945.

In November 1944 Ashford received an order for 1,850 13-ton minerals for the LNER, this being the largest single order the works had yet received. Whether these wagons were of LNER or SR design is uncertain, but their details will be found in Chapter 5. Construction had been underway only three months when Ashford received another massive order from the LNER, this time for 1,500 all-steel 16-ton minerals. Ashford had never built all-steel wagons before, and special arrangements had to be made for their construction. All went well with the main production, but the supply of the pressed-steel doors was in the hands of sub-contractors, and they fell so far behind with their deliveries that a large number of the wagons had to be stored incomplete. The railways were desperately short of wagons at the time, and the problem was not resolved before questions were asked in the House of Commons; whatever the reasons for this fiasco, it was not Ashford's fault.

Just 14 days after Nationalisation, Ashford received its largest order ever, for no fewer than 3,250 open goods, again for the LNER; this was subsequently reduced to 2,230 but it was still the largest single order that Ashford ever received. It has been said that Bulleid was personally responsible for obtaining these orders from his old company (and so he may have been), but there is no doubt that, by this time, Ashford had established its own reputation far beyond the confines of the Southern Railway, and in due course this was rewarded with many large orders for BR's new standard wagons.

Above:
Plate 208 'Warwell' No 19, one of the 25 built by Lancing in 1943. Dimensions: length over headstocks 43ft, width 8ft 3in, bogie centres 35ft, bogie wheelbase 5ft 9in. Livery is probably khaki brown with white writing. In 1950 the Southern Region purchased six wagons of this type (Nos DS3146-51, to Diagram 1903) for conveying locomotive boilers. *R. Chorley collection*

Left:
Plate 209 This photograph was taken to assist in the erection of the 1,000 open wagons produced as kits for the Army in 1941. There were 792 parts in each wagon, and each set of parts was said to take an average of 37 minutes to produce. For its part, the Army claimed to be able to assemble them at the rate of one every 45 minutes. From examples which survived in Israel it is known that their running-numbers were prefixed 'SR' and that their plated tonnage was 11 tons, rather than the 13 tons that might have been expected. Apart from this they were absolutely standard Diagram 1375s of the period. *Kent Arts & Libraries*

Below:
Plate 210 On the grounds that the Southern Railway built this, the authors could not resist it. Officially it was referred to as a 'Dummy gun truck'; presumably for this role it was fitted with a telephone pole as a barrel! Otherwise the intention was that it be used to block strategic points by being derailed, and this photograph was taken at Farnham prior to a demonstration of such a derailment. As can be seen, it is a 12-ton mineral, filled with concrete and provided with an extra axle to take the additional weight. How many of these wagons were produced is not known, but one of the authors recalls that there were half a dozen or so at Havant alone, so their numbers may well have run into three figures. They were authorised for dismantling in September 1944. *R. Chorley collection*

Appendix 1

Basic Details of Southern Railway- and British Railways Southern Region-designed Wagons, also Pre-Grouping Designs Built by SR

SR Diagram	Vehicle Type	Capacity (tons)	Average Tare	Building Period	Running Numbers, etc	Total Built	Notes	Page
1316	Eight-plank Open Goods	12	6-19	10/24-1/25 10/25-12/25	9141-9240 (Steel underframes) 9241-9340 (Wooden underframes)	100 100	LSWR design (See Vol 1 page 24 for details)	27-8
1317	Four-plank Dropside Stone Traffic	15	7-1	11/26 8/33-9/33	61029/30 61121-35	2 15	LSWR design (See Vol 1 page 29 for details)	114-5
1319	Five-plank Open Goods	10	5-12	1930/1	5043-62	20	Rebuild of LSWR design (See Vol 1 page 27 for details)	—
1320	Eight-plank Open Goods Bulk Grain	12	6-6	1931	8042/8/59/87/120/227/95/315/549/620/ 60/822/75/926/999004/39/199/224/37	20	Rebuild of LSWR design (See Vol 1 page 27 for details)	—
1347	Five-plank Open Goods	10	5-14	2/23-3/23 10/25-11/25	14401-70 'Rebuilds' (SECR order) 19079-228 'Rebuilds'	70 150	SECR design (See Vol 3 pages 62-6 for details)	27
1355	Seven-plank Open Goods	12	6-6	6/23-7/23 2/26-6/26	14897-996. (SECR order) 28501-29000	100 500	SECR design (See Vol 3 pages 62, 66 and 102 for details)	27
1362	Five-plank Open Goods Propeller Cases	10	NR	5/41-7/41	5071-5120 (Ex-Diagram 1369, reverted to same 1/45-5/46)	50	Conversion of LBSCR design (See Vol 2 page 14 for details)	149
1369	Five-plank Open Goods	10	5-16	12/23-1/24 2/24-4/24 5/24-4/25 6/25-7/26	25934-26058. 'Partial Renewals' (LBSCR order) 26059-183 'Complete Renewals' 27462-711 'Partial Renewals' 18729-19078 'Partial Renewals'	125 125 250 250	LBSCR design (See Vol 2 pages 19-22 for details)	27
1374	Seven-plank Mineral	10	5-14	1934	18780 (mainland), 27545 (Isle of Wight)	2	Conversion of LBSCR design (See Vol 2 pages 14 and 21 for details)	55/58
1375	Five-plank Open Goods	12	6-9	1/40-9/48	5153-395/400-572/601- 6450/2-779/801-7122, 11848-13080 13082-494/6-672/84-14032, 38151-388/401-750 NE 262690 etc 'SR' 1-1600? LMS 417610-8074, M360120-263/358-71	SR2861 BR1815 NE400 LMS465	Many minor variations. Many fitted by BR Of the 1600 built for the WD, 144 became LMR stock in 1949	38-42 149-50
1376	Five-plank Open Goods Shock absorbing	12	8-10 8-1	4/40-6/40 6/40	38389-94 38395-400 AVB	6 6	AVB by BR	38
1377	Eight-plank Open Goods	12	6-16	10/38-12/39	37401-38150	750	Most uprated to 13 tons. Many fitted AVB by BR	29. 37
1378	Eight-plank Open Goods Cable Drums	12	NR	1937-57	Various		Conversion of Diagram 1379 Also found on Diag 1899	29, 33 37
1379	Eight-plank Open Goods	12	6-18	1/26-5/33	29001-36950	7950	Most uprated to 13 tons. 1500 built by contractors	29/30
1380	Five-plank Open Goods	10	6-0	4/30-7/31	9341-9640 9641-56/8-739/41/3-6/ 8-51/3-983/5-10013/15-55/7-79/8/13- 137/9-73/5-94/6-20-5 10206-7/9-56	900	Officially 'Rebuilds' using second-hand LSWR wheels, axleboxes, buffers etc	29, 31/2
1381	Eight-plank Open Goods	10	6-13	3/32-8/34	10258-302/4-8/10-77/9/80/2-96/ 10298-410/2-8/22-5/7-32/4-8/40-57 10700-41/3-8/50-5/7-68/70/1/3-8/80/ 10782-5/7-90/2-6/8/801-8/10/1 10459-64/6-86/8-577/80-632/4- 10640/2/4-7/9-55/7-9/61/3-77/9-99- 10814/6-20/2-4/6-31/3/4/7-42/4-6/ 10848/9/51/3-68/70-4/6-905/8-11	600	Officially 'Rebuilds' using second-hand SECR wheels, axleboxes etc	29, 32
				9/34-11/35	26200-6/9-12/4-36/8/40-59/61-76/8-96/ 26298-38/13-411/3-6/9-24/6-53 26455-98/500-613/5-54/6-80/2-6/8-718	500	Officially 'Rebuilds' using second-hand LSWR wheels and axleboxes etc	

SR Diagram	Vehicle Type	Capacity (tons)	Average Tare	Building Period	Running Numbers, etc	Total Built	Notes	Page
1382	Container Truck	12	6-9 5-11	6/32-7/33 7/32	39001-25/51-250 'Conflat A' AVB 39026-50 'Conflat B' AVB; from 1935 'Conflat A'	225 25	Most uprated to 13 tons Most uprated to 13 tons	47-51
1382A	Container Truck	12	6-8	11/35	39251-350 'Conflat A' AVB	100	'Rebuilds' 12 ton. Most uprated to 13 tons	47
1383	Container Truck	14	8-16 NR	10/32-1/33 12/32-5/33	39501-75 'Conflat D' AVB 39576-650 'Conflat C' AVB; from 1935 'Conflat D'	75 75	Most uprated to 15 tons Most uprated to 15 tons	47, 50, 62
1384	Seven-plank Mineral End door	12	6-4	8/33-10/33	40001-200	200	Most uprated to 13 tons	55-6
1385	Eight-plank Open Goods	10	7-13	10/33-11/33	36951-37050 AVB	100	'Rebuilds' second-hand LSWR wheels and axleboxes etc. Most uprated to 13 tons	29
1386	Eight-plank Mineral	20	8-19	12/33-4/35 12/39	40201-980 41001-200 (40201-300 loco coal) 41201-9 (Rebuilt from milk-traffic underframes)	980 9	Most uprated to 21 tons Most uprated to 21 tons	55, 57
1387	Eight-plank Open Goods Train Ferry Wagon	12	7-10	5/35	36352/5/69/99/409/26/62/92/502/ 36556/76/601/5/10/39/42-3/70 36686/7/90/733/842/61/ 36873/86/8/90/913/41 AVB, WP	30	All uprated to 13 tons Converted from Diagram 1379	29, 34
1388	Eight-plank Open Goods Train Ferry Wagon	20	10-1	4/36	40981-41000 AVB, WP	20	All uprated to 13 tons	29, 35
1389	Five-plank Open Goods	13	NR	1/43-196?	7116-20, 38418-28/32+one other.	18	AVB conversion of Diagram 1375 Many others converted by BR to AVB	39-42
1390	Eight-plank Mineral with bottom doors	13	7-3	1945 1945/6	41210-309 LNER 267100-268949 (LNER Diagram 192)	100 1850	 No bottom doors on the LNER wagons	29, 35 55/8-9
1391	Five-plank Open Goods	14	5-11	9/45	6780	1	Experimental triangulated underframe	39, 42/4
1392	Five-plank Open Goods Shock-absorbing	12	8-2 8-10	2/49 1/49-3/49	14033-51 14052-70 AVB	19 19	Most converted to AVB by BR	39, 43
1396	Five-plank Open Goods	8	5-1	1927	28316-9 AVB	4	Lynton & Barnstaple line (See Vol 2 pages 96 and 103 for details)	28/9
1398	Eight-plank Open Goods	12	7-7	12/35-7/37	37051-400	350	Most uprated to 13 tons	29, 33/36
1399	Container Truck	12 13	6-9 6-12	9/38 7/40-7/47	39351-400 AVB 39401-50/651-955 AVB	50 355	 Most uprated to 13 tons	47, 52-4
1400	Eight-plank Open Goods	10	6-14	8/36-11/37	10912-41/3/5-93/5-11108/10-20/ 11122-4/6-9/31-76/8-87/9/92-5/7 11298-302/4-98/400/1/3/5-90/2-501/ 11505-8/10/3-651/3-92 11694-7/9/700/2-29/31-3/5-8/ 11740-6/8-9/51-6/8-61/3-70/2-3/5 11776-84/7-9/91-8/800-1/3 26719-901/3-7030/2-247/50/2/4-7/ 27259-60/2/4-7/9/71/4-8/80/3-7 27291/3/6-9/301/4-5/7-11/5/7-9/ 27322-6/8-32/4-42/55-50/2/4-8 27362-71/3/6-84/6-94/6-404/6-417	1400	Officially 'Rebuilds' using second-hand wheels etc Starting in 1939 many rebuilt to 13 tons Many converted to AVB by BR	29, 33/6
BR1/016	Three-plank Open Goods Dropside	13	6-4	11/49-12/49	B457100-99 BR Pt Lot 2061 [SR Nos 3941-4040 allocated but not used]	100		39, 42/5
BR1/033	Five-plank Open Goods Dropside	13	6-17	12/49	B457000-99 (Renumbered B483650-749. BR Pt Lot 2061) [SR Nos 4901-5000 allocated but not used]	100	Ordered 8/47 as 21-ton minerals. Order amended to open goods 7/48	39, 42/6

SR Diagram	Vehicle Type	Capacity (tons)	Average Tare	Building Period	Running Numbers, etc	Total Built	Notes	Page
BR1/034	Five-plank Open Goods	13	6-10	1950	B477050-649 BR Lot 2153	600	Southern Region-designed,. Ashford-built	39, 44
BR1/035	Five-plank Open Goods Shock-absorbing	12	8-14 8-1	1950	B720425-924 AVB BR Lot 2154 B720925-721224 BR Lot 2155	500 300	Southern Region-designed,. Ashford-built	39, 44
1408	Covered Goods	10	7-3	1923 1923	Between 42233 and 44275 (LSWR order, LSWR Nos carried) 44276-325 (LSWR order, LSWR Nos carried)	50 50	LSWR design (See Vol 1 pages 30 and 37 for details)	60-1
1409	Covered Goods	10	7-3	7/24-9/24	43326-425 (LSWR order, LSWR Nos allocated)	100	LSWR design (See Vol 1 pages 30 and 35 for details)	60-1
1426	Covered Goods	10	6-17	12/25-1/26	47101-200	100	SECR design (See Vol 3 pages 71 and 74 for details)	60-1
1427	Covered Goods Ventilated	10	7-1	1923	45617-9/21-3 AVB	6	SECR design (See Vol 3 pages 71 and 87 for details)	60-1
1428	Covered Goods	12	6-18 7-17	5/29-9/31 6/30-7/35	45908-46107, 47201-300/401-550 47301-400/551-976 AVB	450 526		60-2
1428A	Covered Goods	12	7-17	6/35-7/35	47977-48276	300	Officially 'Rebuilds' but 12 ton capacity	60-1
1429	Covered Goods	10	6-17 7-11	11/31-3/32 2/32-3/32	44427-649/51-85/7-97/9-718/994-45041/562-91 46108-90 46774-46923 AVB	450 150	Officially 'Rebuilds' using second-hand LSWR wheels and axleboxes etc	60-2
1430	Covered Goods Train Ferry Wagon	12	NR	3/35-4/35	45918/23/5/6/9/32/3/40/2-4/9-51/3/ 45964/6/71/3/5/8/9/81/3/5/8/90/1 46003/4/24/8-9/31/4/6/44-5-54/6/61/ 46063-6/8/70/2-3/7/9/84/6-94/7-9 46100/3/7 47203/6-7/10/2/6-7/ 461234-6/8/44/8-9/51/7-9/65/6/8/74-99 47300/1/6/9-11/6/8/9/21/414 AVB WP	100	Converted from Diagram 1428	61/3-4
1452	Covered Goods	12	7-0 7-9	1/45-12/49 9/49-12/49	49952-94, 50901-51000/351-500, 54251-500, 56501-57010 B752350-789 [SR Nos 57022-181 allocated but not used] B752790-753099 AVB [SR Nos 45480-555, 46191-228/92-327 allocated but not used]	BR440 BR310	SR1053 54251-500 AVB Most of remainder converted to AVB by BR	61/5, 70-1
1454	Covered Goods	12	7-12	11/43	65980	1	Single-radius roof	61/5/9
1455	Covered Goods	12	7-4	5/42-4/44	44719-82/4-835/9-51/3-67/9-92/ 44794-958/60-88, 45042/103/5-76 45178-96/8-220/2-60/5-321, 54001-250, 59101-250, 65281-979 65981-66130, GWR144269-918, LMS521140-289/3290-539	SR1783 GWR650 LMS400	Most converted to AVB by BR	61/5/8
1456	Covered Goods	8	6-6	1927	47042-5 AVB	4	Lynton & Barnstaple line (See Vol 2 pages 96 and 103 for details)	60-1
1457	Covered Goods Isle of Wight	10	NR	1935	46924-6 WB	3	Conversion of Diagram 1528 (See Vol 2 pages 26 and 36 for details)	—
1458	Covered Goods	12	7-9	5/36-5/41	47001-100, 48277-49951, 59251 60000, 64921-65280	2885	At least 67 sold to WD. Some built VP, AVB provided later The vast majority of those built prior to 1/39 [48277-49426] had normal planking, the remainder '2+2'	61/4/6-9
1459	Covered Goods Biscuit traffic	12	NR	8/36-3/38	48333-6/54/5/77/8/669/90-2/ 48777-91/4-8/802-6/9-12/39-43/6-9 49039-44/59-63/75-92/173-93	100	Diagram 1458 modified (BR 'PARTO') internal partitions fitted	61/6
1460	Covered Goods Egg traffic	12	8-2	11/37-6/38	48323/59/980, 49168	4	Diagram 1458 modified	61/6

SR Diagram	Vehicle Type	Capacity (tons)	Average Tare	Building Period	Running Numbers, etc	Total Built	Notes	Page
1476	Refrigerator Van	10	9-18	9/28	50494-50499 AVB	6	LSWR order, SR design	72-3
1477	Insulated Van	10	9-10	2/31-3/31	50500-74 AVB	75		72/6-7
1478	Banana Van	10	9-0	8/35-12/35	50575-774 AVB	200	Insulated van with steam heat	72/8/9
1479	Banana Van	10	9-7	4/38-7/38	50775-899 AVB	125	Insulated van with steam heat. Originally intendeed to be Diagram 1458 covered goods with normal planking	72/9
1482	Meat Van	8	8-6	11/26	51171-95 AVB	25	LSWR Design (See Vol 1 Pages 38 and 41 for details)	72
1486	Meat Van	10	9-6	1/31-2/31 4/34-6/34	51196-220/41-90 AVB 51291-315 AVB	75 25		72/4-5
–	Fish Van Isle of Wight	10	7-8	1931	44945/6 and possibly one other	2/3?	Diagram 1433 re-lettered (See Vol 2 page 29 for H172 details)	—
1502	Cattle Truck	8	7-14	1923	51846-51870 VP (LSWR order)	25	LSWR design (See Vol 1 pages 47 and 51 for details)	80
1515	Cattle Truck	10	7-2	11/23-12/23 7/25-6/28	52769-52818 VP (SECR order) 52819-81, 53391-627 VP	50 300	SECR design (See Vol 3 pages 92 and 99 for details)	80-1
1529	Cattle Truck	10	8-8	4/30-3/39	53629-53844/6-928 AVB [53845 not built]	299		80-3
1530	Cattle Truck	10	8-8	10/47-11/47	52268-578 AVB	251	Some entered traffic with VP only	80/4-5
BR1/351	Cattle Truck	10 & 12	8-8	10/49-12/49	B891250-399 AVB BR Lot 2064 [SR 1 Nos 52001-150 allocated but not used]	50	First 128 quoted as 10 tons, remainder 12 tons	80
1547	Goods Brake Van	25	25-0	1922/3	20 of 55075-99 LSWR order	20	LSWR design (See Vol 1 pages 54 and 64 for details)	86
1549	Goods Brake Van	20	19-15	1917/8	55100-55119 (Built 1918 for WD. Purchased 1924)	20	LSWR design (See Vol 1 pages 54 and 61 for details)	86
1550	Bo Goods Brake Van	25	25-0	5/36-8/36	56282-56306 AVB	25	Underframe built Lancing, body built Ashford	86
1560	Goods Brake Van	25	25-0	11/23-12/23 1/27	55476-95 (SECR order, SECR Nos allocated) 55496-55515	20 20	SECR design (See Vol 3 pages 103, 118 and 120 for details)	86-7
1561	Goods Brake Van	17	16-8	9/38	55180-55182 AVB	3	LBSCR tender underframe ('B2X' class)	86, 94
1570	Goods Brake Van	20	20-0	1946	56060 (LMS731742, LNER260948, GWR35927)	1	RCH specification for a goods brake van Design prepared by the LMS	86, 99
1576	Goods Brake Van	20	20-7	1923	55917-27 (LBSCR order, LBSCR Nos carried)	11	LBSCR design (See Vol 2 pages 38 and 45 for details)	86
1578	Goods Brake Van	25	25-0	4/28-10/29	55516-8/22-5/31-3/5/6/40/1/6-50/ 55552/4/6/8-65, 55943-92	80	Left-hand duckets. Diagram 1560-type underframe	86-8
1579	Goods Brake Van	25	25-0	10/29-11/33 1/40-7/42	55519-21/6-30/4/7-9/42/5/ 55551/3/5/7/66-85, 55993-56022/61-260 56307-494	270 188	One end window. Normal planking Two end windows. '2+2' planking	86/8-9 86, 90/1
1580	Bogie Goods Brake Van	27	27-13	9/33 3/34-1/35	56263 AVB 56261/2/4-81 AVB	1 20		
1581	Goods Brake Van	15	15-0	8/34-9/34	55675-724	50		86, 93-4
1582	Goods Brake Van	25	25-0	11/47-11/48	55121-70/621-74	104		86, 96/7
1583	Goods Brake Van	15	NR	5/48, 7/48	(Conversion of Diagram 1581 for Canterbury & Whitstable line)			86
	Goods Brake Van	25	NR	10/41 3/42	WD11002-21 AVB WP WD11022-41 AVB WP. Two of these became M360327/8	20 20	Diagram 1579 with minor differences	86, 148-9
–	Goods Brake Van	10	10-3	1933	56044/7-9 WP	4	Conversion of Diagram 1541 (See Vol 1 page 57 for details)	—

154

SR Diagram	Vehicle Type	Capacity (tons)	Average Tare	Building Period	Running Numbers, etc	Total Built	Notes	Page
1597	Bogie Bolster Wagon	40	18-9	1923/4 4/26-9/26	57833-52 (LSWR order) 57853-82	20 30	LSWR design (See Vol 1 pages 68 and 69 for details)	100-1
1598	Bogie Bolster Wagon	40	21-3	1/37-4/45	57883-987 (57883-907 renumbered 64622-46 in 1945)	105		100-2
1599	Bogie Bolster Wagon	40	20-9	6/46-10/46 6/64-1/48	57988-58039 64738-54 [64738-54 also allocated to Diagram 1787]	52 17		100/3-4
1661	Road Vehicle Truck	10	5-12	1923	15 of 60423-545 (LBSCR order, LBSCR Nos carried)	15	LBSCR design (See Vol 2 page 53 for details)	105
1681	Machinery Truck	20	9-3	10/23 5/28 7/42-8/42	61048-59 Well wagon 'Mac B' (SECR order) 61086-98 Well wagon 'Mac B' 61151-72 Well Wagon 'Mac B'	12 13 22	SECR design but none actually built by that company. Most uprated to 21 tons	105-7
1682	Well Truck	20	12-17	1/44-6/45	61101-10, 64600 'Flatrol'	11		105/10-3
1690	Bogie Well Truck	40	NR	11/27	61099, 61100 'Crocodile Wagon'	2	Built by Charles Roberts & Co	105/8-9
1691	Snowplough	18	10-7	12/29 12/48	S1, S2 S3, S4	2 2		114
1712	Shunting Truck Clapham Junction	–	9-9	6/31	61322/3 VP	2	LSWR tender underframe ('A12' class)	114/7
1713	Tar Tank Isle of Wight	15	NR	1929	61381/2	2	Reconstruction of Isle of Wight Railway tar tank	—
1714	Bogie Shunting Truck Dover Train Ferry	–	–	7/35	61324/5 AVB WP	2	LBSCR carriage underframe	114/8
1715	Shunting Truck	25	10-0	1/39	61326/7 VP	2	LBSCR tender underframe ('C2' class) Bournemouth West	114/8/20
1716	Six-wheel Tar Tank Isle of Wight	17	NR	1947	61384/5	2	LSWR tender converted ('A12' class)	—
1717	Bogie Shunting Truck	–	NR	11/47	61328/9	2	SR carriage underframe	114/7/20
1744	Two-plank Ballast Dropside	12	5-15	7/23-8/23	62427-86 (SECR order)	60	SECR design (See Vol 3 pages 138 and 141 for details)	121
1748	Ballast Plough Brake	20	20-5	1932	62030-2 AVB	3	SECR design built by Charles Roberts & Co (See Vol 3 pages 138 and 150 for details)	121, 132
1749	Ballast Plough Brake	20	20-12	1/49-4/49	62857-64 AVB	8	Development of Diagram 1748	121, 132
1760	Ballast Brake Van	20	NR	8/28-1/29 3/37-12/37	62840-6 VP 62847-56 VP	7 10	Diagram 1576 rebuilt (See Vol 2 pages 38 and 46-48 for details)	121-2
1771	Five-plank Ballast Dropside	20	8-16	6/28-10/28	61945-62004 AVB	60	Built by Birmingham Railway Carriage & Wagon Co	121/4
1772	Bogie Ballast Hopper	40	19-5	10/28-2/29	62005-29 AVB	25	Built by Metropolitan Railway Carriage & Wagon Co	121/5
1773	Four-plank Ballast Dropside	15	8-11	2/37-4/37	63001-50	50		121/7/8
1774	Bogie Ballast Hopper	40	20-10	12/36-1/37	62033-54 AVB	22	Development of Diagram 1772, built by Metropolitan-Cammell	121/6
1775	Bogie Ballast Hopper	40	19-10	5/47-12/47	62055-74 AVB	20	Development of Diagram 1774	121/9
1787	Bogie Rail Wagon	40	22-0	7/46	64738-48	11	Also found on Diagram 1599 for Robel cranes	100
1899	Eight-plank Open Goods Cable Drums	12	NR	Not known	Various	60+	Diagram 1378 modified	37
BR1/570	Steel-sided Ballast Dropside 'Lamprey'	20	10-7	1951	DB991000-20 AVB (BR Lot 2065, SR Nos 63051-91 allocated but not used)	21		121/8/20
SR	Vehicle Type	Capacity	Average	Building	Running Numbers, etc	Total	Notes	Page

Diagram		(tons)	Tare	Period		Built		
BR1/570 cont				1951	~~DB991301-20 (BR Lot 2102)~~	20		
				1951/2	DB991141-300 (BR Lot 2241)	160	991141-240 allocated to Eastern and North Eastern Regions 991241-300 allocated to Southern Region	
BR1/585	Bogie Ballast Hopper 'Walrus'	40	20-9	1954	DB992481-530 AVB (BR Lot 2411)	50	Modification of SR Diagram 1775	121/8
BR1/589	Bogie Ballast Hopper 'Whale'	50	23-10	1966/7	DB982350-439 WB (BR Lot 3591)	90	Development of Diagram BR1/585	121/131
BR1/590	Bogie Ballast Hopper 'Sealion'	40	21-14	1970	DB982440-539 WB AVB (BR Lot 3723)	100	Development of Diagram 1775	121/31-2
				1972-4	DB982568-927 WB AVB (BR Lot 3802)	360		
BR1/591	Bogie Ballast Hopper 'Seacow'	40	21-0	1971	DB982540-64 WB VP (BR Lot 3724)	25	Development of Diagram 1775	121/31-2
			21-2	1971	DB982565-7 WB VP (BR Lot 3777)	3		
			21-2	1981/2	DB980000-250 WB VP (BR Lots 3966 and 4010)	251		

Notes:
Dates sometimes varied between the various copies of the Wagon Registers, so the month is quoted as a 'best guide'.
NR=No Record. There was no entry recorded in the Wagon Register or on the Wagon Diagram

Appendix 2

Southern Railway Wagon Transfers to the Isle of Wight

SR Diagram	Vehicle Type	Year Transferred	Totals	Running Numbers
1369	Open Goods	1924	20	26119-23/31-45
1369	Open Goods	1925	6	18988/9/95-8
1369	Open Goods	1926	50	18980-7/90-4/9, 19000-17/33/4/60-75
1369	Open Goods	1927	68	28321-88
1369	Open Goods	1928	70	28389-458
1369	Open Goods	1929	75	28253-300/459-85
1369	Open Goods	1930	75	27721-95
1369	Open Goods	1931	86	27796-881
1369	Open Goods	1937	1	64392
1369	Open Goods	1947	6	27882-7
		Total	457	
1379	Open Goods	1948	48	27890/1/5-9/ 27900/4/6/10/14-48
1379	Open Goods	1949	40	27888/9/92-4/ 27903/5/7-9/11-3 27949-75
		Total	88	
1374	Mineral	1934	1	27545
		Total	1	
1433	Covered Goods	1929	8	46941-8
		Total	8	
1434	Covered Goods	1930	5	46932-5/8
1434	Covered Goods	1931	8	46927-31/6/7/9
		Total	13	
1436	Covered Goods	1927	12	46963-74
1436	Covered Goods	1928	7	46950-6
1436	Covered Goods	1929	7	46940/57-62
1436	Covered Goods	1930	1	46949
1436	(M&T van)	1939	1	437S
		Total	28	
1527	Cattle	1927	3	53374-6
1527	Cattle	1928	1	53371
1527	Cattle	1929	2	53372/3
		Total	6	

SR Diagram	Vehicle Type	Year Transferred	Totals	Running Numbers
1616	Single Bolster	1928	10	59037-45/7
1616	Single Bolster	1930	5	59048-52
1617	Single Bolster	1928	5	59033-6/46
		Total	5	
1641	'Cartruck'	1927	4	60561-4
		Total	4	
1661	'Cartruck'	1928	12	60565-76
1661	'Cartruck'	1929	4	60577-80
1661	'Cartruck'	1930	3	60581-3
		Total	19	
1713	Tar tank	1947	2	61384/5
		Total	2	
1352	Ballast	1924	18	62885-902
1352	Ballast	1931	2	62903/4
		Total	20	
1751	Ballast	1927/8	18	62905-22
		Total	18	
1755	Ballast	1947?	10	62792/8/801/4/5/ 628710/1/6/7/20
		Total	10	
1541	Goods Brake Van	1925	1	56044
1541	Goods Brake Van	1927	2	56045/6
1541	Goods Brake Van	1928	3	56047-9
1541	Goods Brake Van	1930	1	56050
1541	Goods Brake Van	1931	2	56051/2
1541	Goods Brake Van	1932	3	56053-5
1541	Goods Brake Van	1938	2	56056/7
		Total	14	
1542	Goods Brake Van	1948	1	56058
		Total	1	

Note: There was no offical record of the transfer of the Diagram 1755 ballast wagons to the Isle of Wight, but they were undoubtedly there and are believed to have been transferred in 1947.

Appendix 3

Southern Railway Wagon Stock Totals as on the First of January of each year (not including Isle of Wight or Lynton & Barnstaple stock)

Type	Cap.	1923	1924	1925	1926	1927	1928	1929	1930	1931	1932	1933	1934	1935	1936	1937	1938	1939	1940	1941	1942	1943	1944	1945	1946	1947	1948	1949
Open Goods	6T	12	10	6	16	16	9	8	8	7	6	3	2	2	12	10	2	2	2	-	-	-	-	-	-	-	-	-
"	7T	137	126	122	114	108	98	77	60	48	38	30	20	16	12	10	-	-	-	-	-	-	-	-	-	-	-	-
"	8T	3059	3013	2904	2865	2818	2546	2280	2151	1974	1898	1847	1771	1647	1514	1362	986	652	462	356	311	291	265	230	156	100	69	26
"	9T	-	12	9	6	4	2	2	1	-	-	-	-	-	-	-	-	-	-	-	-	-	-	-	-	-	-	-
"	10T	15281	16579	16050	15828	15396	14709	13611	12508	11763	11283	10933	9885	9292	8862	8957	9132	8980	8782	8757	8594	8477	8243	7769	6805	5900	5169	4499
"	12T	3013	3613	3685	3813	5089	6932	8440	9526	10823	11611	11986	12257	12206	12239	12377	12410	12592	11798	10305	8847	7417	5840	4639	4023	3390	3033	2669
"	13T	-	-	-	-	-	-	-	-	-	-	-	-	-	-	-	-	-	1227	2941	4403	5833	8470	10370	10643	10869	10511	11696
"	14T	-	-	-	-	-	-	-	-	-	-	-	-	-	-	-	-	-	-	-	-	-	-	-	-	-	-	1
"	15T	50	50	50	50	50	50	50	50	49	49	49	49	49	49	49	49	49	48	48	48	47	47	47	45	41	35	29
"	20T	-	-	-	-	-	-	-	-	-	-	-	-	-	-	20	20	20	20	7	4	3	3	3	2	2	1	1
"	21T	-	-	-	-	-	-	-	-	-	-	-	-	-	-	-	-	-	-	13	16	16	16	16	17	17	18	18
"	25T	1	1	1	1	1	1	1	1	1	-	-	-	-	-	-	-	-	-	-	-	-	-	-	-	-	-	-
Open Goods Shock	12T	-	-	-	-	-	-	-	-	-	-	1	1	1	1	1	1	1	12	12	12	12	12	12	12	12	12	12
Road Van Trucks and (from 1932)	8T	1	1	1	1	1	1	1	1	1	-	-	-	-	-	-	-	-	-	-	-	-	-	-	-	-	-	-
Container Wagons	10T	401*	438*	433*	424*	418*	401*	355*	300	257	214	186	155	132	120	113	104	95	93	93	90	88	86	81	64	44	33	26
"	12T	27	-	-	-	-	-	-	17	10	8	57	254	252	352	352	352	402	402	417	417	213	92	58	55	53	51	51
"	13T	-	-	-	-	-	-	-	-	-	-	58	-	-	-	-	-	-	-	-	-	389	509	645	648	651	703	703
"	14T	-	-	-	-	-	-	-	-	-	-	150	150	150	150	150	150	150	149	149	132	93	56	17	10	10	10	10
"	15T	-	-	-	-	-	-	-	-	-	-	-	-	-	-	-	-	-	-	-	-	-	10	10	10	10	10	10
"	20T	-	-	-	-	-	-	-	-	-	-	-	-	-	-	-	-	-	-	-	149	149	132	139	139	139	139	139
Stone Trucks	10T	7	7	7	7	6	6	4	3	3	3	3	3	3	3	3	3	3	3	3	3	3	3	3	2	3	2	2
"	12T	17	17	17	17	17	17	15	12	10	9	9	5	4	4	3	3	3	3	3	3	3	3	3	3	3	2	2
"	15T	11	11	9	8	10	10	10	10	9	9	9	22	22	22	22	21	21	21	21	21	21	21	21	21	20	18	18
Cattle Trucks		1504	1543	1502	1526	1477	1515	1435	1314	1341	1309	1230	1142	1104	1062	998	959	912	924	914	897	890	871	839	764	695	879	793
Covered Goods Vans		4129	4125	4157	4117	4088	3983	3752	3782	3679	4121	4364	4388	4449	4643	4973	5266	5366	5484	6331	7079	7723	8529	8450	8830	9196	9115	9022
Refrigerator Vans		397	396	395	395	394	394	385	347	315	280	237	204	194	190	188	180	175	175	175	173	173	172	172	167	162	159	156
Insulated Vans		-	-	-	-	-	-	-	-	-	97	131	152	160	161	161	164	169	167	167	167	167	167	167	160	149	146	137
Meat Vans		191	190	180	173	191	184	154	133	119	183	180	171	190	188	184	182	181	178	178	176	175	171	169	166	160	159	157
Gunpowder Vans		40	40	40	40	40	40	39	38	38	38	38	38	38	38	38	38	38	38	38	37	37	35	35	35	33	29	26
Banana Vans (ventilated)		-	-	-	-	-	-	-	-	-	-	-	-	-	151	200	200	325	325	325	325	325	320	320	319	319	319	319
Brake Vans	6T	99	99	99	99	99	99	99	98	98	93	93	91	89	88	85	85	77	77	-	-	-	-	-	-	-	-	-
"	7T	4	4	2	2	2	2	2	2	2	2	-	-	-	-	-	-	-	-	-	-	-	-	-	-	-	-	-
"	9T	29	29	29	18	14	7	6	4	2	2	1	1	1	1	-	-	-	-	-	-	-	-	-	-	-	-	-
"	10T	745	702	647	615	586	554	482	388	290	226	183	147	126	113	103	97	85	76	73	67	65	61	56	49	46	42	32
"	12T	-	-	-	-	-	-	-	-	-	-	-	-	-	-	-	-	-	-	-	-	-	-	-	-	-	-	1
"	13T	-	-	-	-	-	-	-	-	-	-	-	-	-	-	-	-	-	-	-	32	42	46	49	56	60	60	60
"	15T	-	-	-	-	-	-	-	-	-	-	-	-	-	-	-	-	-	-	-	-	-	-	-	2	2	3	3
"	17T	194	205	225	225	225	227	222	220	220	220	220	219	218	216	215	199	195	195	194	193	193	190	185	177	159	138	122
"	20T	100	136	140	140	150	158	201	252	301	378	474	508	508	508	533	533	533	533	578	578	686	719	719	719	719	735	823
"	25T	-	-	-	-	-	-	-	-	-	-	-	-	-	-	-	-	-	-	4	5	7	9	10	11	13	15	20
"	27T	-	-	-	-	-	-	-	-	-	-	-	-	-	-	-	-	-	-	-	-	1	1	2	2	2	2	2
Timber Trucks	6T	380	347	320	298	277	258	227	223	201	196	194	185	154	102	71	43	27	15	13	11	10	10	9	5	3	2	2
"	8T	87	76	72	67	63	55	40	27	14	11	7	5	4	1	1	-	-	-	-	-	-	-	-	-	-	-	-
"	10T	480	501	518	525	530	533	502	471	428	391	357	310	269	271	264	255	250	244	239	232	223	212	158	104	64	34	17
"	12T	51	51	51	51	51	51	51	51	51	51	51	51	51	51	51	51	51	51	51	51	51	51	40	8	6	5	8
"	13T	-	-	-	-	-	-	-	-	-	-	-	-	-	-	-	-	-	-	30	30	9	30	40	42	44	44	86
"	40T	50	56	70	70	100	100	100	100	100	100	100	100	100	100	100	100	100	100	122	138	159	177	180	232	232	232	231
Batten Trucks	12T	612	609	600	585	573	523	452	374	305	278	241	196	163	144	116	100	100	100	100	100	100	100	100	100	100	100	122
"	15T	11	11	11	11	11	11	10	8	8	8	8	8	8	8	8	8	7	7	7	7	7	8	7	5	5	5	10
"	20T	2	2	2	2	2	2	2	2	8	8	8	8	8	8	8	2	2	2	7	7	7	6	5	5	5	4	4
Well Trucks		22	34	33	32	31	31	42	40	36	35	34	34	34	35	32	31	31	31	31	30	19	8	14	16	15	14	14

Southern Railway Wagon Stock Totals

Description	Cap.	1923	1924	1925	1926	1927	1928	1929	1930	1931	1932	1933	1934	1935	1936	1937	1938	1939	1940	1941	1942	1943	1944	1945	1946	1947	1948	1949
"	21T	1	1	1	1	-	-	-	-	-	-	-	-	-	-	-	-	-	-	-	-	30	35	36	36	36	36	36
"	30T	-	-	-	-	-	-	-	-	-	-	-	-	-	-	-	-	-	-	-	-	-	-	-	-	-	-	-
Crocodile Wagons	40T	4	4	4	4	4	4	4	4	3	3	3	2	2	2	2	2	2	2	2	2	2	2	2	2	2	2	2
Glass Trucks		-	2	2	2	2	2	2	2	2	2	2	2	2	2	2	2	2	2	2	2	2	2	2	2	2	2	2
China Clay Wagons		20	4	-	-	-	-	-	-	-	-	-	-	-	-	-	-	-	-	-	-	-	-	-	-	-	-	-
Mineral Wagons	6T	3	-	-	-	-	-	-	-	-	-	-	-	-	-	-	-	-	-	-	-	-	-	-	-	-	-	-
"	8T	159	-	-	-	-	-	-	-	-	-	-	-	-	-	-	-	-	-	-	-	-	-	-	-	-	-	-
"	9T	14	-	-	-	-	-	-	-	-	-	-	-	-	-	-	-	-	-	-	-	-	-	-	-	-	-	-
"	10T	2144	176	128	76	40	24	17	14	13	11	9	7	5	3	3	2	2	2	2	24	24	24	22	19	15	12	8
Mineral Wagons	12T	2376	1876	1873	1862	1784	1580	1431	1139	933	781	693	804	632	559	530	494	441	413	379	315	261	209	159	134	98	81	62
"	13T	-	-	-	-	-	-	-	-	-	-	-	-	-	-	-	-	-	4	21	75	123	161	180	267	248	247	247
"	15T	59	59	59	59	59	59	53	48	44	40	39	36	35	33	31	29	20	17	17	17	17	14	12	8	5	3	3
"	20T	-	-	-	-	-	-	-	-	-	-	-	4	531	980	980	980	489	326	283	188	114	91	87	80	75	74	73
"	21T	-	-	-	-	-	-	-	-	-	-	-	-	-	-	-	-	491	663	704	801	875	898	901	908	913	914	915
Aeroplane Trucks	4T	-	2	2	2	3	3	3	3	3	3	3	2	-	-	-	-	-	-	-	-	-	-	-	-	-	-	-
"	10T	-	5	5	5	5	5	5	4	3	-	-	-	-	-	-	-	-	-	-	-	-	-	-	-	-	-	-
"	12T	-	2	2	2	2	2	2	2	2	2	2	2	-	-	-	-	-	-	-	-	-	-	-	-	-	-	-
"	20T	9	11	2	2	2	1	2	2	1	2	2	2	-	-	-	-	-	-	-	-	-	-	-	-	-	-	-
Open Flat Trucks		-	-	-	10	10	8	4	2	2	2	2	2	-	-	-	-	-	-	-	-	-	-	-	-	-	-	-
Shunting Trucks		-	-	-	-	-	-	-	-	-	-	-	-	3	5	5	5	5	7	7	7	7	7	7	7	5	7	-
TOTALS		36096	35331	34531	34236	34822	35307	34707	33871	33621	34060	34142	33473	32989	33106	33427	33358	33154	33260	34145	34659	35447	37029	38092	35987	34778	33345	32392

* From 1924 to 1929 8 10 & 12 ton totalled together

Appendix 4

Southern Railway Container Stock Totals

Description	Diagram	Class	Capacity	1929	1930	1931	1932	1933	1934	1935	1936	1937	1938	1939	1940	1941	1942	1943	1944	1945	1946	1947	1948	1949
Large Open	3023, 3024	D	4t	-	-	-	-	-	-	-	-	-	25	25	25	45	44	69	69	69	69	69	69	69
Large Open	3003	DM	3t	50	80	80	80	80	77	71	64	57	56	54	53	53	50	50	50	50	50	NK	45	40
Small Open	3006	G	2t 10cwt	-	-	-	40	40	40	40	40	40	40	40	40	40	39	39	39	39	39	39	39	39
Small Open	3009, 3010	C	4t	-	-	-	110	110	109	109	109	109	109	109	109	109	108	108	108	108	NK	NK	92	70
Large Covered Non insulated	3004, 3011, 3018, 3019, 3021, 3022, 3025, 3026	K BC BD BK	4t	-	-	50	50	100	100	100	100	150	200	200	200	200	200	225	252	312	NK	NK	420	420
Small Covered	3017	BS	4t	-	-	-	-	-	-	6	6	6	6	6	6	6	6	6	6	6	6	6	6	6
Small Covered	3027	A	3t	-	-	-	-	-	-	-	-	-	-	-	-	-	-	-	-	-	3	78	78	78
Small Covered	3005/20	A	2t 10cwt	-	-	-	10	10	7	7	7	22	32	32	32	32	32	32	32	32	32	32	32	32
Small Covered	3007	A	2t 10cwt	-	-	-	2	2	2	2	2	2	2	2	2	2	2	-	-	-	-	-	-	-
Large Covered	3001, 3002, 3013, 3016, 3029	F BN	3t 10cwt	100	150	150	275	275	290	390	389	412	438	438	488	486	481	481	481	481	NK	NK	456	446
Insulated Large Covered	3015	FX	3t 5cwt	-	-	-	-	-	10	10	10	10	10	10	10	10	10	10	10	10	10	10	10	9
Small Covered	3014	AF	2t 10cwt	-	-	-	-	-	3	3	3	3	3	3	3	3	3	3	3	3	3	3	3	3
Large Covered	3008	BN	3t 10cwt	-	-	-	-	2	2	2	2	2	2	2	2	2	2	2	2	2	2	NK	1	-
Large Covered	3012	BM	2t 10cwt *	-	-	-	-	10	20	20	20	20	20	20	30	30	38	38	48	48	48	48	48	48
Totals				150	230	280	569	629	660	760	752	833	943	941	1000	1018	1015	1063	1100	1160	NK	NK	1299	1260

* Capacity 3 tons from 1940
Note: NK totals not known

Appendix 5

Southern Railway Departmental Wagons (not including the Isle of Wight or the Lynton & Barnstaple line)

Description	1923	1924	1925	1926	1927	1928	1929	1930	1931	1932	1933	1934	1935	1936	1937	1938	1939	1940	1941	1942	1943	1944	1945	1946	1947	1948	1949
Loco Coal	NK*	318	316	288	333	339	159	172	189	179	152	136	141	141	130	NK*	128	128	117	106	94	76	NK*	NK*	NK*	NK*	NK*
Ballast Trucks (4-ton)	NK*	-	-	-	63	45	45	36	34	25	3	2	1	1	1	-	1	-	-	-	-	-	-	-	-	-	-
Ballast Trucks (6-ton)	NK*	-	-	-	77	74	70	67	60	33	2	2	1	1	1	1	1	-	-	-	-	-	-	-	-	-	-
Ballast Trucks (7-ton)	NK*	-	-	-	188	175	144	132	114	102	87	75	60	44	37	NK*	-	-	-	-	-	-	-	-	-	-	-
Ballast Trucks (8-ton)	NK*	-	-	-	82	73	55	48	77	74	68	55	46	46	45	NK*	70	67	67	67	67	66	NK*	NK*	NK*	44	34
Ballast Trucks (10-ton)	NK*	1049†	1078†	1052†	278	276	272	265	254	244	229	210	183	182	181	NK*	154	144	141	139	137	135	NK*	NK*	NK*	92	72
Ballast Trucks (12-ton)	NK*	-	-	-	152	152	152	152	152	152	152	152	152	152	152	152	152	152	152	152	152	152	152	152	152	152	152
Ballast Trucks (15-ton)	NK*	-	-	-	112	111	111	111	110	110	110	109	108	108	107	NK*	152	150	150	150	150	149	152	152	152	135	128
Ballast Trucks (20-ton)	NK*	-	-	-	44	44	104	104	104	104	104	104	104	104	104	104	104	104	104	104	104	104	NK*	NK*	NK*	94	94
Ballast Trucks (40-ton)	NK*	-	-	-	20	20	21	45	45	45	45	45	45	45	64	67	67	67	67	67	67	67	NK*	NK*	NK*	87	87
Ballast Brakes (8-ton)	NK*	-	-	-	11	9	9	9	9	9	9	9	8	7	6	NK*	2	2	2	2	2	1	NK*	NK*	NK*	-	-
Ballast Brakes (10-ton)	NK*	71	71	71	51	56	52	51	51	50	50	50	47	44	42	NK*	35	30	29	27	27	27	NK*	NK*	NK*	24	22
Ballast Brakes (15-ton)	NK*	-	-	-	2	2	5	5	5	5	5	5	5	5	5	5	5	5	5	5	5	5	NK*	NK*	NK*	4	4
Ballast Brakes (20-ton)	NK*	-	-	-	7	7	12	14	14	14	17	17	17	17	17	NK*	27	27	27	27	27	27	NK*	NK*	NK*	25	24
Bogie Rail Trucks (20-ton)	NK*	-	-	-	12	12	12	12	12	12	12	12	12	13	13	NK*	12	12	12	12	12	12	12	12	12	12	12
Bogie Rail Trucks (30-ton)	NK*	44	44	12	12	12	12	12	12	12	12	12	12	12	12	12	12	12	12	12	12	12	12	12	12	12	12
Bogie Rail Trucks (35-ton)	NK*	-	-	-	6	6	6	6	6	6	6	6	6	6	6	6	6	6	6	6	6	6	6	6	6	6	6
Bogie Rail Trucks (40-ton)	NK*	-	-	-	14	14	14	14	14	14	14	14	14	14	14	NK*	39	39	39	39	39	39	NK*	NK*	NK*	49	56
P&C Trucks	NK*	6	6	6	6	6	6	4	3	3	3	2	1	1	1	NK*	-	-	-	3	2	1	-	-	-	-	-
Rail & Sleeper	NK*	141	141	141	141	140	129	129	126	123	111	102	95	91	85	NK*	72	71	71	71	70	70	NK*	NK*	NK*	61	60
Travelling Crane	NK*	60	60	62	63	63	60	55	57	56	56	59	56	56	54	NK*	56	54	55	55	56	61	NK*	NK*	NK*	68	69
Dock (Southampton West)	NK*	-	-	-	222	214	222	228	227	116	99	96	121	121	146	NK*	224	224	222	206	226	215	NK*	NK*	NK*	233	246
Dock (Newhaven West)	NK*	-	-	-	4	4	4	4	4	4	3	3	1	2	2	NK*	2	2	2	2	2	2	NK*	NK*	NK*	2	70
Bogie Well Trucks	NK*	-	-	-	-	-	1	1	1	1	1	1	1	1	1	1	1	1	1	1	1	1	NK*	NK*	NK*	1	-
Boiler Trolleys	NK*	-	-	-	-	-	-	9	9	9	9	9	7	6	5	5	5	5	5	5	5	5	5	5	5	5	5
Open Wagons	NK*	102	104	110	37	36	24	48	81	70	60	56	60	79	88	NK*	86	90	92	91	99	106	NK*	NK*	NK*	156	162
Tank Wagons	NK*	78	78	82	83	73	70	76	68	62	62	59	63	58	66	NK*	70	69	68	68	70	70	NK*	NK*	NK*	72	77
Timber Trucks	NK*	23	23	12	10	12	12	17	16	15	14	11	9	8	6	NK*	2	16	16	16	16	16	1	1	1	1	1
Yard Wagons	NK*	237	243	246	342	328	333	320	315	286	294	294	308	307	302	NK*	321	338	341	346	358	389	NK*	NK*	NK*	340	337
Stores Vans	NK*	28	28	29	51	54	55	55	49	70	76	82	89	87	93	93	93	93	100	114	134	155	NK*	NK*	NK*	154	267
Spunge Cloth Vans	NK*	11	11	11	11	11	11	12	13	12	14	15	15	17	15	NK*	16	16	16	16	16	16	NK*	NK*	NK*	20	20
Brake Vans	NK*	NK*	NK*	NK*	5	5	5	6	5	5	3	4	4	5	5	NK*	6	4	4	4	4	4	5	5	NK	8	8

Note NK* Totals not known

Note † All ballast wagons totalled together 1924-6

Over the years, the description of some Departmental vehicles varied, and some cannot be traced with certainty. The above table includes the vast majority but excludes a few miscellaneous wagons. The wartime updating of many 12- and 20-ton wagons has been ignored in the interests of simplicity.

Appendix 6

Isle of Wight Wagon Stock Totals

Description		1923	1924	1925	1926	1927	1928	1929	1930	1931	1932	1933	1934	1935	1936	1937	1938	1939	1940	1941	1942	1943	1944	1945	1946	1947	1948	1949
Open Goods	5T	-	1	1	1	-	-	-	-	-	-	-	-	-	-	-	-	-	-	-	-	-	-	-	-	-	-	-
"	6T	34	35	33	33	24	-	-	-	-	-	-	-	-	-	-	-	-	-	-	-	-	-	-	-	-	-	-
"	8T	170	158	149	148	132	115	82	54	26	9	1	1	-	-	-	-	-	-	-	-	-	-	-	-	-	-	-
"	9T	64	64	61	61	53	42	29	12	-	1	1	1	-	-	-	-	-	-	-	-	-	-	-	-	-	-	-
"	10T	166	164	178	184	230	277	321	377	431	489	457	452	451	451	451	451	451	449	449	449	449	449	449	449	449	455	411
"	12T	21	21	21	21	21	20	16	7	6	1	-	-	-	-	-	-	-	-	-	-	-	-	-	-	-	-	-
"	13T	-	-	-	-	-	-	-	-	-	-	-	-	-	-	-	-	-	-	-	-	-	-	-	-	-	-	-
"	15T	-	-	-	-	-	-	-	-	-	-	-	-	-	-	-	-	-	-	-	-	-	-	-	-	-	-	48
Covered Goods	6T	12	12	12	12	12	12	7	10	13	21	21	21	21	21	21	21	21	21	21	20	20	20	20	20	18	17	9
"	8T	20	20	20	16	13	27	27	30	27	27	27	27	27	30	30	30	30	30	30	30	30	30	30	30	25	25	12
"	10T	29	29	29	18	15	9	8	10	7	7	7	7	6	3	3	3	3	3	3	3	3	3	3	3	3	3	3
CattleTrucks		11	11	11	10	10	9	8	10	7	7	7	7	6	2	2	2	2	2	2	2	2	2	2	2	2	3	2
Tar Tanks		3	3	3	3	3	3	2	2	2	2	2	2	2	2	2	2	2	2	2	2	2	2	2	2	2	2	2
Timber Trucks		22	22	21	22	21	19	20	20	23	20	20	20	20	20	20	20	20	20	20	20	20	20	20	20	20	20	20
Road Van Trucks		-	-	-	-	-	4	16	20	23	23	23	23	23	23	23	20	15	15	15	15	15	15	15	14	14	14	14
BrakeVans		6	6	6	9	8	10	11	10	9	11	13	13	13	13	13	13	13	13	13	13	13	13	13	13	13	12	12
Totals		563	550	549	542	546	538	542	555	566	611	572	567	563	563	563	558	555	553	553	552	552	552	552	551	544	548	531

Isle of Wight Service Vehicles Totals

Description	1923	1924	1925	1926	1927	1928	1929	1930	1931	1932	1933	1934	1935	1936	1937	1938	1939	1940	1941	1942	1943	1944	1945	1946	1947	1948	1949
Ballast Wagons	3	3	21	21	21	39	35	35	35	19	19	20	20	20	20	20	20	20	20	20	20	20	20	20	NK*	30	30
Loco Coal Wagons	1	1	1	1	8	8	8	8	8	12	12	12	12	12	12	12	12	12	12	12	12	12	12	12	12	12	12
Mess & Tool Vans	4	4	4	4	4	2	2	3	4	4	4	4	4	4	4	4	4	4	4	4	4	4	4	4	7	8	8
Travelling Cranes	3	3	3	3	3	3	3	3	3	3	3	3	3	3	3	3	3	3	3	3	3	3	3	3	3	3	3
Match Trucks	-	-	-	-	-	-	-	-	-	-	-	-	-	-	-	-	-	-	-	-	-	-	-	-	-	-	2
Boiler Trolley	-	-	-	-	-	-	-	-	-	1	1	1	1	1	1	1	1	1	1	1	1	1	1	1	1	1	1
Yard Wagon	-	-	-	-	-	-	-	-	-	-	-	-	-	-	1	1	1	1	1	1	1	1	1	1	1	1	1
Stores Vans	-	-	-	-	-	-	-	-	-	-	-	-	-	-	-	-	-	-	-	-	-	-	-	-	-	4	6
Tank Wagons	1	1	1	1	1	1	1	2	2	2	2	2	2	2	2	2	2	2	2	2	2	2	2	2	2	2	2
Dpt Brake Van	-	-	-	-	-	-	-	-	-	1	-	-	-	-	-	-	-	-	-	-	-	-	-	-	-	-	-
WorkmanŌs Coach	-	-	-	-	-	-	-	-	1	-	-	-	-	-	-	-	-	-	-	-	-	-	-	-	-	-	-
Petrol InsŌ Car	-	-	-	-	-	-	-	-	-	-	-	-	-	-	1	-	-	-	-	-	-	-	-	-	-	-	-
Totals	8	8	27	27	28	45	42	51	53	43	43	44	44	44	44	44	44	44	44	44	44	44	44	44	47?	61	66

Note: NK* 10 Diagram 1155 20-ton ballast hoppers were transferred to the Island in 1947 or 1948 on a date not recorded. The crane match trucks, of which there were two, were counted as part of the crane until 1949.

Lynton & Barnstaple Line Wagon Stock Totals

Description		1923	1924	1925	1926	1927	1928	1929	1930	1931	1932	1933	1934	1935	1936
Open Goods	4T	8	8	8	8	8	8	8	8	8	8	8	8	8	8
"	6T	1	1	1	1	1	1	1	1	1	1	1	1	1	1
"	8T	4	4	4	4	4	8	8	8	8	8	8	8	8	8
PlatformTrucks	8T	2	2	2	2	2	8	8	8	8	8	8	8	8	8
Covered Goods	4T	6	6	6	6	6	6	6	6	6	6	6	6	6	6
"	8T	-	-	-	-	-	2	2	2	2	2	2	2	2	2
Brake Vans		3	3	3	3	3	3	3	3	3	3	3	3	3	3
Totals		24	24	24	24	24	32	32	32	32	32	32	32	32	32

Lynton & Barnstaple Line Service Vehicles Totals

Description	1923	1924	1925	1926	1927	1928	1929	1930	1931	1932	1933	1934	1935	1936
Traveling Cranes	-	-	2	2	2	2	2	2	2	2	2	2	2	2
Totals	-	-	2	2	2	2	2	2	2	2	2	2	2	2

There was alsao one crane match truck, counted as part of the crane. The line closed 1936 and the rolling stock was sold.